Wind in the Rock

Wind in the Rock

Ann Zwinger

Harper & Row, Publishers

NEW YORK, HAGERSTOWN, SAN FRANCISCO, LONDON

Grateful acknowledgment is made for permission to reprint:

Excerpt from *Master Rabbit* by Walter de la Mare. Reprinted by permission of The Literary Trustees of Walter de la Mare and The Society of Authors as their representative.

Excerpt from *Wilderness and the American Mind* by Roderick Nash. Reprinted by permission of Yale University Press.

Excerpt from *Final Report for Surface Cleanup of Cultural Sites in Grand Gulch* reprinted by permission of the United States Department of the Interior.

Excerpt from the poem "The Striders" by Loren Eisley from *Notes of an Alchemist*. Reprinted by permission of Charles Scribner's Sons.

WIND IN THE ROCK
Copyright © 1978 by Ann H. Zwinger
For information address Harper & Row, Publishers, Inc.,
10 East 53rd Street, New York, N.Y. 10022.
Published simultaneously in Canada by
Fitzhenry & Whiteside Limited, Toronto.

FIRST EDITION

Designed by Dorothy Schmiderer

Library of Congress Cataloging in Publication Data

Zwinger, Ann.
  Wind in the rock.
  Bibliography: p.
  Includes index.
  1. Natural history—Four Corners region. 2. Four
Corners region—Description and travel. I. Title.
QH104.5.S6S94 1978 500.979 78–2176
ISBN 0–06–014209–X

78 79 80 81 82 10 9 8 7 6 5 4 3 2 1

For my mother,
who taught me

But the Parthenon serves no useful purpose either; if we tore it down we could erect buildings to shelter an inadequately housed population . . . And yet man, if he took the trouble, could rebuild the Parthenon ten times over. But he will never be able to recreate a single canyon, which was formed during thousands of years of patient erosion by sun, wind and water . . .

JEAN DORST, *Before Nature Dies,* 1970

The canyon country does not always inspire love. To many it appears barren, hostile, repellent—a fearsome mostly waterless land of rock and heat, sand dunes and quicksand, cactus, thornbush, scorpion, rattlesnake, and agoraphobic distances. To those who see our land in that manner, the best reply is, yes, you are right, it is a dangerous and terrible place. Enter at your own risk. Carry water. Avoid the noonday sun. Try to ignore the vultures. Pray frequently.

EDWARD ABBEY, *The Journey Home,* 1977

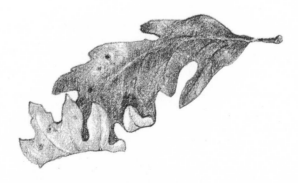

Contents

Wind in the Rock

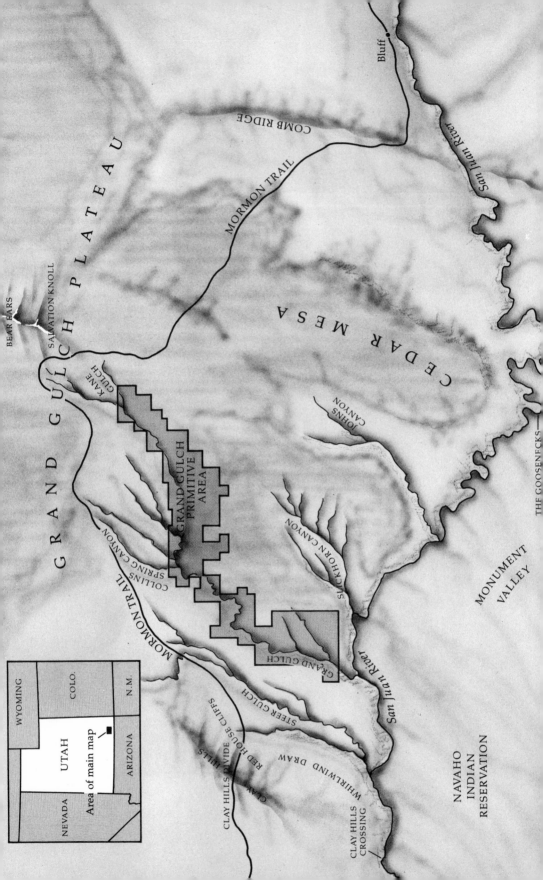

Introduction

1

I first saw these five canyons one April, on a trip down the San Juan River. Their names are as evocative to me now as when I first heard them: Johns Canyon. Slickhorn Canyon. Grand Gulch. Steer Gulch. Whirlwind Draw.

The San Juan River, after rising in the San Juan Mountains of Colorado, runs southward into New Mexico, loops around Farmington and Shiprock, and then flows northwest through the Four Corners area —the only place in the United States where four states meet. Into Utah, it makes one arc past the small settlements of Aneth, Bluff, and Mexican Hat, and then cuts another, more intricate arc through the wilderness of southeastern Utah before joining the Colorado River above Glen Canyon Dam in what is now Lake Powell. The five canyons drain into that second arc, the river's last free-flowing miles, between Mexican Hat and the Clay Hills.

Going downstream that April I wondered about the breaks in the canyon wall bounding the right side of the river. There was a fifty-foot overhang that marked the mouth of Johns Canyon; at its base was a silt-rimmed plunge pool filled with clear water. I walked half a mile or so up Slickhorn Canyon, enticed by the coral-colored fossils locked in the gray limestone shelves. However, by the time I passed the sandy beach of Grand Gulch, I was miserably sick with flu, and Steer Gulch and Whirlwind Draw went by in a blur before we took out at Clay Hills Crossing. Still, I had wondered, what's above and behind that forbidding lip, that limestone stair, that dry waterfall? Wondered, went home, got well, and put the wondering aside in the press of other commitments.

A few years later, by an odd combination of events, I found myself

in southeastern Utah, flying over the Grand Gulch Plateau, which borders the San Juan River on the north, and into which the five canyons
are cut. My husband, Herman, who is a pilot, made the flight one clear
October morning. Beneath the wing, there was not a farm, not a ranch,
not a plowed field, and scarcely a trail—total and remote desolation as
far as I could see. North of the San Juan River is "federal lands,"
administered by the Bureau of Land Management, either as a primitive
area or for grazing or mineral rights. From the look on his face, Herman,
who has become fairly philosophical about taking me to faraway places
with odd-sounding names, must have thought I'd gone bonkers.

The five canyons wander through rough and empty country. Hard.
Unyielding. There are no eastern greens, no gentle contours, nothing
soft, nothing easy. Hundreds of miles of rock scarcely blurred by vegetation, rib and vertebra without flesh, rock the color of dried blood,
earth the color of old leather, scuffed and rutted, gullied and wrinkled.
Most of the time even the sky is hard, such a vibrant, raucous blue, a
color with such an edge to it that it is almost impossible to describe.

Curiosity nudged again. I came home and patched together the
U.S.G.S. topographical maps that cover the area. The maps themselves
indicate the enthusiastic lack of economic interest: there are only 15-
minute series maps, no 7.5-minute quadrangles, the standard size available for most of the United States. On these maps, one inch equals a
mile, hieratic red section lines imposed like a grid over a complex terrain
only sparsely inked with the green overlay that indicates vegetation.
And there are places on the Grand Gulch Plateau map where there aren't
any section lines drawn at all.

The contour lines on 15-minute maps are at 80-foot intervals and,
drawn in brown, resemble scrimshaw; here they are so close on the
canyon walls that I, who am quite nearsighted, must use a magnifying
glass to distinguish the intervals—a 1,000-foot descent can nearly be
encompassed in a quarter inch.

My curiosity about this country intensified. I wanted very much to
get out there and *walk*, explore, discover. To be there. For somehow I
sensed that in this harsh landscape lay challenge; in walking there,
discovery and delight.

And so I went. I discovered that, like all canyons, they have a
powerful sense of direction and this becomes imprinted upon one's way
of thinking: there are upcanyon and downcanyon, and one adjusts to
that simple fact. More than anywhere else I sensed that here one must
fit into the landscape, must know what is there and where, in order to
survive. These canyons, like the ocean and the air, are unforgiving. They

are not places in which to be cavalier or careless. Whatever direction, it's a long way out.

The canyon walls are, for the most part, formidable vertical barriers. The sandstone, limestone, and shale walls are carved either into overhangs or are sheer drops of hundreds of feet or treacherous talus. In most places they are simply impassable. Once down in the canyon, you're locked in. With plants that are thorny, spiny, hostile. Locked in with the potential of sprained wrists or ankles or broken legs for carelessness. With rattlesnakes—the ubiquitous buzztail, sunning on the rock ledge you're about to haul yourself up onto.

In spite of this, after walking there for days, coming home bug-bitten, shins bruised, nose peeling, feet and hands swollen, I feel ablaze with life. I suspect that the canyons give me an intensified sense of living partly because I not only face the basics of living and survival, but carry them on my back. And in my head. And this intense personal responsibility gives me an overwhelming sense of freedom I know nowhere else.

2

One of the odd things about these five canyons is that, although they drain a relatively small segment of southeastern Utah, they are quite different in aspect. The differences lie in their placement on the Grand Gulch Plateau, the altitude at which they begin, the rock through which they cut. The canyons fan out north of the river like fingers on a hand: Johns Canyon farthest east; then Slickhorn; third and longest, Grand Gulch; and last Steer Gulch and Whirlwind Draw, the westernmost.

Taking the farthest tracing of the broken blue lines that indicate intermittent streams on the U.S.G.S. maps, Grand Gulch begins far up on Elk Ridge, its blanket of trees made possible by an altitude of 6,800 feet, which enables it to garner slightly more rainfall than the lower canyons. It does not truly become a canyon until it cuts into the massive Cedar Mesa Sandstone that blankets the plateau; then the entire canyon is entrenched in this sandstone, walls sometimes 500 feet or more high. It was named by a group of Mormon missionaries who traversed the Grand Gulch Plateau in 1880 and had to find a way around the head of this forbidding canyon. Grand Gulch is the largest of the San Juan's tributary canyons, and its 53 miles to the river proved a formidable deterrent to their crossing.

The Cedar Mesa Sandstone has weathered into large overhangs and shelters. These, combined with an open canyon floor in some reaches, a gentle gradient, and reliable water, provided places of habitation for the prehistoric Anasazi Indians who populated the plateau and at various periods utilized the canyon for living and farming and storage and burials. A multitude of prehistoric sites and their accompanying rock art lend to Grand Gulch a unique presence.

The Grand Gulch Plateau stretches over part of the Monument Upwarp, a tremendous low dome some 35 miles wide and 100 miles long that stretches from the Colorado River on the west to Comb Ridge on the east, and from the junction of the Green and Colorado rivers on the north to near Kayenta, Arizona, on the south. The upwarp elevates earlier ocean-laid sediments high enough to be incised by the two easternmost of the five canyons.

These older rock strata appear downcanyon in both Slickhorn and Johns, which is on the crest of the upwarp. Slickhorn was named after a distinctive herd of longhorns that ran in the canyon; Johns, after John Oliver, a rancher who kept cattle there. Fossiliferous gray limestones of the Pennsylvanian Age Hermosa Formation give specific character to the lower reaches of both canyons. In this dry climate limestone is a resistant rock that terminates both canyons in a spectacular series of stair-steps—walkable steps in the case of Slickhorn, descending to the San Juan River, and giant untreadable steps in the case of Johns, permitting no access to or from the river.

Red Halgaito Shale, which separates Cedar Mesa Sandstone from the gray limestones, is thin in Slickhorn, but in Johns, in the mid to upper reaches, forms a slanting red base for the vertical ivory sandstone walls above. Johns is the only canyon that has a broad alluvium-filled middle reach, the canyon walls a mile apart here. Because it is on the crest of the upwarp, it must cut deepest to reach the river, a drop of some 2,800 feet in 12 or so miles, and in doing so exposes the Honaker Trail Formation, the oldest rock in the immediate area.

Flanking Grand Gulch on the west is Steer Gulch. Steer Gulch quirks through flatter country but also drops off precipitously as it reaches the river. Here steers, culled out of the herd grazed on the plateau, were kept prior to being driven to market, hence its name. The westernmost canyon is Whirlwind Draw. Whirlwind begins at about 5,600 feet on the flank of the Clay Hills, the western boundary of the Grand Gulch Plateau. Named because of the dust devils that whirl up it in the spring, it drops quickly from the escarpment of the Clay Hills to a flat sandy terrace with few trees, running through low wandering banks, picking up little gullies along the way. Scarcely six miles long, Whirlwind ends at the San Juan River in a succession of impassable dry sandstone waterfalls.

None of these canyons bear perennial streams. Although there are springs, they are few and far between, and Steer Gulch and Whirlwind Draw have none. The canyons run with water only after a good rain, often in flash floods that clean off the stream bed and scour the walls and bore out the potholes a sand grain deeper and cascade over the usually dry waterfalls, and burst over the cliff walls like the jets from a dozen firehoses.

3

I would like to think that I could be set down blindfolded in any one of these canyons and know where I was when I could see: in the sandy reaches of Whirlwind Draw with the brilliant chunks of petrified wood washed down from the Clay Hills, or on the broad and open area of Johns, threaded with cattle trails, or beneath the overhangs of Grand Gulch, or upon the elegant limestone steps, inlaid with reflecting pools, of Slickhorn Canyon. I think in less than a mile of walking I would know. For, beyond the obvious physical characteristics, one begins to have a feel for each canyon itself—its way of going, its way of defining the sky, its way of turning, that belongs to it alone.

That kind of aware walking brings rewards. There is nothing vicarious or secondhand about walking there; instead, I have an exhilarating sense of immediacy. I'm not watching it or reading about it, I'm here, right *now,* experiencing it. When I crawl across a foot-wide ledge with nothing below, nearly nauseated with fear; when I claw up a sandstone wall, plastered against its abrasive curve; when I heave myself onto the top rim to see a view of such splendor that wonder washes away all my apprehension about getting back down; when I do what I knew I could not do—then I have a heady taste of glory.

To me there is an enchantment in these dry canyons that once roared with water and still sometimes do, that absorbed the voices of those who came before, something of massive dignity about sandstone beds that tell of a past long before human breathing, that bear the patterns of ancient winds and water in their crossbeddings.

Here I find something of necessity. Were I to discover that I could not walk here again, something essential would be missing from my life.

The chief obstacle to traverse is Grand Gulch, which divides the plateau into an eastern and a western part. Though less than 1,000 feet deep, its walls begin with a vertical drop of 30 to 60 feet and continue downward as a series of undercut steps 10 to 40 feet high and 5 to 10 feet broad, impossible to descend, even on foot, except with great caution and at wisely chosen places. Throughout its course the parallel canyon walls wind in and out as a series of closely placed meanders and rise almost vertically from a floor which in few places exceeds 500 feet in width. No trails cross Grand Gulch. Access to its floor from the east is impossible except at one point. From the west it may be reached by an artificial trail near Dripping Spring Gulch, at Collins.

A. J. EARDLEY, *Physiography of Southeastern Utah,* 1958

The country here is almost entirely solid sand rock, high hills and mountains cut all to pieces by deep gulches which are in many places altogether impassable. It is certainly the worst country I ever saw, some of our party are of the opinion that a road could be made if plenty of money was furnished but most of us are satisfied that there is no us[e] of this company undertaking to get through to San Juan this way.

PLATTE D. LYMAN, *Journal,* December 1, 1879

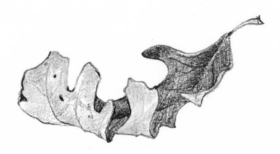

Lower Grand Gulch

1

Grand Gulch, so named by the Mormon pioneers who came, freezing and hungry, long behind schedule, across its extensive and formidable upper reaches in 1880 on their way to colonize southeastern Utah, is the main canyon draining the Grand Gulch Plateau. The canyon drops roughly 3,000 feet in its course and has the most gentle gradient, albeit with some dry waterfalls, of the five canyons. Nevertheless, Grand Gulch carries water from some 1,000 square miles down to the San Juan River, often in flash floods that richochet off the terraced banks and canyon walls.

The floor averages 300 to 500 feet lower than the plateau above, so it is somewhat warmer and milder there, and the cold air drainage that sinks down most other canyons is absent. The canyon walls absorb the sun's heat and radiate it at night, further tempering the difference between night and day. Thus the growing season is slightly longer on the canyon floor, probably some 145 frost-free days, compared with about 130 on the plateau top. In the canyon grow a wider variety of plants: Gambel oak, singleleaf ash, huge cottonwoods and willows, sedges and bulrushes and other water- and shade-loving plants, along with the ubiquitous prickly pear, sagebrush, and rabbitbrush.

For nearly six hundred years, between the prehistoric Anasazi Indians and the Mormon missionaries, no one inhabited this country. If some itinerant trapper or wandering Indian had been here, he left no written record that could be passed on.

Everyone went either south or north of the lower San Juan River, which had been named by Fray Alonso de Posadas in 1686 after St. John. Fray Alonso had been in New Mexico many years as a missionary; his maps and reports were used by the Spanish explorers of the seventeenth

Cliffrose *(Cowania stansburyana)*

and eighteenth centuries. In 1776 Fathers Antanasio Dominguez and Velez de Escalante set out on the Old Spanish Trail looking for a way to the missions of California. On their outward journey they made a great loop to the north and returned home by a great loop to the south, not having found any passage to California. Their avoidance of the lower San Juan suggests that the region was well enough known to be considered impassable by the fathers and their company.

A brief fur trade existed in the Southwest in the 1820s and 1830s. Permits to trap in New Mexico had to be obtained from Manuel Armijo, the governor of the territory, who was not cordial to Americans (1821–1845 was a period of Mexican rather than Spanish rule). Mexicans themselves did little or no trapping, leaving the field open to clandestine operations by American trappers. Two trader-trappers, William Wolfskill and Ewing Young, worked the upper San Juan River in 1824–25, and it is thought that Young perhaps went farther downstream.

Unlike St. Louis, which was home base for the American fur traders working the upper West, and which had newspapers that reported comings and goings, Taos and Santa Fe, where the Southwest trappers outfitted, had none. Spanish reports spell American names phonetically, which makes them difficult to decipher. The yearly rendezvous of the trappers in the Green River country to the north, which provided so much documentation about the fur trade, never became established in the Southwest. As a consequence only meager data exist for the southwestern trade. Wolfskill and Young are credited with having made the first complete traverse of the Old Spanish Trail to California, following Escalante's route part way north, crossing the Colorado and Green rivers near present-day Moab and Green River, Utah, but extensive records of their trapping activities have yet to be found and may never have been written.

First scientific knowledge of the Southwest dates from the mid-nineteenth century when, as a result of a treaty between Mexico and

Utah snowberry *(Symphoricarpos oreophilus utahensis)*

the United States, the area became part of this country. The Gold Rush of 1849 focused attention on routes west. Lieutenant J. C. Ives, in 1857–58, exploring navigability of the Colorado River from its mouth upstream, crossed the Colorado Plateau and reported "impassable obstacles" and that "ours has been the first, and will doubtless be the last party of whites to visit this profitless locality." Only Captain John M. Macomb, with the Corps of Topographical Engineers, traveling from Santa Fe northwest to the Needles area in 1859, came anywhere near the lower San Juan River canyons. His small group climbed to a breathtaking view of the confluence of the Green and Colorado rivers, and on their return to Santa Fe went east, turning south at the Blue Mountains, thus skirting the eastern boundary of a wilderness that remains just as wild today. Both military and railroad surveys of the mid-1800's pointedly avoided the lower San Juan River.

James White, who claimed he ran the lower Colorado River through the Grand Canyon and more than likely didn't, did go some way down the San Juan, but how far it's difficult to tell. He wrote to his brother, September 26, 1867: "i Went prospeCted with Captin Baker and gorge strole in the San Won montin Wee found vry god prospeCk but noth that Wold pay then Wee stare Down the San Won river wee travel down a bout 200 miles then Wee Cross over on Caloreado and Camp."

2

It was for the heroic Mormons to make the first recorded crossing of this unknown country in 1880. Reasons for this journey, which was to result in colonization of southeastern Utah, were multiple: Indians had been raiding Mormon settlements in southwestern Utah and the church believed that a settlement in the southeastern part of the state would help to stabilize the situation as well as cut off some of the outlaw traffic in the area. Peaceful coexistence with the Indians was encouraged; Brigham Young had found it cheaper "to feed than to fight." In addition, non-Mormon cattlemen were moving into the San Juan area from Colorado and New Mexico, a cause of much political concern to the Mormon hierarchy. Mormon colonies farther north in the San Luis Valley were finding it too cold, and it was hoped that a settlement farther south would prove more comfortable as well as more productive. In the words of the church, "this forbidding corner must be colonized."

A Mission was "called" in the spring of 1879 to explore and establish a route from western Utah to the San Juan country and to remain there, waiting for the main contingent that would follow the next fall. The 36 explorers, including two women and eight children, set out across northern Arizona to a bleak and unknown countryside. The route through Arizona was desperately dry, and the Navajos were not friendly. While some of the scouting party remained at what they hoped would be the new settlement, the others returned by a northerly route along segments of the Old Spanish Trail. Both the route out and the route back took a minimum of six weeks, and the returnees, while reporting positively on the new region, recommended finding another way to get there.

Before the main group of colonizers left, word came of a time-saving shortcut to their destination, through the town of Escalante, across the Colorado River, and along the north bank of the San Juan River to the settlement area. Without checking out the report, the band left in October, 1879, under the leadership of Platte D. Lyman. Coming from different settlements in Utah, some 250 Mormons with 83 wagons and more than 1,000 head of livestock rendezvoused where the road ended some 40 miles southeast of Escalante.

Scouts sent out ahead came back with a report that the country ahead was impassable for wagons. By this time, return was cut off by snows in the high country. The company voted unanimously to forge ahead. Building a road as they went, they reached the rim of the Colorado River in December, and there they found a possible descent through a notch in this river's west wall, a notch that was to become known as Hole-in-the-Rock.

It took six weeks of work in bitter cold weather to blast, chip, chop, scrape, and bludgeon a passageway three-quarters of a mile long down to the river two thousand feet below. All wagons and stock were maneuvered down safely, and by the end of January, 1880, all were across the Colorado River without mishap.

Going up the eastern bank was not as horrendous as the descent through Hole-in-the-Rock, but it was still forty difficult miles from the Colorado River to the Clay Hills Divide. Hairpinning down the eastern flank of the Clay Hills, the Mormons found themselves blocked by the formidable slot of Grand Gulch and had to veer north. One of the scouts, George Hobbs, gave an overgenerous evaluation of canyon walls that indeed must have seemed monstrous if you were trying to get across: "We chose a route going almost due east, but had only gone a

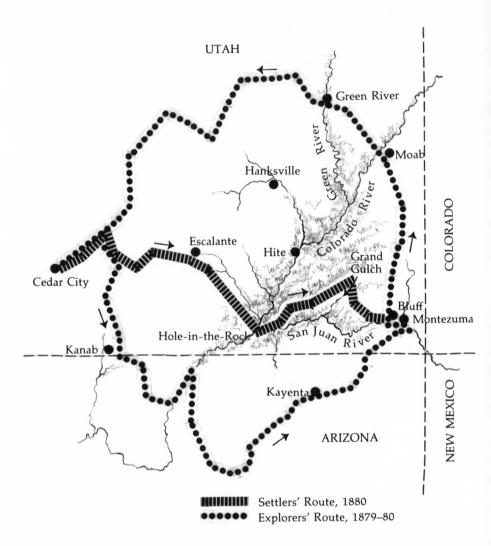

Mormon Routes 1879–1880 Adapted from David E. Miller, *Hole-in-the-Rock Expedition* (Salt Lake City: University of Utah Press, 1959)

few miles when we were cut off by the Grand Gulch, which in many places was inclosed between perpendicular walls from one to two thousand feet high."

On March 10, Platte D. Lyman, entered the same estimate in his journal: "We found gulches with perpendicular banks 1000 feet high running from the extreme north 30 miles into the San Juan on the south, but by going around the head of these we can make a passable road by following an old indian trail. There is plenty of grass and some water most of the way." Lyman's optimism was short-lived. Temperatures dropped, eight inches of snow fell, and five days later he wrote: "Last night was the coldest night I ever experienced it was impossible to be comfortable in bed or anywhere else."

And the fingers of Grand Gulch pushed them still northward until they traveled unknown country, wagons strung out for thirty miles, livestock in duress. If it wasn't the snow it was the mud that fouled wagon wheels, solidifying into great thumping lumps. The scouts rode weakened horses that left bloody hoof prints in the snow. Unsure of the route on one bitter, lung-frosting day, one of the leaders climbed a knoll from which he at last could see the familiar landmark of the Blue Mountains; that knoll is still marked on maps as Salvation Knoll. They turned southeast, crossing Cedar Mesa, dropping down toward Comb Wash, reaching the San Juan River, rounding the south end of Comb Ridge, and thence to Bluff. And in all that lacerating journey there was not one death—and three healthy births!

Their journey ended in April, 1880, and four years later they abandoned the Mission because no one could make a living there, what with the lack of rainfall, Indian problems, and the treacherousness of that muddy San Juan River.

The foolhardy route that exhausted humans and stock remained in use for a year longer, with traffic in both directions, until a better crossing was established at Hall's Crossing twenty miles upstream from Hole-in-the-Rock. The reason for traveling it in the first place must have been an uncommon faith in the Mission and a near total ignorance of what kind of country they were venturing into.

I walked part of the old Mormon trail one gentle autumn morning, shivering with the knowledge of how cold it must have been that winter of 1880, how fearsome this eternal piñon-juniper woodland that blocks the view and appears to go on forever and ever. Fragments of trail still remain, just wagon-width wide, hacked through the brush, debris from tree-cutting shoved off to the side, tree stumps still showing the old ax marks. It's a gnarled trail, taking the path of least resistance, not bulldozed in a straight line like a modern road. Even after a hundred years the ground is still largely clear and raw, the usual matting of needles and juniper berries padding the ground only on the periphery.

And the view down into Grand Gulch, that tortuous uncrossable canyon which forced such a cruel passage, is just the same as it was a century ago—a canyon whose depth and size and ruggedness the Mormons could only commemorate as "grand."

3

My own approach to Grand Gulch is a pleasant one, via the San Juan River in a warm September nearly a century later. I'll be on a boat trip with good friends and guides, Patrick and Susan Conley, but I will leave them at Grand Gulch and meet another guide, Frank Nordstrom, and walk out for four days up the canyon. Frank Nordstrom is a pediatrician from Farmington, New Mexico, who has walked these canyons for years. Needless to say he is a superb guide; to walk this country you have to be.

The anticipation is heightened by the logistics of getting gear together for both a backpack and a river trip. Not that the two are mutually exclusive, but one scarcely needs a bathing suit in the canyons or a backpack on the river. A wool shirt on the river provides warmth even if wet; a down jacket in the canyon is lighter in weight but no good if soaked; a rain suit to row in, a poncho to walk in; and the list goes on and on. I suspect the quintessential backpacker personality finds pleasure in the fine tuning of repacking, reaching perfection with just the right amount of usable gear in the least amount of space with the minimum amount of weight.

The river trip is one of the most delightful I've ever made, serene or exciting, depending on whether we drift between thousand-foot-high walls or scout and run white water. But the last few miles between Slickhorn Canyon and Grand Gulch are against a setting sun which polishes the water surface to an unbearable glare. By the time we debark my face feels frozen in a permanent squint.

The next morning we enter lower Grand Gulch, up and over a thirty-foot ledge that requires a push-pull scramble to ascend. Walking is tedious because boulder heaps and log jams block Grand Gulch's lower reaches. Much of the plateau above is slickrock, canted like a shallow funnel toward the canyon. Even a scamper of rain upcanyon sheets off and quickly focuses into Grand Gulch in flash floods that roar like freight trains and sweep up everything in their path. When a massive flood comes through, log jams twenty feet high or more are created at narrows in the canyon. Debris interweaves in the weft of the logs, forming effective dams, enduring until a bigger frog-choker loosens the plug and breaks it out. The cowboys, who used this canyon as a natural corral, used to burn them out.

Working through this debris is hard going and I think wistfully of the river, where you progress easily with no more than the twitch of an oar. We have eight hard miles to walk, scramble, and climb before the first known water.

So far, the signs are not propitious. This summer marks a second year of drought in the Southwest. It wouldn't take much to turn this land into total desert. As it is, it is not quite desert: a precarious balance just this side of it; eighty percent of the land has no vegetation whatsoever. This canyon country, for all its tough exterior, is fragile. More rainfall and there would be more vegetation to hold the soil in place, dying and rotting to form soil. Less rainfall and little erosion occurs, and the equilibrium of a desert is established. But at ten inches of average annual rainfall, which comes in a few sudden heavy showers, this terrain is most subject to erosion. Torrential downpours rip off the top layer of sand and rudimentary soil and flush it down the canyons.

Only in the relatively few springs, tucked away in canyon corners, or in potholes in the slickrock, momentarily filled after a rainstorm, is there water. And this can be notably and terrifyingly unavailable just when one needs it most. Dr. T. Mitchell Prudden, a medical doctor from Columbia College with a passion for the Southwest and for archaeology, who explored this country in the early 1900s, warned: "Here is elemental life, here is genuine freedom; but these exalted states are not to be won without strict conformity to the inexorable requirements of the land. Water is often very scanty, and usually, to the uninitiated, very hard to find; and the ignorant and foolhardy can readily die from thirst."

As we progress upcanyon, signs of water continue more negative than encouraging. Open sandy channels, that are usually damp enough to provide a firm surface, are dry and the loose sand is difficult to walk through. Where a pool once was is marked now only by a damp slash of silt, kidney-shaped or tear-shaped, sometimes tantalizingly shiny. When wet, many of these reaches are treacherous quicksand; when damp, the fine silty sand or plain silt is mucilaginous. As it dries the silt cracks and then curls upward. The whole lexicon of mud and silt curls embellish the canyon floor. I hate to step on them but there's no place else to put a foot down and I reason that they will disintegrate of their own accord soon enough in this dry heat.

After some six hours of heavy walking with only brief rest stops,

I am cheered by the promise of "the perfect pool" that lies in pristine splendor just a mile ahead, up a small side canyon. The turnoff is reached, the innumerable steps and turnings negotiated. The pool is just around the corner. I can almost smell the water. I have nearly finished my bottles of drinking water, which now sloshes around inside of me instead of my pack, but the weight on my feet is the same.

We round the corner. The gray rim of the pool lies just ahead, glimpsed behind a low screen of boulders and junipers. I keep looking for the water. What water? There is none. *None.* Instead there is dry, hard gray limestone.

For eighteen years, Frank Nordstrom says, always water in this pool. I feel a nudge of uneasiness: in eighteen years water always here. *Always* water. "What if we don't find water?" I hear my raspy voice asking, disembodied, as if from somewhere else.

A moment's silence. "In that case, we make a dry camp, get up at first light, and hightail it out." I think of that Mormon exploration party, coming across this country, making one dry camp after another, cattle in duress, humans rationing what they had, digging wells in the sand, mouth dry down to the lungs, always wondering if there was water ahead. I know that feeling now, in the pit of my stomach as well as in my dry throat.

We drop our packs, take empty water bottles and lunch, and walk upcanyon, hoping to find water. With my pack off, I feel light-footed as well as light-headed, only dimly conscious of the sinuous curve of the sandstone walls, the loveliness of the canyon, the beauty of the day.

We round a good many curves looking for water. Big pools that are regularly filled are as desiccated as my mouth. Warm gray rock paves the bed of the channel, marked with wavering white lines where receding water left a salt edge, stained lavender above. Rushes and willows along the bank delineate the edges of these absent pools. A single paintbrush still blooms, a stab of vermilion next to a narrow-leaf rabbitbrush. Back and up the bank there is mostly rock, great sloping slabs with drifts of sand in the hollows. The resident lizards scatter at our approach. In the shadows, a soft breeze cools. A jet goes over, filling the canyon with a rumble that echoes a long time after. Then the rustling of the cottonwoods and dry grasses takes over, such a gentle whispering. And then silence, such stupendous silence. In this quiet my concerns take on perspective: if there is water around the next bend, good. If not, we walk out. So be it. There is no choice and in such acceptance lies serenity.

We round a sandstone wall and there they are: tiny pools, one after another, hyphenating the slickrock, shining with water. But it takes a good thirst to overcome a natural and lifelong reluctance to drink out of a pool that could best be described as turbid dishwater. I sweep away the surface film with my hand and dip out a cup of water and wait for the sediment to sink to the bottom. And wait. Upon closer inspection, the sediment does not sink because it is swimming, a whole school of daphnia—minute crustacea. I empty my cup and repeat the exercise. And once more again. Then without another thought I simply down it, daphnia and all, figuring it is going to be a lot harder on them than on me.

Lunch never tasted so good. I am awash with a sense of well-being, of joy in living, of being here, at this time, this place—a quart of water, some protein, a little fat, and a lot of salt, and my body responds gratefully and my spirits soar right into euphoria.

For most of the time, one disciplines oneself to ignore the discomfort of being hot or tired or having sore hip bones or swollen hands or being hungry, thirsty, or all together all at once. I may write about them later but at the time they are simply set aside, and it is probably this ignoring of basic misery that makes a backpacker. Someone once characterized backpacking as the most miserable way he could think of of getting from Point A to Point B. I wouldn't go that far, but I do know that if you stopped to inventory where you hurt, you likely would not continue, having discovered that you are not only a masochist but a fool as well. But when salt restores the electrolytic balance, when water cools the insides as well as the brow, when food refurbishes the body's cells, when time has been spent off one's feet and a heavy pack is a mile downcanyon, then there follows a tremendous rush of well-being, a physical sense of buoyancy, all out of proportion to the time and place.

Frank walks upcanyon to investigate any further water possibilities; a guide's knowledge of water may sometime be the difference between safety and danger. I walk back downcanyon alone. My footprints run counter to the wave-patterned sandy channel bottom. Slightly darker silty sand shadows the troughs, loops pointing upstream, accentuated with a sprinkling of small pebbles, most of them angular. Where the channel turns, it is dug deeper against the wall, which rises, protective, a massive wall that holds up the sky, absorbs the sun, and radiates it back at night.

A breeze tendrils around the corner, the advance of a light wind hollowing up the canyon, skittering a cottonwood twig with two dry

Singleleaf ash *(Fraxinus anomala)*

leaves attached. It catches in a footprint and holds, the leaf quivering, rustling slightly, and then silence again, a silence so perfect that even a birdsong would interrupt. And then the wind again. Sometimes it starts high and far away, a distant description of canyon spires and curving walls, and I can trace its passage by what it touches—leaf, grass, tree, bough—the sound filling up and coming from behind, blowing up the canyon, now in a flurry of insistence, raking the small leaves and sticks on the floor, pushing them across the sandbar, flapping my shirt, parting my hair, bringing change into the canyon.

I wish I could sit here for eons and watch as these sandstone walls crumble, grain by grain, and fall to floor this dry wash, become rearranged by water and wind, compressed to other cliffs, excavated into other canyons, and feel the wind all the same. The rock changes, the channel changes, the wind just carries air from one place to another, more constant than the rock. The rock is ephemeral, the wind, eternal.

4

The first campsite has to be passed by because it is already occupied by that most basic of all deterrents—a rattlesnake, this one a fourteen-inch midget faded rattlesnake. This small Western rattlesnake occupies many habitats and its color varies accordingly; lightly splotched with brown and gray on a yellowish-tan background, it mimics the sandstone, dappled with shadows, upon which it lies. Rattlesnakes are classed as pit vipers because of the depressions, called loreal pits, on each side of the head behind the nostril, a temperature-sensitive structure by means of which a rattlesnake locates prey, especially helpful for an animal that hunts in the dark. A rattlesnake can pick up the heat radiation of a human hand twelve inches away, which is about the outer limit of its perception. It has pupils with vertical slits rather than round openings. Although primarily nocturnal hunters, snakes often sun themselves, and the vertical pupil avoids eye damage in such bright light by being able to close completely and effectively. A rattlesnake may detect both airborne and substratum vibrations; this one, probably basking in the sun when we arrived, was undoubtedly aware of our approach long before visual contact.

Rattlesnakes are responsible for most of the snakebites in the United States, and 85 to 90 percent of the fatal bites. The bite is exceedingly painful, like being jabbed with a hot needle; if a lot of venom has been injected, a human has a numb sensation around the bite, a tingling around the mouth, and yellow vision. Rattlesnake venom is an extremely complex poison, containing several enzymes and non-enzyme proteins that are separately and in combination extremely toxic. Strikes against humans are most often in the lower leg or hand; against small prey, in the chest or shoulder. The struck animal endures several paroxysms and then falls on its side stunned within two minutes, dead within five. (The human may survive.) The rattlesnake's loreal pits are helpful in locating the victim if it has fallen any distance away. The snake then swallows it whole, head first. A snake's jaws "unhinge" to nearly 180 degrees; the looseness of the jawbones, the large gape, and ribs unattached to a breastbone make it possible to gulp down prey several times larger in diameter than the snake.

Known in Europe as "the serpent with the castanets in its tail" which courteously warned you before striking, the rattlesnake was a natural for banners carried by the colonists, one of the most famous being the Gadsden flag with a coiled rattler on a yellow field, and underneath the words: "Don't tread on me." Beneath the narrow overhang where this rattlesnake has taken shelter comes the soft but unmistakable burr. Not only will I not tread on it, I will not even enter its territory.

5

The second campsite is spacious, oriented so that the sunlight lasts late, with some cottonwoods that are good for hanging laundry on, a small sluggish algae-clotted pool close by for dishwashing. A kind of aureate light illumines the air. Even though the cottonwoods are far from turning, the smaller plants presage fall, seedheads empty on most, drying out, shrinking to essence, a beautiful time of year in Grand Gulch.

Instead of sitting down like a sensible soul and restoring my feet to their proper climate, I walk around the rincon against which we've camped. *Rincón* is a Spanish word meaning nook or inside corner, and is often used in the Southwest to mean a bend of an abandoned meander.

Once the water that cut this canyon ran in the serpentine channel of a meander, making a great looping sweep here. For some reason—such as a steepening of terrain or a greater stream volume—the water eating away on the outer curves of the meander finally cut through the narrow neck which separated the channels and now runs straighter, leaving a D-shaped island of rock. I walk up to the channel floor of the old meander, which remains higher than the bed of the newer channel below.

The whole channel is paved and walled with rock, going up and around. On the ground the Cedar Mesa Sandstone is weathered into rounded pillowlike forms. Thin exfoliated slabs look like three-dimensional U.S.G.S. contour maps—continents and countries, peninsulas and islands, bounded by the concentric lines of elevation notations. The plates are loose and slip off the parent rock at a touch, falling with a soft clank, crumbling on the ground. Freezing and thawing, wind, and lichens accomplish this disintegration. A vibrantly gray-green crustose lichen, with mustard-brown fruiting bodies, intermingles with the more common charcoal-gray lichens, its distinctive color making it stand out in the patch. I feel in another world here, a world set aside, a canyon museum of what was here before.

What makes the walls here so extraordinarily handsome is the bedding of the Cedar Mesa Sandstone—undulating lines sweeping in the kind of reiterated curves one sees in marbled papers or fingerprint whorls. Sometimes the beds simply sweep upward in an open curve; sometimes they undulate, almost scalloped, ending in a swirl. Because some beds were not as firmly cemented as others when the sand became sandstone, they have weathered more, have lost their sand grains to the wind. Series of holes punctuate the boundary lines between beds, dark ovals and rounds like staring eyes, perforations and chains, holes shadowed behind holes, intricate screens and mysterious facades. And on the rim mushrooms and goblins and stone people, as tall as a two-story building, keep watch.

The inclination of these beds, which lie very nearly as they were originally laid, tells that they were deposited as dunes, either by wind or water currents from the northwest. If it were possible to slice through a sand dune today, as it lies on the beach, these same sinuous lines would be revealed, dipping away from the source of the sand. Most of the sandstone crossbedding is at an angle that suggests the sands were worked by wind, and other bedding lies at an angle that suggests they were formed by longshore ocean currents, much as are ocean sand bars today. For here lay the vacillating shoreline of an inland sea. Water currents that brought white sand from the northwest and laid it near the shore could have been replaced when the ocean retreated, now and then, by wind currents that piled the sand up in beach dunes.

I walk on, pushing through a small scrub-oak thicket. My heart stops—that faint burring, the warning ruffle—where is it? I stand motionless. Afraid to move, afraid not to move, the "watch for buzztail" admonishment sharp in my mind. The wind blows, a rabbitbrush rustles, and I realize that *that* was my rattler. Nevertheless, my awareness is sharpened: when one walks alone in this country one takes on a new responsibility for self.

That whiffling rustle is hard to describe, since it varies, being much faster in warmer weather. All I can say is that once you've heard a rattler you stiffen at any sound faintly resembling it. Dry leaves blowing in a certain way, a small animal dashing through the brush, even a beetle on dead leaves can make my heart stop.

The rattles are a series of loosely interlocking three-lobed segments that cover the tip of the tail, so attached that each rattle covers two lobes of the one beneath it (except for the last one, on which all three lobes are visible). The way in which the rattles interlock and their size gradient tend to hold the whole string raised off the ground, saving wear in traveling; when vibrating, they are held almost straight up. The number of rattles does *not* tell how old a snake is; a new rattle is added at each moult, and snakes frequently moult more than once a year, adding the new rattle at the body end. Strings of rattles usually break off after six or eight are formed; it's rare to find a dozen on a wild snake.

The sun is momentarily blocked by a segment of canyon wall, a wall topped with mushroom rocks, all species and each as big as a house: morels, puffballs, russulas, amanitas. The wind still blows, whistling a little, and its cooling is welcome. A still world with only plants timing the season, and yet they too seem timeless, as if this is the way they've been all century long.

I veer around the last corner of chimney rock, on a shelf about forty feet above the base of the canyon. Behind me the sun shatters on the canyon rim, obliterating its outline, like some baroque apotheosis of light. Sunlight still shines on the west-facing cliff, but where I am it is evening, the only temporal notation I feel. The sky to the east holds brilliant blue, bright and flat. Sunlight hits the tiny residual pools below that are embedded in the newer channel; they cast back murky pewter reflections.

The old meander is dry, carved and left with no more water to pound out holes, no more water to suck the pavement clean, dig out roots, push plants aside, tumble the rocks until the whole canyon booms, no more water to carom around its elegantly curved walls. The

Milkvetch pods *(Astragalus lentiginosus)*

new channel below is straighter, more efficient, but it lacks a curvilinear grace.

6

At night, bright starlight highlights the canyon walls. The big prow of the abandoned meander rises ghostly, and to the north two pinnacles of sandstone gleam extraordinarily white. A solitary frog, perhaps washed down in the last big fence-lifter, bleats a plaintive pulsating song.

I sleep in stop motion, watching the light change. At moonrise, as on many other nights in the canyon, almost simultaneously a draft of wind sighs downcanyon. I doze and wake, plagued by a single maddening mosquito. Two bats swoop overhead in the dawn light: I will them down here to consume the pest. I catnap, awakening finally to sunlight and a crisp morning wind.

When I wash my face in one of the tiny pools near camp the walls are reflected and then set shimmering by a bevy of water striders going out in swift angular movements that make expanding circles on the surface, interlocking and slicing through each other. It is another way of seeing oneself, Narcissus-like, upside-down, haloed with water-strider circles.

I become intimately familiar with these pools because I am in charge of scrubbing cups, spoons, and a small blackened pot that will never shine again. The pools remain all year round, although their perimeters expand and contract with the season. Spring-fed, they lie in a line, from an inch to a foot deep, the shallowest at the upper end. In alternate sun and shade, they are warm to the hand except where the minuscule spring, waffling the surface, freshens them. Being partly shaded, they are not subject to the extreme evaporation and heat of small pools in full sun, and the result is a thick broth teeming with every kind of small creature, in spite of the fact that the omnipresent white alkaline lines show the pools are down more than two inches.

Grayed cottonwood leaves mat the bottom, overlaid with the slender pointed ovals of blackened willow leaves. Small patches of bedrock show through the silt, which is etched with a calligraphy of tracks. The whole bottom is creased and lined with comings and goings, and not a straight line to be seen. The bottom of the pool is quilted with caddisfly larva trails—"rock rollers" in local idiom. One trundles along, leaving

Fragrant sand-verbena *(Abronia fragrans)*

the dragline of its case flanked by a delicate webbing on either side made by its feet. There are several, all actively on the prowl, dragging cases perhaps half an inch long, made out of the debris of the pool bottom. A small black snail leaves a narrower, smoother grove. The alkaline water provides the calcium carbonate necessary for shell building. Another has an egg case attached to its back, an ambulating nursery. Other eggs in their gelatinous coverings are plastered on the wall of the pool and on the leaves. Some snails carry on their shells tufts of bright green algae that sway in the water like ostrich-plume fans.

Fingernail-sized tadpoles flicker across the bottom, then lie still, motionless until one moves and a flurry of movement surges through the rest. Perhaps these are the young of the small canyon tree frogs, which lurk on the dry shelf above the pools. Among the tadpoles a water beetle rows his way in crisp diagonals, and a tiny swarm of seed shrimp are counterparts of the swarming midges above my head.

The pool is swept by a pulsating breeze that moves the water surface back and forth. Two wrigglers—mosquito larvae—are transported six inches north, and snap themselves back to the center again. The small flies that alight on the surface slide with the water's undulation. A few big water striders skate swiftly back and forth, undeterred. All the other movements are so small and so delicate or so slow that, by contrast, the water striders look frenetic, striding off with seven-league boots.

The water stills, and reflects the cottonwoods up on the bank once again. Then a sharp gust corrugates the surface in a precise diamond pattern. A very small water beetle swims, valiantly I think, against the surf that breaks into half-inch-high waves near the shore. Even the striders lose ground. The beetle starts out again. The breeze dies, the peaceful ebb and flow of the movement resumes, the water piled up with the breeze retreats, and a cottonwood leaf, floating barely under the surface, drifts by again—a totality of shifting movement as if each flotsam was held to another by an invisible thread, and when the wind pulls on the thread, all are obliged to move in unison.

Canyon tree frog *(Hyla arenicolor)*

Rushes stalk one edge of a pool, some of the stems bent down to the water, catching light in silken shifts up and down their snail-patroled stems. On a dry rock in front of me, blinking golden eyes, looking like a tiny Buddha, is a canyon tree frog, the size of a pocket watch. With padded toes it clings to the rock, like a boss on the stone, the same color of mottled tan. I wonder how long it's been watching me.

Looking up, I have to refocus my whole vision, which has been tuned to minutiae. Out there are monstrous cottonwood trees chattering in the wind and gigantic sandstone walls. They seem lacking in some basic quality: rock is rock, tree is tree, but I miss the animation of a snail, embellished in algae, sweeping across the bottom like a duchess on her way to be presented to the queen.

7

Walking upcanyon, across slanting ledges of bedrock, is like walking up the steps in a fun house. No angle is sensible. Occasionally a late sand verbena, its sticky stem and leaves as covered with sand as sandpaper, or a milkvetch hung with seedpods, graces the way, but mostly there is just sand, sand and rock.

Snugged against the curving wall of another abandoned meander is an Anasazi dwelling. Made of sticks and branches, it is scarcely visible in the patterns of the landscape. I stand looking up at it, twenty feet above, nestled at the base of a huge overhang, so silent, so preternaturally silent. The parabola of the walls, like a huge receiving radar, must hold the memory of voices, a saucer impregnated with so many answers that we will never hear.

In none of these canyons can one walk without the sense of those who walked here before, the Anasazi. The Navajos coined the word "Anasazi"—"ancient enemies"—to describe a people who had already abandoned the Four Corners region when the Navajos entered. The ancestors of the Anasazi came here at least 15,000 years ago; some archaeologists think that there is evidence of some migration 25,000 or even 40,000 years ago. These people came from Asia, across the Bering Land Bridge, probably turning south and coming down the eastern face of the Rocky Mountains. From here some swung further southwest and west, and others went southeast into the Mississippi River Valley and beyond.

The first evidences of man in the Southwest are established as being

13,000 to 10,000 B.P.—"before present." Populations were small so there were infrequent contacts and minimal exchange of information; there was little chance for cultural evolution, and such a culture remained nearly static for a long period of time.

These earliest peoples were primarily skilled hunters—perhaps too skilled. Although there is considerable discussion, some anthropologists suggest that ancient man may have been the primary factor in the disappearance of the megafauna—the big game mammals—that were once common in the West, for their disappearance came quickly. In a brief thousand years or so, at the close of the Pleistocene Era 10,000 years ago, these big animals were gone. Early man often trapped whole herds, and with no means of preservation could use only part of the meat, leaving the remainder to rot and waste.

At the end of the Pleistocene, climatic changes crept in, too slow for a generation to note perhaps, but over the centuries pushing hunters farther and farther, searching for animals that became fewer and fewer as they responded to a drying climate. Large herbivores are the first to go in a deteriorating ecosystem because of their needs for greater space, food, and cover, disappearing far more quickly than small herbivores, which may better weather the shift, as did the rodents and rabbits of the Southwest. The survival level was low for man and involved exploitation of wide areas simply for subsistence. For some 11,000 years man in the Southwest made use of his natural environment and just survived.

In response to the increasing scarcity of large game animals, between 8000 and 7000 B.P., a semi-nomadic culture, called the Desert Culture, developed a way of life that depended primarily on gathering wild plants, and in which hunting contributed only a minor portion of the food supply. But the same kind of intimate knowledge of the environment was involved as in a successful hunting life: a knowledge of plant species, whether they were healthful or poisonous, at what time of year the parts used were available, and where they could be found in quantity.

Characteristic of semiarid regions is a less varied flora but more individuals of the same species, of economic advantage when these plants are being harvested. Most plants had to be collected in competition with other animals, and consumed according to their storage properties: prickly-pear fruit had to be picked immediately upon ripening and used quickly, while dry amaranth seeds could be stored until needed. Plants of semiarid regions generally have seeds (which were used more than any other plant part) that require little moisture to germinate and therefore remain edible longer, and are not subject to the molds and rots that may spoil seeds with a higher moisture content. Available plants, among dozens that were utilized, were piñon, wild grasses (especially rice grass), saltbush, prickly pear, yucca, sego lily, wild onions, and scrub oak.

Constantly responding to small-game migration and the uncertain productivity of various areas, people of the Desert Culture, probably traveling in bands, lived a restless life of seasonal rounds within a territory familiar to them. There were no permanent settlements, no pottery, no agriculture. Life was opportunistic, adjusted to the available. Equipment for such a life style was light, with few tools, each suited to several tasks. Characteristic are baskets and *metates,* stone slabs (which were more than likely left at various sites and not carried) on which seeds were ground. (Metate is an Aztec word that came north with the Spaniards.) These gatherer-hunters also made excellent nets and snares, simple chipped scrapers, and choppers and points. Larger projectile points were crafted for hunting, while smaller, broader points, often with serrated edges, were of use in gathering and preparing plant foods.

The Desert Culture remained an identifiable entity until sometime around 2000 B.C., by which time maize had reached the American Southwest. Although formal agriculture was not yet practiced, the addition of a slightly more reliable food supply presaged a change in life patterns. About A.D. 1, the first fixed housing appeared, signaling a more stable and sedentary, less nomadic life.

The slope below this one-room dwelling is badly eroded and we detour far around the side to climb up. Although there seems to be no midden heap (ancient inhabitants usually simply tossed any waste out the front door and down the slope) it doesn't mean that there isn't one; there has been no excavation here. Or perhaps the dwelling was only used seasonally, the occupants living the rest of the year on the mesa top. Further down to the left are large depressions in the sandy fill that more than likely indicate the burial and storage hollows called cists.

I crawl to the front opening of the dwelling and peer inside. As my eyes adjust to the light I can see that the floor is cut twelve to eighteen inches deep into the ancient hardpan fill of the overhang. The back wall reveals the stripes of different depositions: darker red clay topped with an uneven pebbly layer, capped with fine sediments. There are four corner posts still standing; the front ones are forked to hold the front-to-back rafters. The rest of the roof is still largely in place, eight-inch crosswise beams crossed by another layer of five-inch poles, alternating crosswise and back to front, four layers in all, covered over with bark shreds and weighted down with large flat rocks. The back wall is blackened with the soot from many fires, and much of the surface rock is spalling off. Bat guano is as thick on the back wall as rodent droppings are on the floor. A huge black-faced bumblebee, bigger than a postage stamp, cruises in while I take notes, his buzzing reverberating.

Primitive, yes: but how many of our houses will be standing eight hundred or so years hence?

8

One of the largest sites in Lower Grand Gulch is the well-known Wetherill Ruin, called so for Richard Wetherill, one of the earliest explorers of the canyon, who wrote on the back wall, "Wetherill, 1894."

The overhang opening, nearly three hundred feet long, faces due west. Because Cedar Mesa Sandstone is such a massive cliff-forming rock, and because Grand Gulch's meanders were formed by water cutting, over the millennia overhangs of considerable dimension have formed by sapping, leaving wide hollows like great clam shells. Seepage along the surface of some impervious layers dissolved the cement between sand grains, which blew or fell out, undermining the strata above. Sometimes the layers fell, like leaves of stone, until over time a vast opening was left in the wall. Blocks of sandstone thundered down and still remain in front of many overhangs, where they form a natural palisade and were often used as grinding and sharpening surfaces by the Anasazi inhabitants.

Standing within this overhang, I gaze outward to the slope below, littered with large angular boulders, over the hidden dry streambed, to the sagebrush terrace across the way. Beyond, the high walls of the canyon curve around, a whole circle of pale walls, ingress and egress obscured, with sentinel balanced rocks along the rim. It seems somehow magical, this circle, this encompassing stillness. The wind bustles outside; I almost hear ancient voices in its low, soft murmuring. Within this overhang not a dead leaf flickers, not a grain of sand moves. A woodpecker attacks a cottonwood; the sharpness of its tack-tack-tack startles me.

This is a Basketmaker site, a term coined by Richard Wetherill to describe a civilization whose remains he found beneath those known as

"Cliff Dwellers" or "Pueblos," the later Anasazi peoples. "Pueblo" was the word used by the Spaniards of the sixteenth century to describe the more settled farmers they found, in contrast to the nomadic Indians roaming the area.

Richard Wetherill came west with his parents in 1879, settling near Bluff, Utah. When the runoff from a torrential downpour hit the Wetherill ranch and took most of it downstream to the Colorado River, the family moved north and settled on the Mancos River, near Mesa Verde. The first sighting of the cliff houses of Mesa Verde by a white man (Ute Indians knew they were there but would not go near them because of the spirits) was in 1887 by Richard's brother, Al Wetherill.

Like Mesa Verde, the ruins of Grand Gulch were explored in what has been characterized as a period of "subsidized vandalism": someone would offer to finance a party to go in and dig ruins in return for a share of the findings. No notes were kept, sites were disturbed, stratigraphy was totally ignored, and there were no laws, federal, state, or local, to prevent widespread pilferage. Today the Antiquities Act of 1906 provides federal control of all archaeological sites on federal lands and establishes a permit system for those wishing to dig.

Perhaps a few Mormons had been into Grand Gulch in search of stray cattle, but Charles B. Lang, a young photographer from Pittsburgh, who later accompanied Wetherill, and a companion were the first recorded explorers in the canyon, sometime prior to the winter of 1890–91, when ranchers Charles McLoyd and C. C. Graham of Durango, Colorado, entered. Ranchers in the summer, they could get away only in wintertime to go relic hunting, and they brought out large numbers of artifacts, which were sold and dispersed.

Richard Wetherill had been systematically digging at Mesa Verde and went to the Chicago World's Fair of 1893 to display his findings. There he met Talbot and Fred Hyde, heirs to a large soap fortune. From this meeting developed the Hyde Exploring Expedition, as Wetherill called it, subsidized by the Hydes, supplied and packed by Wetherill. The first expedition got off in 1893. From Bluff, Wetherill led his wagon train northwest, excavating along the way. When he had the Bears Ears, a prominent local landmark, in sight, he turned west toward Grand Gulch, which he described in his journal:

> Grand Gulch drains nearly all the territory southwest of the Elk Mountain from the McComb wash to the Clay Hills about 1,000 square miles of territory.
>
> It is the most tortuous cañon in the whole of the southwest,

making bends from 200 to 600 yards apart almost its entire length or for 50 miles and each bend means a cave or overhanging cliff. All of these with an exposure to the sun had been occupied by either cliff houses or as burial places.

The cañon is from 300 to 700 feet deep and in many places toward the lower end the bends are cut through by nature making natural bridges.

Wetherill had a sense of mission for this first expedition. He wrote to the Hyde brothers early in 1893 that he intended to number every artifact, make plans of the ruins, and photograph the area before lifting a shovel:

> I think you will find this will meet all the requirements of the most Scientific but if you have any suggestions whatever I will act upon them this whole subject or rather the subject of it is in its infancy and the work we do must stand the most rigid inspection and we do not want to do it in such a manner that anyone in the future can pick flaws in it.

Archaeology *was* in its early period in the United States, and even had Wetherill lived up to current standards there would still have been much lacking compared with modern practice.

By March of 1894 Wetherill had worked down to "Graham Canyon," where C. C. Graham had entered Grand Gulch previously and dug out "more than a hundred caves." (Graham Canyon is now called Bullet Canyon and is still one of the main access routes to Grand Gulch proper.) The expedition was disbanded at the end of March. The 1,216 relics that had been packed out and stored at Bluff were repacked into wagons to go back to Wetherill's ranch, where he would spend two months cataloguing and preparing them for shipment to the Hydes.

The Hyde brothers themselves came out to Grand Gulch in July, 1894, and on their return to New York they took all the maps, negatives, and notes made during the previous winter's expedition. In the fall of 1895 the Hydes presented this collection to the American Museum of Natural History in New York. The field notes and maps have been lost, but the field catalogue, as well as most of the collection, survives in the Department of Anthropology at the museum.

The expedition costs for the whole winter's work came to some $3,000. Wetherill paid himself $25 a week and, to keep costs down, furnished pack stock from his own ranch. While Wetherill was away, his ranch suffered from lack of attention; his loss that year was $2,500. When money was not forthcoming from the Hydes to pay his men, they panned for gold along the San Juan River. Sometimes they could bring in $5 a day; working for Wetherill they got but $1 a day.

But on this trip Wetherill found, beneath the level of Pueblo civilization with which he was familiar at Mesa Verde, burial hollows which he recognized as belonging, by virtue of their placement, to an earlier culture. It was one of the first instances of the use of stratigraphy in Southwestern archaeology. He wrote to Talbot Hyde on December 17, 1893:

> Our success has surpassed all expectation. The party is large that I am working but I am in a country that will be snowed in next month so I wanted to get all I could out of it before that time— In the Cave we are now working we have taken <u>28 skeletons</u> and two more in sight and curios [sic] to tell and a thing that will surprise the Archaeologists of the country is the fact of our finding them at a depth of 5 & 6 feet in a cave in which there are Cliff Dwellings and we find the bodies <u>under</u> the Ruins—3 ft below any cliff dweller sign. They <u>are a different</u> race from anything I have ever seen they had <u>feather cloth</u> and baskets no pottery. . . .

He described round or egg-shaped holes dug in the loose sand, walled up with sandstone slabs when necessary and carefully covered over. In these he found bodies of both sexes and all ages, sometimes wrapped in shrouds made of yucca fibers, sandals on their feet, beads around their necks, cedar-bark breechcloths, blankets made of rabbit fur. What most had in common was the large shallow baskets, often as much as twenty inches in diameter, placed over their heads, heads that were not flattened like those of the Cliff Dwellers.

Wetherill listed what artifacts were included in the cists: spear points, fine bone awls with long hooks on the ends, small baskets containing corn and seeds and sometimes ornaments, usually placed near the head. There were sandals, square-toed and finely woven, and sometimes a brand-new pair was included—perhaps to assure an easy journey to the wherever? If an atlatl was entombed, it was found broken and on top of the body.

Basketmakers hunted with the atlatl, a slender piece of hardwood which simply acted as a lever to extend the arm two or so feet farther, as an aid to hurling a small spear. The atlatl shaft rested on the shoulder and had two loops through which the fingers fitted. The main shaft of the spear was lighter and drilled to accept a detachable foreshaft to which a heavy point was affixed. When thrown with the atlatl's aid, the spear was guided more accurately and with more force than if thrown by the arm alone.

Atlatls were once common in prehistoric cultures throughout the world, and while they are more effective than a hand-held spear, aim is neither as accurate nor range as great as with a bow and arrow. Atlatl points were, however, generally more than twice as heavy as arrow points, and their impact was probably quite authoritative and stunning.

Perhaps even more important, Wetherill also observed, out of his experience of several years of digging Pueblo or "Cliff Dweller" sites, what was *not* found in the Basketmaker burial cists: first of all, no pottery; no bows and arrows; no stone axes; a different kind of sandal; no deformation of the head. He surmised that some of these overhangs may not have been used as residences at all, but as storage and burial sites by a people who were partly agricultural but still roamed widely, gathering and hunting, and who used these caves to store precious grain until the next growing season, and the same cists to bury their dead.

Wetherill wrote of "the Basket People" in a letter to Talbot Hyde, who suggested the term "Basket Maker." Dr. Prudden published Wetherill's theory in the June, 1897, issue of *Harper's Monthly* in an article entitled "An Elder Brother to the Cliff Dwellers." In 1902 the American Museum of Natural History *Journal* contained an article on the subject by George Pepper, an archaeologist. Despite these prestigious publications, Wetherill's find was considered a possible hoax for many years and was not verified until 1914, when the Southwestern archaeologist *par excellence,* Dr. Alfred V. Kidder, along with Samuel Guernsey, established the reality of the Basketmakers at a cave in Arizona. By that time Richard Wetherill was dead.

9

Southwestern archaeology came of age with A. V. Kidder, a pioneer in stratigraphy and one of the most beloved and influential scholars in the country. Kidder combined intellect, sensitivity, and a love for the Southwest. After pioneer work on the Anasazi, he left to study the Mayan culture; many years later he returned to the United States and visited Emil Haury, another well-known archaeologist, who was at work in the Southwest. Kidder recorded his reaction: "It was all most upsetting, because for years I had been struggling to get the Southwestern virus out of my system—and here it was back again worse than ever.

And at Haury's diggings good honest Southwestern pottery—not fancy Maya stuff—was coming out of the ground. I had a wonderful time with those sherds, particularly the corrugated ones."

The rapid accumulation of data about the Southwest prompted Kidder to call a conference in 1927 while he was working at Pecos Pueblo in New Mexico. Here the assembled scholars attempted to bring order out of chaos by classifying the cultures with which they were dealing. They set up three periods of Basketmaker culture—Basketmaker I, II, and III—and four of Pueblo—Pueblo I, II, III, and IV (actually the biggest break is between Basketmaker II and III rather than between Basketmaker and Pueblo). The Pecos classification has stood, with adjustments, for fifty years and is the basic framework of Anasazi culture. Richard Wetherill's distinction between "the Basket People" and later cultures has survived as part of the standard terminology of Southwestern archaeology.

Another felicitous occurrence took place at the same time: the development of tree-ring dating, or dendrochronology. This supplied, especially in the Southwest, accurate dating for many of the ruins and a chronology of considerable precision. Dendrochronology was the brainchild of Dr. A. E. Douglass, an astronomer at the University of Arizona, who suspected that the effects of climate would show in tree growth. He designed a corer by which a sample of the tree's growth rings could be extracted.

Each year most tree species add one growth ring; the flow of sap upward in the spring followed by the summer's growth produces large thin-walled cells with a light yellow color. As cold weather approaches the cells become smaller, their walls become thicker. Growth stops for the year and a smooth reddish layer forms at the outside of the growth ring.

In semiarid areas like the Southwest, trees respond with great sensitivity to rainfall. For piñon, ponderosa, and Douglas fir that grow where moisture is marginal, or on dry slopes or in exposed situations, the growth rings reflect the amount of moisture available to the tree for each specific year; fortuitously, these woods were also widely used as beams in Anasazi dwellings. (Juniper often grows too eccentrically for good dating; cottonwood is unuseable because it only grows where there is moisture and its growth rings are quite uniform.)

After Douglass began his work he soon realized that ring patterns could be cross-correlated because of their definite patterning in time; the variable sequence of thick, thin, and medium rings is essentially distinct for any period of a few decades or more. He then developed a master pattern against which a new core could be matched.

In 1929, two years after the first Pecos conference, the initial link was made between a historic and a "floating" prehistoric sequence, with cores from a Southwestern pueblo that extended the chronology to A.D. 700. In the last fifty years the chronology has been extended back to 200 B.C., providing an accuracy of dating for the Southwestern archaeologist that characterizes almost no other research. It is far superior to Carbon 14 dating, which gives a plus/minus reading with a large margin. Some tree-ring series can be dated to the year, sometimes even to the season, in which the building was constructed, although the economical Anasazi builders often re-used timbers, which makes acute archaeological observation a necessity. Recently considerable refining has taken place, documenting precisely what affects tree-ring growth and when, and how individual species react to these various stimuli.

10

Wetherill Ruin was not a permanent living area; there are no blackened patches on the wall that would indicate cooking fires. Unlike most Anasazi overhangs, it faces west and does not receive morning sun. It appears to have been primarily a storage and burial area, with any habitation on a temporary basis. Huge boulders bear smooth depressions which could have been used as massive in-place metates, or grinding hollows. Thin grooves mark where stone tools or sticks could have been sharpened. A typical Basketmaker metate contained an oval depression, indicating that the hand stone, or mano, was worked in an oval or circular motion—as opposed to the linear motion more prevalent in Pueblo times, which left a straight trough. Corn would have been ground on these metates, as well as piñon nuts, berries, and seeds (Anasazi teeth display extreme wear—worn down to the gums at an early age, because of the amount of sand in their stone-ground food).

Because Wetherill Ruin has been thoroughly worked over the years, there is mostly just rock debris left. When found undisturbed, burial cists can yield a wealth of information. In one cave, upcanyon, more skeletons of children than adults were found, each laid away wrapped in a turkey-feather blanket. How precious children must have been to an agricultural society, as opposed to a hunting and gathering group, in which they would have hampered mobility, and how few must have survived. The turkey-feather robes were light and warm. Soft feathers were split down the vane to make them more flexible; rabbit or other fur was cut into thin strips. Both were then wound around fiber cords. The encased cords were then laid parallel to each other and connected by twined cross cords, creating a very warm, very light and open blanket.

In another group of cists great numbers of sandals were found, partially completed. All were worked "off-hand"—that is, without a last, and weaving began at the toe, giving a somewhat crescent shape. Some have been found with the loose ends of the weaving fibers tied in a bunch to keep them from tangling until time could be found to complete the sandals. Finely woven in an over-and-under weave, woven double so that designs on top did not extend through to the raised pattern on the sole, they were tied on by a loop fitted over the toes and another over the heel and arch; various ties attached around the sole and could be wound up and about the ankle. One needs only to look down at the rough-pebbled and cactus-strewn ground to realize the worth of a good pair of foot protectors!

11

A couple of Basketmaker cists in upper Grand Gulch were opened very recently (Wetherill was at that site too, and inscribed his name and "January 26, 1894"). In one was found a bundle of ash splints, ready to be used in weaving a basket. Although baskets were made throughout Anasazi history, relatively few were made after the advent of pottery making, which was much less time consuming.

Basketmaker baskets are exquisitely made. A long coil was formed with a center of one or more firm sticks, such as peeled willow withes, accompanied by a bundle of grass or other fibrous material laid parallel to them. Coiling began in the center of the base, and was sewn together with thin splints of wood or tough bark until the desired size and shape was reached, much as in making a coiled pot. Sewing extended through the coils; sometimes the stitches were interlocked, sometimes laid side by side. The tightness of the weaving was such that some baskets were actually waterproof.

I remember a small basket fragment weathering out of a midden pile, about a square inch worth. I blew off the dirt and held in my hand the work of a meticulous craftswoman (pottery and baskets both, if one

goes by ethnological evidence, were made by women). So firmly woven
was it that I could not finger it apart to see the precise technique,
although a curl of loose splint showed it to have been sewn in interlocking fashion. The splints were scarcely an eighth inch wide, and where
one ended and the next began was a joining so skillful that it was several
minutes before I discerned the fag end.

Other variants of the basic weaving techniques of twining, coiling,
and plaiting, some thirty in all, were used by Anasazi basketmakers to
form utilitarian trays, bowls, carrying baskets, and ceremonial baskets.
Often they were plain. Designs were limited by the geometric character
of the technique itself, and were infinitely more difficult to execute
symmetrically than on pottery. A potter could divide and compartmen-
talize the areas to be decorated when the pot was finished. The basket
weaver had to count off even increments at the beginning and maintain
the symmetry while extra stitches were added as the basket flared.
Decoration tended to be in quadrants, or in a wide band between two
boundary lines. Rims were finished with varying and elaborate braids
that hid the rough ends.

The strength and order of these basket designs provided a ready
example when early pottery was decorated. Much easier to make and
reliably waterproof when correctly fired, pottery replaced the time-
consuming art of basketmaking, but never entirely. Baskets were still
made, although much less frequently, to the end of Pueblo times. Many

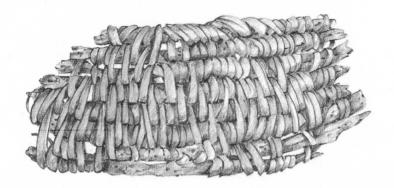

Fragment of Basketmaker III basket woven in stitch-and-wrap, interlocked, on
one-rod foundation, with rim finished in false braid. From Earl H. Morris and
Robert F. Burgh, *Anasazi Basketry, Basket Maker II through Pueblo III* (Washington,
D.C.: Carnegie Institution Publication 533, 1941)

an early pot bears the imprint of the basket that supported it during coiling.

12

I look down the length of the great overhang and see only empty hollows filling in with sliding sand, and a few fragments of pottery. There are no unopened cists here in Wetherill Ruin to yield exciting finds. In 1972 a salvage team worked here, identifying forty-eight loot-ers' pits, and concluded that there were few research possibilities left. They described the tragedy of unregulated pilferage throughout Grand Gulch:

> The cumulative effect of these activities has been the thorough but unsystematic reworking of much of the fill in the cave floor areas at these sites, the creation of numerous pits and backdirt piles in these disturbed areas of cave floor fill, and the scattering about on the surface of the sites of large quantities of cultural material, both per-ishable and non-perishable. This material includes, among other things, human bone, cordage and basketry fragments, and ceramic and lithic debris. . . . The depletion of the cultural resource repre-sented by the sites in Grand Gulch has continued at varying but probably continuous rates since . . . 1891. Observations by Bureau of Land Management personnel and others familiar with the area over a period of time indicate that the depletion process is still continuing at a significant rate through illegal digging, accidental or intentional damage to structural features, and the casual pocketing of surface artifacts. Since its establishment as a Primitive Area in 1970, Grand Gulch appears to have experienced a growth in visitor traffic. While this traffic is not necessarily related to the more serious forms of "pot-hunting" and looting, it does indicate a need for increased atten-tion to be given to the conditions of archaeological sites in the area and to their overall protection.

Every time I stand in this ruin I have the same feeling of disappoint-ment. Beginning as a pot hunter who cleared out sites for personal gain, Wetherill developed a respect and a fascination for the sites he worked, and did do scientific digging as far as it was known in the late nineteenth century, learned how to use a trowel and brush, along with the necessity of keeping notes (albeit skeletal ones) to indicate where he found vari-ous objects *in situ*. Because of this he lies somewhere between the

grave-robber and the legitimate archaeologist, and although the prove-
nance of many objects he carted out of Grand Gulch is blurred forever,
at least most of the objects themselves are preserved and protected in
museums.

Still, how much we could have learned had these sites been left
intact if only for a little longer. With sophisticated interpretation of
tree-ring data, pollen-analysis studies, archeomagnetic dating, and
other esoteric means, plus meticulous mapping and stratigraphic control, modern archaeologists can extract considerably more information.
And how much more will future archaeologists learn, with newer methods and newer insights, from those ruins we leave today? Archaeological sites are nonrenewable resources: once disturbed, they can never be
studied in their original richness again.

13

Across from Wetherill Ruin, but hidden from it by intervening cottonwoods and sagebrush and a turn of the terrace, is an immense panel of
pictographs and petroglyphs, the former painted, the latter incised into
the sandstone wall. There are hundreds of figures, very nearly the whole
vocabulary of Anasazi art, among them stiff-shouldered anthropomorphs (a generic term to cover human figures of all kinds) with
necklaces and hair bobs and headdresses; atlatls, ducks, and birds;
mountain sheep; racks of corn and corn flowers; zigzag serpents.

There seem to be two styles of representation in Anasazi rock art.
One is more naturalistic, the other more formal. The naturalistic human
and animal figures are generally smaller. I remember a very small petroglyph in upper Grand Gulch that haunts me still, as much for the
implied meaning as for the skill of the artist who has chiseled very
simple figures that yet convey action and emotion.

On the left are two human figures; there is something feminine
about one of them, perhaps in the greater suppleness of line. Both
figures reach toward the center of the panel, where a duck, facing right,
is depicted with a child mounted on its back. The child turns, stretching
its arms as if pleading not to be borne away.

In contrast to the poignant relationship between these three human
figures, others on the right, by their verve and movement, seem to be
rejoicing. Although possibly unrelated, these figures seem part of the
whole meaning to me, connected, important. And yet I can't say why:

are they dancing at the return of the child? or at the child's capture? Is it a kidnapping? It is evidently a very old petroglyph because the edges are eroding, the figures themselves are darkening. Nevertheless, the artist bridges the centuries, conveys with great economy of line something palpable, vivid, indelible, and unique.

Quite different in aspect are the large anthropomorphs—human figures presented frontally, drawn with large triangular torsos, small arms and legs, adorned with headdresses and chest ornaments. Yet these hieratic figures often tempt interpretation too. I wonder about the ones, painted in white, arrayed just above my head, a long row of figures rank on rank, with their right hands raised in the same greeting or salute, almost like the Hollywood Indian saying "How!" Was this particular canyon a crossroads where people of different bands came, and did this sign indicate friendship and peace? Or was the raised arm a warning, and the long row of figures an indication of many warriors?

This rock art, across from Wetherill Ruin, is up on a very high shelf, and standing here I can look down on the big alluvial terrace below. Now filled with sagebrush, perhaps once it contained Indian corn, wreathed with bean plants, that on such a day as this would have rustled and glistened in the sunshine breeze.

I am high enough so that a flutter-winged swallow flies at eye level. The sound of the wind is all below. Here all is quiet and warm. Across the canyon it looks as if the clouds stand still and the rim wall moves. As I sit here alone, a canyon wren's descending call arising from the next meander loop down, the wind just off stage, carrying across other walls, I think that this must have been a good place to live. The basics are all here: a place to grow corn, a shelter to protect from rain, a nearby seep for water, the purring of the wind, the coolness of the rocks in shadow, the beauty of the day.

14

After being in lower Grand Gulch for a while, one's eye becomes attuned to every rectangular shadow that could betray a granary or a dwelling door. As my eyes trace the cliffside two dark squares punctuate a narrow overhang. I work up to them, a hundred feet or so above the sagebrush terrace.

Granaries are secreted throughout this whole area, usually tucked away as this one is. Occasionally ears of corn remain, anywhere from three to four inches long, sometimes up to eight, with eight to twelve rows of kernels, small cobs that describe less than optimal growing conditions. But they also describe a life with some measure of security, allowed by a surplus of grain to be stored.

Anasazi maize cobs

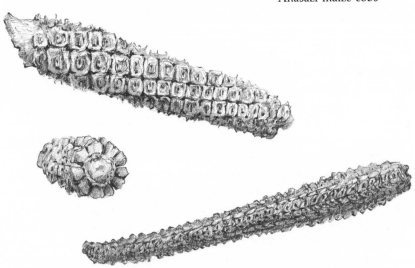

The maize grown by the Hopi Indians today needs a 130-day growing season and it is probably grown in much the same way as that of the Anasazi: several grains are dropped into a deep hole, dug with a stick, to assure the extensive fibrous root system access to deep water. (*Maize* is the proper name for Indian corn and derives from the Spanish *maiz;* the plant itself derives from Mesoamerica.) Maize is one of those unique happenings in the plant kingdom, a plant unlike any other, a single species in its genus, very nearly a single genus in its family, known now only in cultivation. It is a Western Hemisphere grass whose ancestry is still clouded. Wild maize pollen, found in peat layers beneath Mexico City, dates to 80,000 years ago. Genetically a very plastic species, maize through time crossed and recrossed with itself and with another native grass, *teosinte,* which it closely resembles. Ears an inch long were growing in Mexico 5,000 years before Christ; by 3000 or 2500 B.C. maize had spread into the American Southwest.

Male tassels at the top of the stalk shed pollen, which simply drops onto the female parts of the plant below, although it can be wind-carried. Each strand of "silk" is a stigma, receptive to pollen along most of its length. When fertilized, the corn kernel develops and remains attached to the woody cob in double rows, a great advantage to man over wild grasses that shatter when ripe, meaning a large loss in forage. Of the six varieties of *Zea mays* (dent, flint, pop, pod, soft, and sweet), the Anasazi grew primarily flint from the beginning. Flint is a hard-grained maize with very little soft starch, and it grinds into a good cornmeal. Corn, for the equivalent nutritional value, could be grown on smaller segments of land than corresponding wild plant foods.

Actually maize is quite well adapted to dry climates like that of the semi-arid Southwest. The upper side of the leaves contains large wedge-shaped cells that absorb moisture during rains, but shrink in dry weather, causing the leaf to roll upward along the edges. Less surface is available for evaporation, and the lower surface of the leaf, where there is a thicker protective cuticle, is the one exposed. Twenty inches is considered optimum rainfall for maize; the ten inches that fall on the Grand Gulch Plateau provide just marginal growing conditions.

An attractive food like maize was probably easily assimilated into a daily pattern of foraging and gathering, and at the beginning probably played only a minor role in diet, being just another one of many plants ground in the same metates with the same manos. Over time, larger harvests appeared. The best seed could be selected and stored for next year's crop. Instead of subsistence keyed to the vagaries of wild plants, there were what must have seemed miraculous surpluses. And assuredly the Anasazi practiced selectivity, which increased harvest size and nutrition each year.

Corn dried well and could be used throughout the year, providing a needed buffer against an unproductive winter; when heated it popped into a tender and tasty morsel from an inedible hard kernel. It was a reliable source of fats, carbohydrates, a little protein, minerals, and vitamins. However, the seasonal scheduling involved with planting, cultivation, and harvest was a long time in coming. Some two thousand years passed between the first appearance of maize and actual agriculture. When it came it brought massive changes in life style as well as nutrition. Underground storage had been employed for centuries; and now more storage areas were dug; granaries were built to house grain over the winter, constructed with care to be rodent-proof and moisture-proof, hidden away where those who had less would not be likely to find them. A like investment in labor was made for the first housing.

Rain is most needed for corn at the critical times of germination and new growth, and if there is no rain, someone has to carry water. When the grain is ripe, someone has to be there to harvest it. If too many weeds appear, someone has to be there to pull them out. And so a semi-nomadic life gave way to a sedentary one, and the cave walls blackened with the fires of many winters, and more shelters were built, more people lived together, and life must have seemed good indeed.

15

Walking up the canyon I see good places for growing a few mounds of maize in every low terrace. I speculate: Is this where I would plant, or here? Would there be enough water from that seep to fill an olla to water the new shoots? As the sky clots with clouds, I think only of the beneficence of that rain, watering the corn to fill the granary snuggled in that narrow overhang just ahead, ears filled with plump kernels.

I am brought sharply back to the present by the swift narrowing of the canyon, sandstone walls so close I can very nearly touch both sides at once. Thunder mutters. These narrows below Collins Spring Canyon, where we will walk out, are *not* the place to be if there is a rainstorm up on the rim. The sight of a log wedged far above my head goads me into a quicker pace.

Collins Spring Canyon is the only ingress or egress on the west side of Grand Gulch that can be negotiated with any safety. The head of Collins Spring Canyon is reached by a kidney-jolting oilpan-grabber road, used by most travelers in and out. Other accesses to Grand Gulch —Kane or Bullet canyons—are far toward the head of Grand Gulch. Hikers can come down at Polly's Island on the east side, but only after a ridiculous cross-country drive compounded of lost trails and deep sand. One can climb out of the canyon at a few places, although it would be precarious to try to do so with a pack. One emerges onto an expanse of slickrock where there is so little water that traversing the area is sheer lunacy. And furthermore, it's easy to get rimrocked—climbing up is much easier here than getting down. Up there, in that slickrock wilderness, everything has an appalling tendency to look the same.

The drizzle begins, and I put on a poncho as we start the two-mile trek upward. The sight of flotsam and jetsam left by more recent inhabitants of the canyon interrupts my thoughts—rusty baking-powder and bean cans, left by the cowboys who ran cattle in this canyon up until about fifteen years ago, lie in a heap. For Collins Spring Canyon is also the only place to bring cattle into the lower canyon, and the trail we follow upward is an improved version of what must have been a devil-ish descent. With its reliable water source and sheltered overhangs, this was a natural campsite for those early cowboys.

Harve Williams worked for and had an interest in the SS Cattle Company (SS stands for Scorup and Somerville, the main owners of what was one of the largest herds of cattle in the West) and tells about those years in Grand Gulch and Collins Spring:

> We'd put the grain down and put a tarpaulin over it, then put the sand back on it. But them ol' rats couldn't get in there, she was too loose—fill up's hole as fast as he dug. Yea, I've put flour in that Collins cave, left it up t'two or three years. Yes, you c'n keep anything as long as you keep it back away from the rock. If you bury it up close to the rock it'd draw moisture from that rock, but not back out in the cave. A lot of good caves in that country to camp in.

The SS Cattle Company was started by J. A. Scorup and Jim Scorup of Salina, Utah. Nineteen in 1891, young J. A. Scorup wanted more than anything else to be a cowboy with his own herd. In March of that year a Salina rancher asked J. A. to take care of 150 longhorns of his, which were running wild in White Canyon, just north of the San Juan on the east side of the Colorado River; J. A. was to get one-third of the calves born of those spooky wild cattle. With high hopes he left home "with a spare horse, a couple of patchwork quilts, and a dream." Once over in the White Canyon area, he began to run out of food; he put the cattle in a box canyon and hired out to an outfit trailing cattle to Colorado. On his return he was greeted by armed Texans and told to get out of their territory. And stay out.

Dashed, J. A. went back to Salina to tell his employer what had happened. This time he was offered one-half the cattle born. With some ingenuity and "neglecting" to tell his older brother Jim about the Texans ensconced in the canyon, he got Jim to return with him and persuaded other Salina ranchers to entrust him with some three hundred head of their cattle. When they got back to White Canyon, the Texans were still there, so Jim and J. A., eschewing a confrontation, ran their cattle north into such outlandishly wild country that the Texans didn't bother them.

Wild horses competed for forage; mountain lions and wolves went after the calves. The brothers lived like Indians, shooting an occasional deer, burying their supplies in the floors of the big overhangs, sleeping in the shelter of caves. Supplies were three days' ride away, at Bluff, Utah. Once a wild steer ripped open J. A.'s leg and nearly tore off his kneecap; he lashed himself to the saddle and made it those three long days to Bluff to get himself put back together.

The Texans pulled out. The Scorup herd began to grow. When times were hard they practically hand-fed their stock; when competition moved in, they had to spend as much time herding others' cattle off as they did moving theirs to good grazing spots. When they needed money, J. A. would go off and round up wild cattle at $5 a head; one spring he brought in two thousand and deposited $10,000 in the bank. With the money, the brothers bought carefully and increased both the size and quality of their herd, bringing the first registered Herefords into the area. By 1912 their "Lazy TY" was branded on cattle that grazed thousands of acres over San Juan County.

Jim Scorup returned to Salina and married in 1908, commuting the six hundred miles back to the Grand Gulch Plateau until he retired and the outfit was sold in 1918. J. A., however, almost immediately entered into negotiations for a new spread, much to Jim's discomfiture, for he had no intention of returning to ranching. They went back into the ranching business with the Somerville brothers, Bill and Andrew, incorporating as Scorup-Somerville Cattle Company, known locally as the SS.

The winter of 1919–20 was a bitter one for J. A. Not only did his brother Jim die, but the weather on the range was brutal and the company's financial losses were great. Cattle died like flies; to survive J. A. paid $1.50 apiece to have the carcasses skinned and sold the hides for 28 cents a pound. But weather improved, and by 1927 the Forest Service had issued the SS Cattle Company a grazing permit for 6,780 head, the largest permit yet issued in the United States. In succeeding years 7,000 to 10,000 head roamed over close to two million acres.

J. A. Scorup died in 1959. In 1965 the SS was sold to Charles Redd, who divided it into four portions. Redd maintained Grand Gulch, as the Scorups had, as a preserve for specially bred cattle, "the aristocrats." But when Grand Gulch was designated a Primitive Area in 1970, he withdrew his cattle.

San Juan country is still largely cattle country, and Scorup-Somerville cattle still wander over much of it. But that era is nearly gone. Lake Powell covers the crossing where the Scorup brothers struggled to get their cattle across as it also inundates part of Hole-in-the-Rock. Much of the winter range is included within the boundaries of Canyonlands National Park. Those who rode with J. A. are nearly all gone, men who remember well the hardness of the life, men with deep creases at the corners of their eyes from squinting against the sun and picking out a lost calf in the shadow of a sagebrush and chasing wild cows, men who woke up with snow a foot deep on their bedrolls and cooked hot biscuits in a Dutch oven, a way of life gone with the coming of trucks and jeeps, a way of life that is, in many ways, much missed.

16

I stand on the ledge at the top of Collins Canyon and look back and down. The canyon turns, twisting out of sight, screening the gulch itself, as if the only way one is allowed knowledge of what went before is to go down and find out. A thin corner of blue sky catches on a sandstone pinnacle: so different up here, slickrock rolling away for miles, so open, windswept, windtorn. The canyon, sheltered by its cocoon of sun-warmed walls, is to me a halcyon place.

I turn away with regret, feeling freshly molted. Down in the canyon I grew a little, understood a little more, perceived even more, and in so doing split the carapace of time and place I commonly wear. Split it, wriggled out of it, left it there, a stiff and empty shell to be blown away by a canyon wind. The new skin was extra-sensitive, and so I perceived the canyon about me with new eyes, more sensitive touch, emotions closer to the surface, and I walked protective of this as yet unhardened integument.

And now I walk out, having experienced this shucking-off of everyday ways, to return to the everyday world. But for a short while that newly bared skin is too delicate to cope with the noise and the smell and the denser necessities of living. It takes a few days for the new carapace to harden, smooth out, protect again. Until then I feel as vulnerable as the crab skittering across the rock in his new soft clothes or the dragonfly clinging to the sedge stalk and tentatively flexing wrinkled wings.

One of the least frequented and probably also one of the most inaccessible parts of the United States. A great rift in the earth, tortuous and fantastic, with mushroom or toadstool rocks, monuments of standing, seated, and bust figures, hats atilt, and every conceivable form and shape on which imagination seizes or turns into semblances of life. . . . The general course is northeast to southwest, but the hot sun makes one aware that we face in turn every point of the compass.

NELS C. NELSON, *Field Notes,* 1920

For those who like to brave the sun, who do not shun rough fare, are not fastidious in drinking water, and can ride day after day over a rough, baked, almost trackless land, there is a vast region west and north-west from Mancos, reaching over to the Colorado River and beyond which is little visited, full of wild, scarcely explored canyons with many prehistoric ruins not mentioned in the books, quaint carvings on the cliffs and far outlooks from volcanic summits and from the rims of lofty mesas.

T. MITCHELL PRUDDEN, *On the Great American Plateau,* 1906

Upper Grand Gulch

1

I haven't been on a horse since I was fifteen years old and then the horse and I parted company with a mutual lack of esteem. But Pete Steele assures me that Buddy is kind of heart, tolerant, gentle, narrow of girth, and broad of mind.

Pete has been (and is) among other things a uranium miner, a wrangler and rancher, and, that most demanding of professions, a rodeo clown. He now lives in Monticello, Utah, and does commercial packing and guiding. He stops his truck across from the Kane Gulch Ranger Station and I watch from a respectful distance as he unloads Buddy and his own horse.

After the horses are down he unloads his two pack mules. Watching him cinch the packs on tight I am reminded of Nels C. Nelson, an archaeologist from the American Museum of Natural History, who worked upper Grand Gulch in 1920 and who commented about the same procedure:

> To see mules being packed for the first time is liable to elicit considerable sympathy. The tightening of the cinch is accompanied by such grunting and groaning that it seems cruel. But after seeing a mule, in process of being loaded, deliberately, quick as a flash, rear up and throw himself on his back, breaking the packsaddle; watch one lie down repeatedly in an attempt to rid himself of his load; and try in vain to mount one, being kicked in the bargain, one's heart soon hardens.

One of Pete's mules is named Esther, after "a difficult woman with peculiarities," and the other, Jane, the traditional name for a "good mule." Pete says that she was an exceedingly obstreperous and willful mule who kicked and bucked on being packed, but then she got caught in some quicksand and had to be dug out "a time or two so now she thinks people are pretty neat anymore." Pete swears that mules thrive on affection and indeed it seems so with Jane.

Ranger Cynthia Simmons arrives to take our permit, and tells us that we are the ninety-sixth party to go down this year. Now that Grand Gulch is designated a Primitive Area and administered by the Bureau of Land Management in Monticello, a small field station has been set up at the head of Kane Gulch. Records have been kept since the ranger station opened in 1974, indicating gradually increasing usage over the past seasons.

She asks if we have grain, since horses may not graze in Grand Gulch this year because of the drought, and must be kept hobbled or tied up at night so they don't get into the water. She advises that all toilet paper should be burned, and all litter carried out, and that so far this year the litter situation is good in Grand Gulch.

The management of BLM primitive areas is patterned after that of Wilderness Areas as set forth in the Wilderness Act of 1964—to preserve and protect their quality, open them to study and research and to public use and enjoyment that does not conflict with wilderness values. Under the new Federal Land Policy and Management Act of 1976 (better known as the Organic Act) primitive areas become eligible to enter the wilderness system's more permanent Congressional protection. Grand Gulch is being studied for a possible change from "primitive" to "wilderness" status, with the recommendation due to be made in 1980.

2

Much too soon it's time to go. I take a deep breath and heave myself up onto Buddy's back. Since I'm sure I'm going to go right on over in approved slapstick fashion, it is with great relief that I view the world from between Buddy's ears and realize that I am safe and sound, and that it isn't half as high up as I remember. However, I've just been reading Richard Wetherill's notes on his second and last trip into Grand Gulch in 1897 and they provide little comfort: "We had several extra ones [horses] on the way down to use in case of accidents which proved of frequent occurence [sic]. One animal fell off a bridge and broke its neck. Another fell off the trail where it wound about a ledge, going into the cañon, and was killed instantly. Another fell off a cliff with the same result."

Pete takes the lead, trailing Jane and Esther; Buddy and I follow. We ride across a sagebrush flat and then begin the descent into Kane Canyon, which was originally called Wetherill Canyon. A steep declivity comes all at once. I catch my breath: from the height of Buddy's back I look straight down through the stirrups for what must be two hundred feet. Pete has already started down with the mules and I can hear the pack boxes banging on the rocks alongside the trail. Having watched these two mules sashay through slot openings without scraping off a splinter, I realize how narrow the trail is. Trail! It's a footpath, and no horse as wide as Buddy with four legs to worry about can ever negotiate it, Pete's example notwithstanding.

I open my mouth to holler to ask Pete if I can dismount and lead Buddy down when, unsignaled, Buddy begins the descent. The saddle tilts forward at a forty-five-degree angle. Buddy takes the first angle of the switchback in three pieces as if he were a three-car train. I quash my desire to close my eyes. When I go off I want to see where I'm going. I leave fingernail prints in the pommel; my knuckles are as white as my face. I take off half a sagebrush between stirrup and flank. I have visions of one catching on my boot and hauling me off Buddy's precipitous back.

The next sound I hear is Buddy's shoes clacking on the bedrock of the channel. That I am still astride is a matter of some wonderment. I look back up the canyonside and as quickly look back down again— some things are better not known. And so we proceed, down slickrock steps, across alluvial terraces, sometimes up on a bankside, sometimes down in a sandy channel, sometimes on a rock-strewn streambed. Periodically I enjoy looking up and around, something I don't have a chance to do when backpacking. Two blue-winged teal flush out of some high grass. A raven and two red-tailed hawks wheel and dive, almost as if they were playing; there's a misjudgment of distance and speed on someone's part—the raven and a hawk have a near miss and explode outward in the sky.

But then Buddy, as well I empathize, stumbles on the unstable rocks in the streambed and I nearly come unglued from the saddle and so spend the next half hour watching Buddy's footing for him, which he obviously doesn't appreciate but which provides great solace for me.

We reach the junction of Kane with Grand Gulch proper. Like many canyon joinings, this one holds an Anasazi habitation, the largest I've yet seen in the canyons. It is an ideal site, beneath a curving overhang three hundred feet long and twenty-five feet deep, that allows exposure to the east, southeast, and south, benefiting from the early rays of the sun. Unless the rain was blowing, the interior would have been dry. It is high off the streambed, unaffected by flash floods, behind a screen of scrub oak that follows the dripline of the overhang.

Junction Ruin is extensive, and to my pleasure we spend most of the afternoon here (Pete explains that all the major ruins in Grand Gulch have been named in order to make location of accidents, vandalism, etc., simpler). Pete is a knowledgeable and articulate guide, and in addition has a real affection for these ruins and generously shares his knowledge. A self-admitted "Moqui-poacher" of years back ("Moqui" is an old and inaccurate term for Hopi), he became more and more concerned, as he learned about the ancients who lived here, for the survival of these ruins. In consequence he is a dedicated and forceful conservationist.

On the back wall is scratched "J. Wetherill 1920" and "No. 73 AMNH 1920 N.C.N." and "B.T.B.H. 1920." All refer to a survey conducted in 1920 by Nels C. Nelson of the American Museum of Natural History, guided by John Wetherill, Richard's younger brother, and accompanied by B. T. B. Hyde, his mentor. Nelson led this expedition in an effort to identify Richard Wetherill's numbered sites and so document the artifacts in the possession of the museum.

Tucked under the overhang are wattle-and-daub structures, the ceremonial rooms called kivas, some hardpan cists excavated by earlier Basketmakers, ghost walls (the light stripes left between blackened areas where walls once stood), and masonry-walled living and storage structures built by later Pueblo occupants, some twenty constructions in all. Obviously the site was used for a long period of time by both cultures, perhaps the full length of Anasazi occupation. Tree-ring dates show a flurry of building activity in the late 1000s and early 1100s. The presence of Pueblo-period Anasazi is also indicated by pottery sherds executed in specific and datable styles (there are also some sherds that may point to Basketmaker III occupation), trough metates in which grain and seeds were ground in a linear back-and-forth motion, and multi-roomed dwellings with masonry walls. Probably at any one time, in spite of the multiplicity of rooms, no more than one or at most a few extended family based households lived here. In Basketmaker times, at different periods families may have grouped together for seasonal activities such as hunting, but probably they did not live in more permanent communities until later Pueblo times. Small communities such as here were common, but large town-sized settlements developed only in a few places like Chaco Canyon and Mesa Verde.

The walls vary from undressed sandstone slabs, with more mud mortar than rock, to bifacially chipped stones rather carefully laid, cushioned with mud. Although the mortared walls were probably built by men, plastering was likely done by women. Mortar often oozed out between the stones, and handprint impressions are deep, as if trying to shore it up. Sometimes tiny stones are embedded into it in simple decorative patterns. The plastering of finer mud is patted more smoothly. On one wall a hand impression is very clear; my square hand just fits into it—and indeed, at five feet, I must be close to the size of an Anasazi woman.

Later I sit beneath an ancient multiple-trunked cottonwood, tipped over on its side. Where the roots are pulled out of the soil they form a cage in which debris and silt have caught, and the cakes of silt look exactly like Anasazi mortar—lumpy, full of twigs, studded with pebbles.

3

As opposed to the highly dispersed settlements of Basketmaker times, in which each unit had to supply more or less all its own needs, Pueblo society drew together in more permanent aggregations, characterized by greater division of labor and more formally defined social roles. One of the manifestations of this change was the formalized kiva, the round subterranean ceremonial chamber so characteristic of Anasazi culture, a structure that developed out of the semi-subterranean pithouses of early Basketmaker dwellings. *Kiva*, suggested by John Wesley Powell, is the anglicization of the Hopi name for these ceremonial structures. One of the most important adjuncts of Anasazi society, the kiva continues nearly unchanged in use and design in modern Pueblo villages.

Three kinds of rooms—for storage, habitation, or ceremonial use—characterize building complexes in prehistoric Pueblo times, becoming fairly discernible by A.D. 800–900. Blackened walls, metate and meal bins and the residues from grinding, and large numbers of pottery sherds generally signal habitation space. Storage rooms contain large amounts of pollen, with corn, beans, and squash dominating. These rooms are often small and dark, obviously not for living. Ceremonial structures are notable for their standardized circular floor plan.

In early kivas, as in early pithouses, four posts supported the roof beams; these would have been in the way for ceremonies and dancing. During Pueblo II the posts were moved outward, and it would have been only a step from shoring up a leaning support with rocks and adobe, connecting it to the outer wall, to incorporating the support itself as part of that wall.

I look down into one of the three kivas here; since the roof is long gone one can see the floor plan laid out. It is approximately fifteen feet across; a banquette some four feet high surrounds the perimeter; from this, six supporting pilasters rise upon which logs were laid crib fashion (an eight-inch-diameter cottonwood roof beam with stone ax marks remains and the vertical supports were also of cottonwood, which makes dating difficult); the next course was laid across the angles of the beams below, until the opening was small enough to receive parallel logs. The roof this formed was heaped over with bark and brush, with an opening left for access.

On a north-south line bisecting the kiva, I can make out the venti-lator shaft, fire deflector, fire pit, although the *sipapu* is no longer visible. The tiny hole of the sipapu was the symbolic opening in the earth by which Anasazi ancestors were thought to have risen into the sunlight of the upper world from the dark, damp world below. Placed in front of the ventilator shaft that was connected to the outside, the deflector prevented downdrafts from blowing out the fire or gusting ashes all over, and aided in air circulation in the closed chamber.

The wall above the banquette contains about equal amounts of mortar and stone. Once burned out, it was built up again and replastered at least twice after construction. In the original plan, four posts held up the roof and it may originally have been a pithouse; after one fire the more "modern" six pilasters were erected and it assumed the formal characteristics of a kiva.

Used mainly by men of a tribe or group, the kiva had both religious and secular importance. In historic and contemporary Pueblo groups, men traditionally did the weaving and usually did so in the kiva. The important religious ceremonies that tied a group together took place here, and occasionally these included women and children. Originally the kiva may simply have been an extended family or village gathering place, and the first kivas were probably modest semi-subterranean rooms such as those found throughout the San Juan region dating from around A.D. 700. As population grew and specialization developed, and with increasing dependence on a few crops, more time had to be spent developing the ceremonies which propitiated the spirits who would

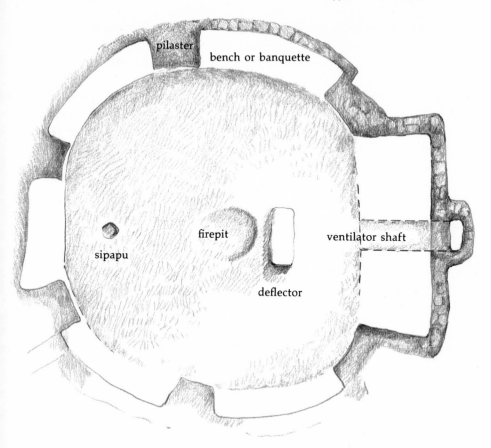

Kiva from Junction Ruin, courtesy of Dr. William Lipe, and John C. McGregor, *Southwestern Archaeology* (Urbana: University of Illinois Press), p. 287

bring rains for those crops, a different pantheon from that of the hunter. And with the formalization of the ceremonial aspects of the kiva came a similar formalizing of its structure, a conservative design that, once developed, continued to present-day Pueblos.

The shift to late Basketmaker and then to Pueblo cultures was most probably the result of new ideas filtering into an area psychologically ready to receive and assimilate them. Trade existed with other areas, and both maize growing and pottery making diffused northward from Mesoamerica into the American Southwest. Although early maize was not very productive and formed only a minor component of diet, by A.D. 500 beans were being grown in the Southwest and farming itself was more productive. Maize is a good source of starch but lacks some of the amino acids necessary to make complete protein. Protein would have been in good supply as long as there was time for extensive hunting, but caring for crops curtailed the time an Anasazi once spent pursuing game. Beans not only improve the soil through nitrogen-fixation, they also contain the important amino acid lysine, lacking in corn. The combination of the two plants would have been an important nutritional breakthrough even without any improvement in strain, and may possibly have been one of those accidental "kicks" that, increasing the survival rate, eventually brought about a change in social organization. At any rate, population did enlarge considerably during the Basketmaker III–Pueblo I period, as witnessed by increasing numbers of habitation sites with a greater volume of artifacts and more storage structures. By Pueblo II times the largest population of the Anasazi era was reached in the San Juan drainage.

Between A.D. 700 and 1000 other new products appeared. Cotton was introduced, much better than yucca or human hair or dogbane fibers for weaving; distinctive pottery decoration and refinements of technique developed. Pottery making did not actually arrive until some two thousand years after maize, but was a craft that dovetailed with the sedentary life demanded by an agricultural existence—easily breakable pottery is almost nonexistent in nomadic cultures. Ring baskets were widely made, while the more time-demanding coil baskets diminished in popularity; the bow and arrow appeared, with points now lighter, as befitted this more efficient and portable hunting tool. The use of hard cradle boards flattened babies' heads into "short skulls," as opposed to the undeformed Basketmaker heads that had rested on more flexible and soft cradle boards.

At this time turkeys were also domesticated. Another of the well-visited sites, Turkey Pen is a few miles down from Junction Ruin. Turkey Pen is so designated for an unusual isolated "jacal" structure, of which only part of the wattle wall remains; it looks very much like a pen. "Jacal" and "wattle-and-daub" are synonymous, a simple building technique utilizing various-sized sticks set in place and tied together with plant fibers, and then plastered over with mud. Where these materials are available it is a commonly used building technique in primitive societies.

Whether or not the "pen" was ever used to house turkeys, the name Turkey Pen may not be too much of a misnomer. Wetherill wrote: "The debris seemed to be too much for us to work in the limited time we had.

Also too filthy. As it was composed almost entirely of desicated [sic] turkey droppings we worked down into them to a depth of 7 feet and did not come to the bottom."

4

I stand at the foot of Junction Ruin's extensive midden heap. Often midden heaps provide excellent clues as to the occupation of the inhabitants. But such loose fill is very subject to erosion, especially from boot pressure as people walk on it.

Some stabilization was attempted here when the midden heap was a foot higher. The stabilization is, to my eye, awkward—some cement tinted the wrong color of pink, which looks as if it had been simply dumped in place. A better suggestion for saving the remainder has been made: channel traffic by means of subtly placed boulders or logs and sacrifice a narrow strip of midden to a path.

Whether to stabilize or not is a thorny question. If done skillfully and discreetly, it probably preserves the site in its near-original aspect. Judgments have to be made on a site-by-site basis. If it means such an alteration of the site that it loses its quintessential character, then some archaeologists feel that more radical responses are called for. One might be salvage excavation, to obtain information before the site deteriorates further; another would be closing the site to unsupervised visitor entry. The worth of the archaeological sites in Grand Gulch is that they *are* here to be learned from, to be understood in all their rich complexity and relation to the natural world around them rather than fragmented, disassembled, and closeted behind glass in an air-conditioned museum. Consequently, the hope is that they can be both protected *and* visited by the public.

All sorts of interesting tidbits protrude from this midden heap: a curved tooth that looks like that of a bobcat, pieces of corn cob, soft cotton string, shreds of bark (used for bedding and diapers), turkey feathers, preserved through the centuries because of the dry climate. Pete stoops down to show me a three-inch piece of string caught in the dirt, a fine hard twist that would have been a good utilitarian cord, made of cotton. A bunch of yucca fibers are tied in a square knot, which the Anasazi used exclusively—a beautiful restoration done in another canyon gives itself away by using granny knots.

A sliver of what looks like straw protrudes from the dirt, and without thinking I finger it loose and hold a shred of what must have been a ring basket made from yucca leaves. Tough fibers extend from the root to the tip of the yucca leaf. Being plentiful here, yucca is often used for cordage and weaving. Ring baskets were fashioned of dried yucca strips, which were soaked and, while pliable, woven into a flat mat. While the mat was still damp it was manipulated into an osier ring and bound and finished with a braided rim.

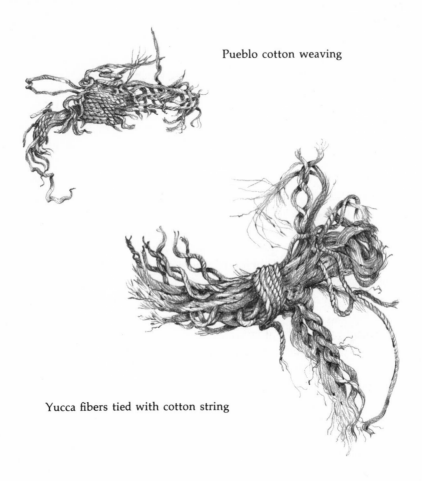

Pueblo cotton weaving

Yucca fibers tied with cotton string

Plain twill weaving (over two, under two) was elaborated with other combinations of over-and-under, black-dyed strips woven in a cross pattern design, and various meander patterns. The latter may look easy but are not because of the way in which a formula has to be established from the beginning to insure an unbroken pattern as the mat grows outward; two anthropologists trying to duplicate some of these patterns found the venture so time-consuming that they completed only one sample in paper strips. Although many ring baskets are finely woven, the technique itself generally gives an open weave. The shape was not subject to variation as that of coiled baskets was, and ring baskets were most likely utilitarian, used for gathering and winnowing.

Ring basket fragments and braided rim (Morris & Burgh)

Hopi "yucca sifter baskets" are still being made in an identical way today, although the occasional maker may substitute a coat-hanger wire for the osier ring.

5

Large pieces of pottery lie on a big flat rock. A wide variety of corrugated ware is displayed, some with rows of corrugations contrasted against smooth bands, others with various pinch patterns. A sturdy handle once garnished a jar or pitcher. A sherd with a hole drilled in it was undoubtedly laced through with yucca fiber or willow splints to a corresponding hole on an adjacent piece, an efficient means of mending a pot or keeping a crack from going further. Pitch was also used for repairing and to restore waterproofness. This gray corrugated ware was probably used mostly for cooking; a whole pot in which the corrugations are arranged in a pattern is a very handsome piece. I have come to enjoy the corrugated ware as much as the decorated work, if not more.

I pick up a large sherd of pottery lying on the ground. Well smoothed, grayish white, it curves only slightly, likely a segment of a large open bowl. Beneath it is a glimmer of brilliant iridescent green: a tiny beetle carapace. I finger the sherd, admiring the evenness of the wall, the smoothness of the surface. The message that comes through my fingertips is that a skilled hand must have made this pot, knowledgeable of technique, sure of touch.

Rising to the west are the Clay Hills and closer by, Halgaito Shale cliffs, only two of many places whence this clay may have come, this peculiar fine-grained material that becomes plastic and workable when mixed with water and permanent when fired. A fascinating material, made up of very fine crystalline structures like minute plates, more or less hexagonal in shape. When fired at a high enough temperature this crystalline structure is destroyed and the individual particles become permanently bonded in an earthenware vessel.

Early potters undoubtedly learned from trial and error. When clay absorbs water, it expands. When it dries, clay cracks with shrinkage. By introducing another, nonplastic substance, called a temper, the shrinkage can be controlled. From using grass and bark in unfired vessels, potters progressed to sand or ground-up sherds or rock. Although temper weakens the paste, it also reduces the amount of water needed to make the clay workable, and therefore reduces the potential of cracking as the vessel dries. Ground sherds, even though they required more labor to process than sand, were obviously recognized in time as a more effective temper, the sharp, irregular grains adhering to the clay structure better than the rounded ones of sand.

When it became leather-hard, and again when completely dry, the pot was polished, important for a smooth finish, since glazes were not usually used. Often, so thoroughly was the surface rubbed at various stages during construction—with a waterworn pebble, a piece of gourd, a sherd, or a bone—that it seems as if a slip must have been used. (A slip is a suspension of fine clay in water, with no temper, which when fired forms a thin coating on the vessel, a refinement of technique that smooths the surface, seals the pores in the clay, and often enhances the color of the finished pot.) And in fact, in such lengthy and meticulous smoothing, the finest particles of clay float to the surface in a very thin emulsion with the water that is used in the process. On occasion, true slips were used.

After drying, the pot was fired. During firing, which is essentially a dehydration process, oxidation destroys the organic impurities in the clay and heat cements the original crystalline structure into a single whole. There must have been many superstitions about firing pots, just

Rocky Mountain beeplant *(Cleome serrulata)*

as there are today. Some potters feel that it is bad luck to watch the kiln. Zuñi potters fear a loud noise might be a "voice" that will enter the pot during firing and shatter it.

The Anasazi undoubtedly did as Southwestern Indians do today, built a simple updraft kiln—often in a beehive shape—when and where necessary. Firing is done with the pottery either in a pit or raised above the ground on rocks or large sherds, and lasts scarcely an hour. The pots must be protected from contact with the fuel, else the surface blackens with a "fire cloud." Present-day Indian potters use sheep dung; more probably the Anasazi, with no large domestic animals, burned juniper wood, of which they had a plenitude. It burns easily and rapidly and makes a hot fire with little smoke, retaining its shape, important in lowering the chance of fuel fall against the pots.

The gray color of the sherd in my hand is due to firing in a reducing atmosphere, when the fuel consumes all the oxygen in the kiln and takes oxygen from the mineral constituents of the clay, a firing technique distinctive to this area. The original color of the clay could have been red or yellow, rust or buff, but when fired in this manner, it turned gray. Such firing dates from the beginning of Anasazi pottery making and was used for hundreds of years. Vessel sizes and shapes, methods and styles of decorating, and the kind of temper used changed with time; the basic coil construction of a pot and its firing, once a reducing method was established, did not.

Under my hand lens I can see the coarseness of the clay; there is even a certain graininess to the polished surface. Yet considerable care was taken in evening the wall. The firing was good, the color a uniform gray, suggesting little fluctuation in temperature. I set it back on the earth; where it lay warm in my hand there is now a cool place.

6

A black-on-white design decorates a piece with a squared-off rim; this rim edge and the design are both characteristic of the pottery style known as Mesa Verde Black-on-White. The pearl-like luster of the white background, the bold and neatly done charcoal-black design are a singular combination.

The present-day Hopi potter first simmers a solution of mustard or beeplant, removes the fibrous remains, and boils the residue down to a thick black syrup. Allowed to dry and harden, it keeps until needed. She grinds a small chunk with water on a special metate, sometimes including a piece of hematite, which adds iron oxide to the paint. If a pot is fired in an oxidizing atmosphere, all the carbon from the plant matter burns out, but in a reducing atmosphere the carbon is not totally destroyed, and during firing it is protected by a thin film of silica, an impurity in the hematite, leaving a bold black design. However, a considerable amount of prehistoric pottery has carbon paint without hematite or other minerals; Mesa Verde Black-on-White pottery, in which the carbon did not burn out, was probably accomplished by, among other things, assiduous polishing.

I pick up a beautiful red-on-orange sherd scarcely more than an eighth inch thick, a fine piece of pottery making. In Pueblo III times, in the Kayenta, Arizona, area just south of Grand Gulch, there was an interest in oxidized ware, where oxygen was present during firing, producing this lovely orange-red. Polychrome pottery of this period is rather rare and uncommonly good-looking, combinations of red and orange and black being particularly stunning.

In all innocence I remark to Pete how lovely it is to have a chance to see pieces of pottery like these out in the open, where one can pick

Mesa Verde Black-on-White (Courtesy American Museum of Natural History)

them up and examine them in hand. And one still has the quick pleasure of discovering a sherd in the sand and putting it out for someone else to enjoy. Pete harrumphs and indicates that he thinks this display is not only pretty meager but of low quality besides.

When he first began bringing people here, he says, there were some really beautiful pieces, large, well painted. But in the intervening years they have gradually disappeared, probably the "Oh, it's so pretty! It won't matter if I take *just* one!" syndrome, and so they've gone, in spite of the Antiquities Act that makes it a federal offense to remove any artifacts.

7

High, high up on the walls at Junction Ruin are mud splats, which occur frequently at these sites, daubs of mud the size of a fifty-cent piece or so, obviously flipped with considerable force. Were they made by children playing, seeing who could get the highest? Or by someone practicing his aim, someone whose food supply depended upon the accurate coordination of eye and hand? There are also handprints, and they appear so often on the canyon walls that sometimes they seem more than innocent glee—a temporal notation? An indication of how many people lived here?

Lower, petroglyphs are chiseled into the wall surface, and in spite of a certain stiffness engendered by the technique, they frequently have great spirit and vitality. A coyote streaks across the sandstone, tail streaming out behind. Two mountain sheep, one above the other, face in opposite directions and seem just to have turned their heads. Some are more geometric: an elaborate yucca design is chipped into the shallow of a boulder, fitting into the irregular confines of the space. Many of these petroglyphs are faint, difficult to see; only in shadow, where the difference in depth can be seen, do they show off well. Full sun obliterates their borders and they are, for this reason, quite difficult to photograph; a flash simply washes out what are at best minimal contours. The alternative of chalking in the contours is an abomination and fortunately has only been done once or twice in Grand Gulch.

To the right, pecked into a dark varnished panel, are human figures, facing each other, dancing to the flute playing of Kokopelli, the priapic humpbacked flute player. Except in this instance (as often in Grand Gulch portrayals) he has no hump, but the flute playing is unmistakable and the dancing figures are lively. Kokopelli is a familiar figure in

Anasazi art and a striking one. Associated with fertility as well as the hunt, he is sometimes represented as a locust, Locust being the musical and curing patron of present-day Hopi flute societies, and clan symbol for the Spider Clan.

Elsewhere in Grand Gulch Kokopelli appears as a combination Pied Piper and St. Francis of the canyons; he stands facing a mountain sheep that looks at him intently—mountain sheep are notoriously curious and I can well imagine one enticed to the sound of Kokopelli's flute. Perhaps Kokopelli enchants him, rendering him easier to kill. On another panel, far down the canyon, a butterfly-like shape takes flight near two atlatls while Kokopelli plays: a charm so that the atlatls would fly (as Pete suggests) "like a butterfly," their aim true, the hunting good?

Kokopelli's popularity is documented on countless walls, beginning in Basketmaker times, but the iconography most surely goes back to sources far to the south. Various medical reasons have been suggested to explain Kokopelli's distinctive attributes, such as bone tuberculosis, which could have caused both his hump and constant erection, a symptom of spinal irritation, but no reason seems as reasonable or as realistic as the postulation of an ancient ancestor, blanket full of belongings or trade goods slung over his shoulder, flute to his lips, wandering between villages like a medieval minstrel, likely a glamorous figure bringing news from exotic places, seducing a nubile female or two along the way. One anthropologist suggests that, in just such a pack as Kokopelli's, corn might have been carried from Mesoamerica.

Kokopelli is also a katchina—a deified ancestor—to the Hopi, and the ceremonies attached to his presence are to say the least ribald, emphasizing his sexual prowess. Such ceremonies are rarely performed now because their bawdy choreography was offensive to early white observers.

But the original Kokopelli still dances on the walls of Grand Gulch in full panoply. Panels with Kokopelli have an enchanting animation, a vivacity, that the hieratic figures lack. I can almost hear the music of his flute, a trifle reedy in sound, but chuckling and full of delightful phrasing, irreverent and rollickingly suggestive.

Other representations are painted on the walls: rabbit tracks, like big exclamation points, hop up the wall; ducks swim in the air, separated by vertical lines; figures, likely male, with hair bobs and necklaces, face the spectator—men wore their hair in bobs like two short pony tails sticking out to the sides, while Anasazi women often wore theirs short, trimming it to use in weaving.

But always the enigma: are they doodles? messages? The keen

observation of natural forms indicates a far from primitive drawing ability, but the haphazard arrangement leaves the modern left-to-right mind at sea. Is there a connection between the dwelling site and the rock art, or were they done separately with no temporal connotations at all?

What I do sense in my own head, is that some cool morning, when there was time, an early resident took stone in hand and chipped out a record of something important—perhaps the visit of a trader from the South, or a ceremony, or the ducks he saw yesterday, or a dance—and left the figures for all to see. And then went on about his business.

8

Boarding Buddy a second time is much easier. But Buddy has discovered that he's carrying a soft heart under a softer head, that allows him to graze along the way. Consequently we lag farther and farther behind. Pete waits patiently for us to come around the bend.

"Make him keep up!" he instructs me.

"But he wants to eat all the time," I reply, which seems perfectly logical to me but must be utter nonsense to Pete, who knows very well that either of us is bigger and more authoritative than a horse that weighs three times as much. "Just give the reins a good jerk and pull his head up," he tells me and starts off again. Esther gives me what I consider a very superior look.

In half a mile Buddy spots a succulent clump of grass. Down goes the head. Up snap the reins. Down goes the head again. This time I wrap the reins around my hand and give them a jerk that I think will dislocate Buddy's neck and, at the least cause him to buck and take off, dragging me with one foot caught in the stirrup. The head comes up, the ears come up. Then he begins walking, although his whole gait is one of weary resignation. And he proceeds thus, a momentarily disciplined horse, until we reach a ten-foot bank that angles up to a terrace. There he breaks into a full canter. I hang on to anything I can hang on to, including a good handful of mane. The pounding of his hooves causes Pete to turn around in the saddle, at which point Buddy stops dead, looks innocent, and begins walking. I could wring his neck.

Still, in spite of Buddy's and my communications problems, April is an exhilarating time in these canyons. Beside me, black brush bears tiny yellow flowers on attractive spiky branches. Grass shoots six inches

Blackbrush *(Coleogyne ramosissimum)*

tall are almost in bloom. New green enlivens the base of encelia tussocks. Yellow parsley is in bloom, fresh leaves close to the ground unbothered by breezes that flick the dry stalks of last summer. Over all a writhing juniper, mostly dead but with one branch still determinedly green, casts a grotesque shadow. Pink-and-white rocks are encrusted with charcoal-gray lichens, not even a fingernail thick; where pieces have scabbed off, the rock beneath is fresh salmon pink.

The three dominant colors in this landscape are rosy beige, charcoal gray, and olive green. There are occasional dashes of bright green, but otherwise the landscape color is very subdued. Of gray there are lichen, desert varnish, dead stalks and tussocks, juniper and bitterbrush branches, and driftwood. Grays are often in intricate shapes, from snaggy twisted branches to the pointillist dots of lichens to desert varnish stripes. Olive green is rounded or fan-shaped: the roundness of pine-needle clusters on piñon, or the shape of the whole tree across the way. But mostly the streaked and blotched warm beige of Cedar Mesa Sandstone, swirled and layered, holds the world together. From here two-thirds of the world I see is sandstone.

Far ahead virga draw curving fingers across the sky, curtains of rain that do not reach the earth below, common in the Southwest. Weather is coming in, from almost due south. Soon no sun shows at all, and I button up my wool shirt, zip up a windbreaker over it, and pull on gloves. Spring in the canyons is not necessarily warm and balmy. It's just as likely to be reluctant and annoyed with having to put in an appearance, maybe wishing it had stayed in bed a little longer.

As we ride on downcanyon, I admire the crossbedding in the sandstone wall that defines the right side of the channel. I note a sharp demarcation line: below, the sandstone is pale and clean; above, it's the weathered mouse gray Cedar Mesa often becomes. The line is at eye level as I sit astride Buddy. Suddenly the realization dawns: this is the height at which flash floods tear through here!

Flash floods have been a fact of life in this canyon for untold centuries. A 1953 survey party noted that they had to resort to "time-consuming stadia traverses" because of the difficulty of crossing canyons, and "such traverses could not be made in the deep canyons cutting Grand Gulch Plateau because of the growing danger from recurring flash floods." Pete tells me you can hear a flash flood roar as it comes racing downcanyon. Although there are floods in this canyon big enough to perch foot-diameter logs on a shelf twenty or thirty feet aboveground, most are smaller and not so long-lived; high flow seldom lasts long although during that time water velocity is quite high.

The bore of a flash flood carries twigs and branches and other debris, swept off the slickrock and picked up off the canyon floor. Rocks roll in the turbulent water, knocking and pounding together. Dr. William Lipe, an archaeologist who maintained a summer field station for many years on Cedar Mesa, tells of six- to eight-foot sandstone slabs banging around in flash flood down a tributary of Grand Gulch. The color of the water is invariably red with mud and silt. After the storm, chunks of the bank which have been wetted fall off in successive plops into the streambed to be swept away in the next flood. A single flash flood can carry away much more ground than would result from months or even years of a small stream's regular flow. After the water sinks into the sandy soil, all that is left is ripple patterns in the sand, debris woven into shrubbery along the banks, and small ephemeral pools that evaporate to shiny patches of silt.

Herbert Gregory, a U.S.G.S. geologist who must have loved this country, for he did so many years of field work here, acutely observed the vagaries of weather and described the environment that engenders flash flooding:

> The sudden violence of the showers in a country almost barren of soil and vegetation results in a maximum amount of run-off, for little of the water soaks deeply into the ground. The falling rain gathers almost immediately into rivulets and gulleys, which carry it swiftly into the larger drainage channels. During heavy storms sheets of water cover much of the surface and roll along to some depression or plunge over the cliffs as a nearly continuous waterfall. In the canyons a turbulent, swollen flood of dirty, débris-laden water quickly appears, where before there may have been not even a trickle, and the waters may rise several feet in almost as few minutes. In narrow sections of the canyons the water may reach a height of 15 or even 20 feet above the canyon floor, and in many places it is dangerous to be caught during a heavy storm. To one not acquainted with the plateau country it is surprising to see the tumbling, noisy "wall of water" advance swiftly down a dry watercourse at a time when the immediately surrounding country is bone dry.

9

The horses' hooves ring on bedrock pavement and we traverse a reach of canyon where raw dirt walls tower thirty feet above us. Pete remembers when there was alluvial fill on the bottom of the wash and the walls were not nearly so high.

There have been other erosion cycles in the canyons, depending upon local conditions and rainfall. Archaeological excavations show a period of alluvium deposition that suggests that some areas of the

Boxelder *(Acer negundo)*

canyon during Pueblo times were marshy; the presence of so many ducks, and occasionally other waterfowl, in prehistoric petroglyphs and pictographs tends to uphold this. There have been other cycles since, but the predominant one of the present seems to be erosion.

Much cutting is extremely local. In the narrows of this canyon, log pile-ups, packed with debris, can form very effective dams. Such a dam downstream would have allowed silt and sand during certain periods to fill in behind it. When the dam broke, a new stream channel would have been established by the new steepness of the bed. In all the side canyons we enter in this reach of upper Grand Gulch, evidence of such adjustment is clear. That ground level was originally much higher is brought home after we scramble up bank after bank to where rock paintings and dwellings now stand isolated far above the streambed, and access to dwellings that clearly once were entered nearly on grade becomes difficult to impossible.

We explore more pictographs, more ruins, each of which seems to be up a higher, steeper wall than the last one. Back in one little V of a small tributary canyon, where the walls warm and reflect their heat into a narrow slot of ground, spring is much farther on its way. Drifts of tiny white mustards bloom. The boxelders are leafed out. As with most plants growing here, prehistoric Indians made full use of them: the sap was boiled to form sugar; the inner bark was boiled to make a decoction used as an emetic; pipe stems were fashioned from twigs; the wood, burned to charcoal, was used for body painting.

The boxelders are raining boxelder bugs. About half an inch long, the adults are dark gray with conspicuous red lines, making a W on their backs. We must have come just after an emergence; boxelder bugs hibernate in hollow trees or other sheltered places and often appear in masses on warm days.

The young bugs, bright vermilion, hatch from red eggs laid in cracks of boxelder tree bark. They emerge in the spring, when they feed on the fresh foliage. They will become marked with black when they are about half grown. Now they pepper the ground like paprika.

10

Richard Wetherill came back to Grand Gulch a second and last time in 1897, funded by a wealthy "Harvard scamp," George Banks, and his tutor, C. E. Whitmore, who were looking for a little educational adventure and were willing to spend a little money to find it. Unlike the mild winter of Wetherill's first trip, this was a typically bitter Grand Gulch winter and the expedition remained but a month. When the temperature dropped below freezing, all the day's glass plate negatives were spoiled. They found no grass, and the forty pack animals, forced to subsist on inadequate vegetation, became weak and thin. There were frequent accidents with the animals. One night in the snow Wetherill worried about the mummies left exposed and got up to rescue them, asking his new wife where she'd like him to put them. "At the foot, Mr. Wetherill. At the foot of the bed." And there they leaned all night.

Up a narrow canyon spattered with blood-red penstemons is one of the sites Wetherill dug on this trip. This is a complex and fascinating site, one which had been dug out even before Wetherill; the names of C. C. Graham and Charles McLoyd of Durango are scratched on the wall as well as that of James Ethridge, who was here with Wetherill in 1893. Heavy looting over recent years (fifty-two looters' pits have been tagged) has left the site in a precarious state: walls are in danger of collapse, scattered dirt and open holes are an invitation to more vandalism.

Until a few years ago, the mesa immediately above this site was easily accessible to vehicles; that ingress has since been closed off. But, even without vehicular access, many of the archaeological sites in Grand Gulch are vulnerable; it's impossible to protect every single one, especially those on the periphery that are more easily reached and most vulnerable to vandalism. A change in public attitude would be the most effective cure for vandalism, and the BLM attempts to provide this by interpreting the value of these ruins to visitors as they come through the Kane Ranger Station (it goes without saying that looters are not likely to make use of the main entrance). In some cases helicopter patrols can spot both looters and their parked vehicles from the air in time to apprehend them, but the courts are generally unnecessarily lenient, and those who walk the canyons for peace and quiet take vigorous exception to the intrusion of the helicopters.

Wetherill, who dug here in both 1894 and 1897, penciled a description of this site that is skeletal but accurate:

> The cave is on the N. or N.E. side of the Cañon and opens very
> little above the bottom of the Arroya. But in the Central and Western
> part a talus from the roof has filled it up 30 or 40 feet upon this this
> [sic] small detached houses are built and between the Rocks and Cliff

Firecracker penstemon *(Penstemon eatonii)*

are the few Pot holes dug out by us. The Cave is 200 ft long, 50 ft
high and 50 deep at center. These measurements of course depend for
correctness upon where we amagined [sic] the Cave began and ended
— This is the only cave in the Cañon. It has a small Cliff house in cleft
higher up—
  The face of the Cliff on the north side is covered with painted
pictures In Red, Yellow, Green, Brown & White. We failed to get a
negative of them.

One of these large figures painted in red is striking: emphasis is made
of the breasts and the portrayal is clearly of a woman. A tiny figure is
positioned between her legs in breech-birth position. Among the many
reasons for wall paintings must have been commemoration of unusual
or frightening events—as such a birth certainly would have been.

The figure beside her, also outlined in red and done in the same
style and scale, has two slashes in the side. And here Wetherill did find
a mummy with a gash in its side, sewn up with a braided cord of human
hair. In a letter to B. T. B. Hyde, February 4, 1894, Wetherill described
what he found:

> It is a very old man cave dweller. He was cut in two at the loin
> and abdomen, or rather the skin is, and sewed together again with a
> string at least an eighth of an inch in diameter, with stitches one half
> inch apart. It seems most horrible to me. The face seems to indicate
> pain. The hands are clutched on the cut upon the stomach.

Some of what Wetherill found and removed from this cave to ship
East is listed in a letter to Hyde, dated January 24, 1898; he is enumerat-
ing the contents of a single shipment:

> I have shipped to you to-day one Barrel by Express, weighing 107
> pounds—at 12½ cts per pound—and a valuation of $500.00 costing
> .75 or 1.00 more—This Barrel Contains 169 sandals, 18 Jar Rings, 44
> Baskets and material for making. 3 ears of corn 2. Bags of Corn and
> 1. Package of Corn and Beans. 2 Bunches of Herbs. 2. Feather Blankets
> 3. pieces of feather blanket. 1. Feather skirt. 1 Bunch Cedar Bark rope.
> 2. Bunches Cedar bark tinder. 5. pieces Mt. Sheep Skin. 1. Piece Buck
> skin. 1 Buck skin String. 1 Buckskin bag containing Azurite. 4 Pieces
> Cotton Blanket 23 Bunches Turca [sic] material—See balance on other
> sheets—in all 361 numbers.

As we head downstream to the mouth of Bullet Canyon, Buddy for
the time being has given up grazing and trots along behind Esther.
Esther takes umbrage and attempts to pull up alongside Jane in a wide

place in the channel. Jane turns and gives Esther what-for. Jane is *first* mule and not likely to let anyone forget it.

When we set up camp for the evening, Pete asks if I would answer a question for him: "When I asked if you would like to camp up at that last site, you said no. How come?"

I hadn't really thought of it, but there was a coldness there—easy to explain because the canyon was in shadow. Still, I had felt an uneasiness that hadn't even seeped into consciousness until Pete asked. It was just a place where I didn't feel comfortable; a certain edge of violence was there, of pain perhaps, of tragedy.

"Me, too," Pete confesses. "That is *one* place I don't ever want to spend the night!"

11

When I wake up to eternity I'd prefer it to be just like this: under a venerable cottonwood just leafing out, sunlight sliding down the canyon wall, the soft rustle of dried cottonwood leaves on the ground, a canyon wren caroling, and then the silence of an April morning.

I hear the clang of Pete setting the lid on the Dutch oven. We've had fresh biscuits morning and night on this trip, and add to that some delectable apricot jam that Jackie, Pete's wife, made from their own apricot tree, and I think perhaps Buddy's doleful look when I climb on his back is because of my ever-increasing weight. Backpackers certainly don't carry cast-iron Dutch ovens and quart jars of jam!

As I butter my fifth and last biscuit, I look up to see a bird in the bush opposite—bigger than a junco, smaller than a robin, white breast, bright orange wash on the sides, head so dark brown as to look black; a gorgeous rufous-sided towhee, red eye a-glitter. It is a bird of open brush, its brilliant color making it seem hand-painted, fastened to a bush in a diorama.

A double-door granary is visible from where we sit. Pete tells me that one hard winter in the gulch, when feed was very scarce, cowboys found enough maize in the Anasazi granaries to tide their horses over.

I pack up my duffel after breakfast and neaten up where I slept, which in this case means messing up: kicking back the rocks that anchored my ground cloth, scuffling the leaves and twigs where it lay, smoothing out the hollow in the sand. Then while Pete packs Jane and Esther I sketch an early milkvetch with lavender and white flowers.

Longleaf phlox *(Phlox longifolia)*

We've come down some 1,220 feet so far, and using the rule of thumb that the temperature changes four degrees for every thousand feet, we seem to be crossing first-bloom thresholds and find many flowers in bloom here that were just in bud at the beginning. Drawing these milkvetches as the sun warms my back I realize in what an optimum place they grow.

There may be better ways to start the day but I sure can't think of any.

12

We dismount and file up a side canyon. The walls get closer together, and I have that queasy feeling that precedes a rock walk. Every time Pete reassures me that "it's not bad" I know it's going to be worse than ever. And this time, not only going up is bad, but access is across a narrow, narrow ledge under a low overhang.

After crawling through this, around a turn a wall blocks entrance to the site. In it is a narrow keyhole door. On the inner side of the door are two loops. Defense: a rock slab was emplaced, a sturdy stick slid behind it held in place by the loops; it would have been nearly impregnable. Looking down I realize that the valley floor must have been about twenty feet higher centuries ago, but this site is still a respectable leg-breaking distance above, and anyone who wanted to come up here had better have been "friend."

These fortified entryways to nearly inaccessible ruins began to appear in Pueblo III times between A.D. 1100 and 1300, especially in the 1200s. A larger proportion of the dwellings were built down in the canyons themselves, secreted away in small side canyons, or tucked in overhangs far above the main canyon floor, much less accessible than mesa-top sites or even such sites as Junction Ruin. They are more defensible and often smaller in size. Other entryways we climb up to have peepholes, each canted to a different approach. Although shooting an arrow through these apertures would have been difficult, anyone approaching would have been both well observed and vulnerable. Along with these defensible sites went an abandonment of the more open Pueblo II sites and a migration to the larger population centers of Arizona, Colorado, and New Mexico.

Up here, in this impossible slot of rock, a wattle-and-daub granary is built up against the curve of the back wall, its slab doorway miraculously intact. I poke my head inside and wait for my eyes to become accustomed to the darkness. And what I see is the most exquisite possible job of tying willow sticks. A channel of mud was laid around the bottom; wet willow wands were tucked into it and wedged into place against the ceiling—if not done this way, when the branches dried and eventually shrank, they broke the seal. These withes, each a uniform thumb's thickness, still fit perfectly into every indentation in the rock ceiling, snug and precise and tight.

Five horizontal branches are lashed to the uprights with yucca fibers, the tie run through and around from the outside, where it is tied in a neat square knot. Mud was plastered over the entire exterior, making a complete seal. Any grain stored here was safe from weather and rodent. And raider.

With the examination of this meticulous structure I strike the word "primitive" from my vocabulary. This is truly fine work. I curve my hand around the heavy rim of mortar that finishes off the doorway; its smoothness and roundness bespeak refinement, fastidiousness, pride in workmanship, an elegance of touch.

A falcon glides down the canyon below, a sleek, slender projectile on noiseless wings. As we start down, a cold crescent moon cuts the sky. Up on the ledge it was comfortable, the rocks emanating warmth and protection. Going down into the streambed is like opening the refrigerator door. Perhaps the chill is part psychological, for these sites, on such precarious hard-to-reach ledges, suggest a different way of looking at life. Instead of sunshine and openness there are secretiveness and furtiveness; instead of a radiating peace there is a pervasive uneasiness; instead of the laughter and shouts of voices past I so often hear in the back of my mind there is the silence of desperation.

13

Shortly after 1300 the Anasazi were gone from these dwellings, leaving their maize in many of the granaries as if they were coming back. They were gone from the Cedar Mesa and the Grand Gulch Plateau, from the whole Four Corners area, having moved south to the drainage of the Little Colorado River or southeastward to the Rio Grande, where there was reliable water and where the Spaniards, looking for the mythical "Seven Cities of Cibola," found their descendants nearly three centuries later in the pueblos we know today.

The fortified sites have been pointed to as evidence of invasion from the outside such as occasional raids by nomadic Athabascans coveting food crops of the Anasazi. Current evidence suggests that Athabascans did not reach the Southwest until the 1400s or 1500s.

There is little evidence of warfare, and when the Anasazi moved, they went to open valleys in less defensible locations. The answer to the question of why they left does not lie in simplistic single factors but in a web of circumstances, complex and interwoven, psychological and sociological as well as environmental.

What seems the more likely reason for fortified dwellings and obscure granaries is internal squabbling and crop failure. Tree-ring evidence documents a deteriorating environment in the thirteenth century. The regular summer rains of Pueblo II times were less reliable. Pollen studies of granaries show a decrease in domestic pollens and an increase in wild food pollens. Crop failures must have become more prevalent, and corn fulfilled less and less of a role in diet, decreasing harvests implying lower nutrition.

At the beginning of such a period some "permanent borrowing" might easily have occurred in the interests of not starving, and with it a general air of mistrust; fortification-like entry walls would have protected both dwelling and granary. And many solitary granaries turn up on incredible ledges that must have required the agility of a spider to get to. Who knows what psychological stresses accompanied the diminution of nutrition, what distress followed the discovery that one's food was only as safe as the caching of it.

An emphatic change in effective moisture patterns had already occurred around A.D. 1150, and tree rings are much narrowed for the period between 1276 and 1299. Although tree rings generally are most responsive to lowered winter moisture, refined studies are beginning to show that other moisture was lacking also. Germination of seeds and young growth that depended more on stored soil moisture than spring rains were hampered by drier winters. When summer precipitation was abnormally low, crop failure resulted; when abnormally high, arroyo cutting took out alluvial flats and other near-stream acreage. Without winter moisture, springs and seeps would have been affected. Repeated flooding and/or overirrigation could have deposited so much alkali that the soil was no longer amenable to crops.

When the beneficent rains of summer came no more, a whole way of life was profoundly affected. And for twenty-three years, from 1276 to 1299, they endured devastating drought. But there had been droughts years before, some more severe than these, and one has to ask why this one destroyed such a resilient and resourceful population. Perhaps overpopulation and climate change worked together to defeat the tenacious Anasazi. The major population increase that began in Pueblo II times provided a larger labor force for agriculture and the time for specialized duties. But with limited acreages for farming, and more people farming, the less the return for each individual. The population became too large for the carrying capacity of the land under anything but optimal conditions—conditions which may well have existed in earlier Pueblo times. With a period of greater moisture such as that between 1000 and 1150 when summer rains were particularly beneficial, the Anasazi had spread far out into the marginal farmlands (some of which appear to have been abandoned some five hundred years previously because of insufficient moisture).

When population exceeds the carrying capacity of the land, there tends to be an increase in both the mortality rate and migration outward. One by one, family by family, people began to abandon outlying areas and drift southward and eastward. Without sufficient manpower to carry out all the previous functions of the settlement, those remaining were also forced to migrate. As a military wife who moved many times, I wonder if they left this canyon with reluctance, pausing, hand on doorway, for one last look inside, or if they simply went without a backward glance, leaving metate and mano, bowl and jug, point and chopper, thinking they would return.

Some may have joined larger settlements like Mesa Verde, where the environment remained favorable a little longer. But such a large site tolled its own death knell: the concentration of population could have come close to exhausting local resources, or, at the very least, put a heavy strain on them. Cutting massive numbers of trees for ever-increasing housing left bare ground open to erosion. With the removal of plant cover, small game would also have moved out of the area. Although the Anasazi utilized wild foods, replacing natural ground cover with a single crop, maize, opened that ground to more rapid erosion when that crop failed. Irrigation works would have been of little use without the water to supply them. Closer living conditions and meager sanitation could promote disease and sickness, and increase contact with disease-carrying animals such as rats and their plague fleas. By 1400 even the large population centers had disbanded. The Anasazi were no more.

And no one came here for nearly five hundred years to break the silence of the stones, to shadow the doorways that looked like empty eyes out on empty canyons, to sift the midden heaps drifted over with the silt of centuries or to peruse the petroglyphs staring down blindly from high walls—the time of comings and goings, all gone.

14

Yet, before it all fell apart, there must have been good living here, before the mistrust, the hunger, the fear, the bad times. Living in these sunshine-streaked canyons must have been infinitely preferable to being a serf in rainy, cold, miserable England!

My favorite site, up a close-walled side canyon, gives me just that feeling of time in the sun. Nothing here has been excavated, stabilized, or much rearranged. Very large pieces of pottery suggest that this site is still comparatively unvisited, and I sit here with a sense of time uninterrupted between then and now. There are no peephole walls here, no inaccessible ledges, no sense of threat or uneasiness, no attempt to prevent entrance, but just a low, sloping rock pavement for children to run on, a bench to sit on, a place to make pottery, a wall on which to cut petroglyphs, and perhaps, even a place to dream.

To reach this site we contour up a gentle sandstone slope at whose foot is a permanent spring. The sandstone, richly crossbedded, curves up to floor a wide, generous ledge. A V in the rock forms a trough across which remnants of a small check dam remain. If it was built up to the lip of the pour-off, a considerable reservoir of water would have been impounded, right on the doorstep.

Rising above this terrace is a sheer sandstone wall, a lovely warm beige. Within it is a small overhang. At the dripline of the overhang a strawberry cactus blooms, flowers a rich, velvety red, petals gilded with pollen, forecasting sweet-tasting "pitayas," the fruit that tastes like strawberries. A small conical granary is cosseted against the back wall. The imprint of the slab door still shows in the mudded door frame, which is spun with shining cobwebs that shimmer at my breath. Another small masonry room is still partially roofed, half-filled with a pack rat's nest. It is attached to a slab granary, constructed with big flat stones laid on edge, characteristic of Basketmaker construction. It must have been difficult to get them balanced this way, but it was done and done well. The topmost flagstone leans against a jag in the rock roof that holds it solid.

Where the floor of the overhang slopes downward, a low ledge of rock provides a comfortable place to sit, even and level. Seated here, beneath the overhang, I look out to the terrace—full of piñon and juniper, bluegrass stems shining in the morning breeze, daisies in bloom

Strawberry cactus *(Echinocereus triglochidiatus)*

among yellow parsley, big frowzy bushes of sagebrush, narrow-leafed yucca, buffaloberry; yellow evening primroses as big as teacups, brilliant scarlet paintbrush and rice grass and Mormon tea—a lovely warm crescent filled with glorious blooming, and beyond, the green treetops of the draw below. Oriented to the sun, this terrace is an April garden. Here, more than anywhere else, I have the feeling of an open, warm, peaceful world, of sunlit living that was industrious and useful and satisfying to those who lived here.

The flagstone granary and the gray pottery sherds, of a type known as Chapin Gray, indicate this overhang was occupied early; the masonry, that it was occupied for a long time. A sherd sits heavy in my hand, a good quarter inch thick, only crudely smoothed. Because the temper was coarse, irregular pieces were dragged across the surface during smoothing, leaving tiny triangular troughs. I hold the sherd flat in one hand and rub the surface, feeling what an ancient potter knew.

Sitting on this low bench, legs out straight, sun warm on ankles and knees, I too dream. I think probably I would have been a potmaker had I lived then, grinding the clay, winnowing the clay particles in this reliable breeze, pulverizing the temper, mixing it all with water until it felt just right to the hand, letting it age, then this morning, a good morning to make a jar, waiting for the sunshine to creep closer to warm my hands so I could work more easily. While I wait, I go down to the spring and fill my gourd dipper with water. While waiting one works. I waste nothing. Not even time.

I would take up the basket my mother made, of such fine weaving, in which I once gathered plants and carried them home, but now so worn. So worn. Good now only for holding the beginning pot. I don't even know how to make as fine a basket anymore. I set it firmly on the ground, in a little depression, and pat out a disk to fit in the center.

Next I fashion a coil, not too thick, not too thin, rolling it to evenness between my palms. As my mother taught me. It fits around

Yellow evening-primrose *(Oenothera brachycarpa)*

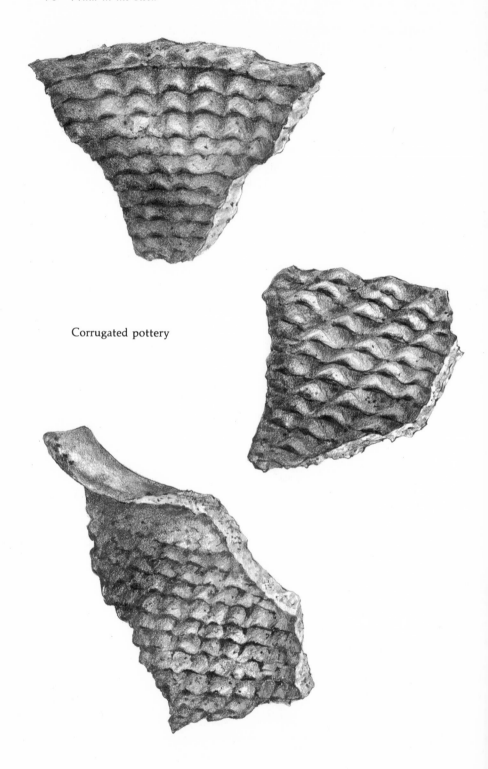

Corrugated pottery

the base and I pinch it on carefully, being sure the joining is firm. I form another coil and add it, in a ring, pinching it carefully and neatly. As my mother taught me. When it is hand deep, I take my mother's piece of gourd and, holding one hand against the outer wall, scrape the inside wall smooth. I dampen my fingers and rub them over the concave interior. I want it to be very smooth, this pot. To be even. To go on the fire and not crack. Then the outside—but no, the jar says no, wait.

I feel the satisfaction of the form taking shape between my hands. I look out over the terrace, everything visible, everything lucid. My world within these comforting walls, behind this screen of juniper. I pinch the last coil on. Again I take the piece of gourd my mother used to finish the smoothing. Then something in the pot speaks to me. Speaks to my hands. Along each coil I press the clay between thumb and forefinger, making a crimp, and another, until I have gone around once, and then another row, and another, trying to align each tiny pointed scallop with the one below, winding it upward, filling the whole surface with a fine-shadowed crosshatching. Such a pleasure in the doing.

And I feel joy. I might have no word for "joy" but that is what I know. Contentment. The pot will be good and useful. Easy to hold on to, firm in the hands. Good to look at. I set it aside to dry.

The day is beautiful. There is a little clay left. I waste nothing. With happiness in my fingers, I begin another bowl, a tiny one. As my mother taught me.

The stream draining Johns Canyon has a fall of 60 to 75 feet at its mouth, though no water was flowing from the canyon on August 5, 1921, when it was passed. Beneath the fall there is an elliptical pool 70 by 100 feet filled with clear water, which was utilized by the party for drinking and bathing. The water in the pool had clarified by the settling of the mud to the bottom.

H. D. MISER, *The San Juan Canyon, Southeastern Utah,* 1924

In longitudinal profile the floors of valleys in the San Juan country are very uneven. The floor of many a canyon is a series of steps, some of them bare ledges, over which the stream progresses by rapids and waterfalls separated by stretches of steep or flat gradient. In general the steps in tributary streams are more numerous and higher near the headwaters and near their mouths, thus making the generalized stream profile a curve steep at both ends.

HERBERT E. GREGORY, *The San Juan Country, A Geologic and Geographic Reconnaissance of Southeastern Utah,* 1938

Johns Canyon

1

I stand on a knife edge of rock, testing the morning wind, feeling as a falcon must just before it's ready to cast off and soar. At my feet, goldenweed wreathes the rock crevices, and five hundred feet below, two small side canyons, grinding their way southward, meet at the foot of this promontory. The wavering sandy lines of their dry streambeds are interrupted but once by the green of cottonwood and willow. In contrast to the somber green piñon-juniper blanket that covers the Cedar Mesa Plateau, from which these lateral canyons descend down into Johns Canyon proper, the white Cedar Mesa Sandstone canyon walls shine clean, looking as if they had been bitten out—I remember how Cedar Mesa looks from the air: a dark green jigsaw puzzle with the canyon heads like missing pieces, rock layers looking like the layers of plywood. (Incidentally, there are no cedars on Cedar Mesa; "cedar" is a local name for juniper.)

From the end of this wind-fretted promontory I can see two miles down the throat of Johns Canyon, where the walls are wider and the floor is leveled off, filled in with alluvium. Down there on that flat, cattle can be run if there is enough water both for them and to promote a good growth of grass; still, around here it takes a minimum of fifty acres per head.

Looking that far down the canyon, the even-floored reach looks deceptively gentle and flat, easy to walk on. Distance lends enchantment. I doubt that I will ever forget the misery of my first trip into Johns Canyon over that same terrain. Our youngest daughter, Sara, was home on spring break; our guides were Frank Nordstrom and his son, Dave, also home on vacation.

Over the previous year I somehow had added 15 pounds to my normal 105-pound weight. One doesn't think about the strain those surreptitious extra pounds cost you, but you would *never* put 15 useless

Goldenweed *(Haplopappus acaulis)*

pounds in your backpack. Furthermore, I had forgotten what the extra weight of a pack does to your feet. No matter how well boots are broken in with regular hiking, that additional 25 to 30 pounds sends flexible feet, such as mine, elongating toward the walled boot toe. I finished the trip with three purple toenails.

The erratic paths snaking up the canyon, laid out by obliging cattle, were a nightmare. Cattle pulverize the soil so that to follow their trail means sinking deep into an unresisting medium that gives no support. Leg muscles strain in an abnormal stride. Slogging is what it is. And, what's more, hot slogging, even at the end of March.

The streambed up which we eventually walked was little better. But here the sand was combined with rock-studded reaches. Not nice river cobbles with smooth surfaces laid firmly in the streambed, but a hodgepodge of rough, angular rocks, as many unstable ankle-knockers as stable ones, and these latter more often than not laid on edge so that a boot sole must land and balance on half an inch.

This kind of walking is, of course, merely annoying under normal conditions. But put twenty-five to thirty pounds on your back and things change. A turned ankle at normal weight is just that; with a backpack a turned ankle becomes a sprain that you have to limp out on for five miles. Here, walking demands a constant wariness. Of course, if you're twenty years old, six feet tall, and male, these concerns probably never reach consciousness. But my stride is short and I found my whole concentration focused on staying upright. I saw few flowers (unless I was trying to keep from stepping on one), enjoyed no butterflies, took only vague note of birdsong, looked not at weather or cliff or sky or tree, but only proceeded numbly, computing all the way the safest and best, the easiest and most efficient, and wondering how soon the next rest stop would be.

Somehow I got through that trip, and when I was able to think sensibly again and walk without limping, fifteen pounds came off in a hurry. And I became a dedicated runner.

2

So it is with a lot more energy and enthusiasm, and infinitely more comfort, that I walk up Johns Canyon in June, a year later, with our eldest daughter, Susan, and Frank Nordstrom. Frank leaves his truck beneath some old cottonwoods. Remnants of John Oliver's corral, a root cellar, a disintegrating fence, are mute evidence of tragedy forty-odd years ago. Johns Canyon is named after John Oliver, who with his brother, Bill, ran cattle here in the 1930s. Their presence was contested by an unsavory character named Jimmy Palmer. Not much over five feet tall, he lugged two pistols that reached almost to his boot tops. By the time he arrived in the San Juan area, he had already murdered his father-in-law, with whom he had run a floating cockfight operation.

In the Blanding area he had been stealing horses and wanted to keep his stolen stock in this canyon, having built a trail out the upper end of one of its tributary side canyons. He threatened the Olivers, who were not about to move. Palmer came back with a shotgun and blasted John Oliver in the face, and then shot Bill Oliver's grandson, Norris Shumway. He piled the bodies into the Olivers' old truck, and was said to have dumped them over the cliff and headed out for Arizona. Sometime later he was captured and imprisoned in Texas, where he died in jail.

3

We unload gear, distribute lunch, and add four pounds of water to our packs. Last winter was extremely dry, with minimal snow in the high country. This spring the drought continues. The little creekbed close by is bone dry. New green shoots colonize its loose sandy bed, drought-resistant plants which may not even survive the summer.

The cottonwood trees are abuzz with huge beetles that alight on the leaves and take off again immediately in a frenzy of flying, garlanding the trees with movement. They remind me, in size and in their lumbering but swift flight, of the June bugs of my Indiana childhood that blundered up against the screen doors in the summertime. And indeed these goldsmith beetles belong to the same family.

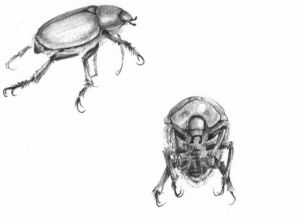

Goldsmith beetle *(Catalpa lanigera)*

Nearly an inch long, the beetle's back is brassy yellow with darker chrome yellow head and thorax, mahogany-colored legs, and short clubbed antennae. Underneath is a fuzz of short white hairs—hence its specific name, which means "woolly." If too abundant, goldsmith beetles can completely defoliate a tree. Primarily daytime insects, they glint like flecks of sunshine as they fly. The one in my hand, with its hooked tarsi—the end segment on its legs—sticks like Velcro for a moment to my palm, then lifts off like a 747 of the beetle world.

Leaving the shade of the cottonwoods, we prepare to walk the five miles or so to where water has been reported by a local helicopter pilot who occasionally patrols the area. My pack is too heavy to swing over an arm as one slings on an overcoat, so I do it the easy way: prop it against a tree trunk, sit down and work my arms through the padded straps, and *then* get up.

We walk upcanyon to the first branching, hoping to find water early. The canyon rises very gently here, and the walking, aside from the fact that hot sand radiates heat upward, is relatively easy. In past centuries tons of alluvium were carried into the upper canyon, flushed off the plateau above; were one to dig down, there would be the witness layers that would tell how big the floods were that laid it here: layers of cobbles from big water, layers of sands and silts from gentler floods.

Here the thousand-foot-high canyon walls are wide-spaced, nearly a mile across from rim to rim. The top half of the walls is of Cedar Mesa Sandstone, which underlies the Grand Gulch Plateau. Fresh breaks are pale cream and here it weathers to a golden tan. Streaks of desert varnish, like pennants, slide down its face.

Desert varnish is a patina characteristic of areas with meager rainfall. Rain water dissolves minerals from the soil on the plateau above. Depending upon the contour, the runoff tends to follow established patterns, century after century. Silicon, aluminum, iron, and manganese in solution drip down the rock, and it is mainly the oxides of the last two that leave the dark brown or charcoal-black ensigns.

Hollows and notches where the minerals from runoff have accumulated tend to be darker and shinier. Probably most of the varnish was deposited at least 2,000 years ago. The West had been in a fluvial period, with consistent heavy rains, since just before the time of Christ, and archaeological evidence suggests that a considerable amount of desert varnish was laid down during this time. The streaks, wider at the top, sometimes follow the contours under the overhang, describing the curve of the cliff as well as a former climate. A few cliff faces, newly sapped off, are fresh and clean, but all the older ones are pennoned like a medieval castle wall prepared for a tourney.

The lower half of the wall is a red-brown slope of Halgaito Shale. Paler blocks of sandstone stud the talus slope. Even though they look as if they might topple any minute, they've been there for centuries and more than likely will be there for many more. When sandstone overlies a weaker rock, as the Cedar Mesa Sandstone overlies the Halgaito Shale, the moist shale weathers and fractures and falls away, undercutting the massive sandstone above. Without support the sandstone tends to break at joint lines, falling off in massive slabs.

Some 270 million years ago shallow warm seas covered this area, the fluctuating shorelines of which extended in a band roughly southwest to northeast across Utah. These red shales, named for Halgaito Spring near Mexican Hat, Utah, document that pulsating shoreline. The shales were once muds and silts, carried in by slow streams, sorted by leisurely currents, compacted over the millennia to form thin-bedded rock stained a deep reddish brown that today contrasts with the pale sandstone above. The source for these red iron-rich sediments was the Ancestral Rocky Mountains, a range which lay to the northeast much as the present-day Rockies do.

On top of the red shales wind and water currents brought in from the northwest clean white sands, which were laid on top of the red shales and covered hundreds of square miles. So widespread is this sandstone that it has come to be known by different names in different places: in the Grand Canyon it is known as Coconino Sandstone; in Dinosaur National Monument, farther north, it is known as Weber Sandstone and forms the prominent landmark called Steamboat Rock; here, it is known as Cedar Mesa Sandstone.

4

Between sand grains are interconnected air spaces through which water can move, seeping down through cracks and joints, flowing out near the contact line of permeable sandstone with impermeable shale. Here most of the reliable springs occur and we are counting on them. But at the first known upcanyon spring in Johns Canyon there is no water, an eventuality that I've become quite apprehensive about in these dry years.

In this region of ten inches or less annual rainfall (in these drought years, about half that much), most of the water trundles but momentarily down the little dry gullies and is inhaled by the sand. Much of the water from a quick shower evaporates. Only a good cloudburst leaves any appreciable amount of water to gather in potholes, or seep into the ground to replenish the springs that normally flow from the canyon walls. Certainly the rain showers of summer scarcely wet the rock; they at best permeate the sandy soil for only a fraction of an inch, adding little to the ground water. Springs have little relation to the perennial drainage system of the area.

The mechanics of ground-water replenishment are known; the time lapse is less well known. Likely most of the water for these life-saving springs comes from the percolation of melting snow into the permeable rocks as well as into rock cracks and crevices. It would be interesting, indeed useful, also to know in what direction underground water funnels (other than down) and how long it takes to reach the spring itself. Judging from the last snowless winter and the dry water sources this spring, one suspects the effect to be rather immediate.

This knowledge adds an edge of anxiety to walking further upcanyon, and I try not to think about having to walk all the way back to the only water we can be sure of—that in the truck. I sneak a look at my thermometer. I wish I hadn't. It's 92 degrees Fahrenheit in the shade.

The streambed we follow is dry, rocky, and narrow, not very promising. Under an overhang there are two small pools with scarcely enough water to cook dinner, and a concentration of inhabitants in them that makes a cup of water contain more wrigglers than water. My need for protein at the moment isn't *that* strong. White salts limn the pools' highwater marks—lacy lines of alkali deposited as the pool evaporates.

I am finding the midday June heat extremely debilitating. I finish off my quart of water. The air is so dry that one never seems to perspire, feeling only a flushing of skin and an incredible thirst. Even the hardy buffaloberry bushes, usually an aluminized green and as drought resistant as any shrub out here, have branches of browned leaves. But another third of a mile ahead we find better pools, sufficient for cooking and cleaning up, and just a little further, a small plunge pool.

Where we finally drop our packs the canyon walls have closed in, scarcely a hundred yards apart. On the far side is a fifty-foot perpendicular wall, then talus for another fifty feet, topped with more wall notched with overhangs, ruddier in color than the sandstone usually is. On the near side, where we're camped, the shale wall is crumbling and slumping. Big chunks have sagged off very recently, leaving piles of shale flagstones beneath an overhang that otherwise would be a nice place under which to wait out a rain shower.

The turning of the canyon here provides a charming campsite, although to my weary eye almost anything except straight-up vertical would be fine. Tonight I could sleep on a bed of nails and never know it.

5

The farthest-up pool, which is deep enough to submerge in, is total heaven. The water is neither cool nor warm, just pleasant, a boon for hot feet and tired shoulders and sore hip bones.

I sit on a submerged rock near the edge of the pool, inundated to my chin, and discover the delights of being on eye level with the water striders. All one ever sees from the top is the slender dark brown body, short front legs, and the long middle legs used like oars. From this view I get a flash of the white underside. They rest quietly near the pool's edge until some movement of the water surface sends them skittering. Water-repellent pads and hairs on their legs spread their weight so that they are easily supported on the surface film.

Under water, a water beetle clings for a second to my foot, air bubble gleaming like a pearl, then darts on. At the water's edge, a dozen empty carapaces hang, quivering with the light breeze, on a boulder. Damselflies, needing a place to metamorphose from their water-bound nymph stage, found it here as they crawled out of a still pool. Time and again, beneath the water, they had grown, split the confining cuticle, and had become more of what they were before. But this time it was different: wings, held close to the thorax, twitched and throbbed with new messages—no more molting beneath the film that separates water from air but up through it, breaking the elastic confinement, clutching and clinging to someplace firm, feeling tendrils of air currents instead of water, a delicate flexing, a swallow of air, an increase in pressure, the old cuticle splitting along predetermined lines of weakness, then stepping out of that safe house, head out first, then thorax, then threadlike legs, stepping on dry instead of wet rock, wings still folded and damp, only the claws hard and able to lock into the rock—a new world, a new being, resting on the edge of blue wings and black body. I imagine them, a *corps de ballet* of damselflies, stretching, limbering, then off to the brief dance of summer.

Thankful now that the sunlight is still warm, I air dry off. Like a lizard I sun on a flat warm rock and feel a great lethargy. The lazy notes of Susan's harmonica weave into the sound of summer wind in the cottonwoods. I wonder that I was ever hot, ever tired, ever anything but at peace with this best of all possible worlds.

6

After dinner, the air has cooled and the evening is pleasant. I sit facing the shale wall, where that recent slide dumped half a ton of rock into the streambed. The outside of the curved channel is more subject to the force of the water tearing against it. And tear it does: mute evidence of past floods lies tangled in bushes six feet off the streambed bottom. On the inner side, where I spread my sleeping bag, a sand bar has been built up over the years—or in one good flood.

The curve of the dusty bed in itself is elegant, slipping around a slender cottonwood. But dry as a bone. Sprays of tamarisk, a scrub oak in early green, are full of dried shreds of branches where the last flash flood boomed through. And will again. In a couple of decades. Or centuries. Or day after tomorrow.

I awake to a lovely cool breeze at five-thirty, with a canyon wren trilling and the first fly of the day cruising by. A thin high overcast wefts the lozenge of visible sky. Although a full moon lit the sky last night, I never saw it because the canyon walls are too high, too close, and run in the wrong direction.

Early mornings in the canyon have a distinct quality; they are a time I cherish. Out here there is time to watch the day begin, hear the small secret sounds that no one else is awake to hear, time to watch the light change, to anticipate the coming day, all the good hours stacked ahead. Cool dawn, in these dry canyons, is a time of rare perfection, fresh beginnings, infinite peace, total awareness unimpinged upon by the necessities of the day. I sleep with my notebook by my head and, when I get home, find that more entries are written at dawn than at any other time. I lie on my back, arms behind my head, sleeping bag up to my chin, watching, watching the day begin.

One bat dives erratically after whatever insects may still be out or just coming out (all Southwestern bats are insectivorous). Others still remain high, flickering across the narrow arc of sky. Except for hesitant faraway birdsong and a marauding fly, there is a silence so pure that I can hear the tiny ticking sounds that the bat's wings make as it swoops just over my sleeping bag.

That fitful flight—the dives checked in midair, the short sideways darts—make it possible to identify a bat even when it feeds early in the evening among a flock of swallows. Its exquisite maneuverability enables it to snap up the insects whose unpredictable flutterings are meager protection against such a hunter. A bat's wings, an unfurred double membrane stretched between and enclosing elongated "finger bones," contain an intricate system of blood vessels that are like a radiator in cooling the blood during the strenuous activity of flight. A fine nerve network also threads the wings, probably associated with a sense of touch. The absence of fur reduces drag and permits more efficient flight. Bats use their wings much as a bird does, and like birds have strong pectoral muscles for flight; but unlike birds they do not have bones with interconnected air spaces for lightness but are of the same basic structure as other mammals, even though they are the only ones able to fly. I suspect from the size and the flight pattern this is a little brown bat, one of the most common and plentiful in the Southwest, with a measured air speed of between twelve and twenty-two miles per hour.

All this efficiency is necessary for an animal capable of grabbing a small insect every six or seven seconds; little brown bats have been found with over a thousand mosquitoes and gnat-sized insects in their stomachs, the catch of a single summer night. A swallow may fly through the air with its mouth agape, catching whatever is unfortunate enough to be in the way; a bat catches the insect in a scoop formed by the wing membrane near the tail and then transfers it to its mouth. A bat, with its calculated chase, undoubtedly harvests more than the swallow—the bird depends upon eyesight, the bat upon its ears. Above me, the bat's flight seems to web the sky, sewing an invisible net from cliff to tree to cliff.

At the end of the eighteenth century an Italian scientist suspected that in bats hearing had replaced seeing as a method of locating prey, but could not establish this with experimental proof. Not until 1940, when an electronic apparatus was developed which could pick up sound frequencies outside the range of human hearing, were bats discovered to be emitting sound, and lots of it. Further experiments have refined the original findings: little brown bats issue a series of squeaks of about 2 milliseconds duration, from 10 per second when simply cruising to 60 per second when locating, in a frequency range from 40,000 to 100,000 cycles per second; they are able to make rapid changes in frequency so that they utilize both pulsed sonar and frequency modulation when echolocating.

At first I think it is the clicking of the wings I hear, but the longer I watch the more the sound varies and doesn't fit the flight pattern. Because of the bat's proximity and the extreme quiet, the faint tick must be the component of a bat's transmissions that a human ear can just hear. I'm inordinately pleased—I feel privy to some arcane new knowledge that belongs only to me this early morning.

But all of the bat's sounding skill would be of little use without the ability to receive the sound that's been bounced off an object—in nature, a minute insect or two; in experiments, wires as fine as human hair. A bat's ears are large for its head size, meeting over the nose, and probably act like parabolic reflectors, magnifying the sounds they pick up. Auditory portions of the brain are enlarged for more efficient sound perception. The bat's brain, far more sophisticated than the most advanced radar, can rapidly interpret auditory signals and complex sound patterns. Although bats hunt mainly by echolocation, sounds made by the insects themselves may alert the bat, focus its attention, and give it something to home in on.

But this great physiological adaptation of the bat to efficient hunting is matched by that of some species of crepuscular moths. Some of these have large organs of hearing located in the thorax and occupying a considerable part of the body; these are sensitive to bat sounds and warn the moth of approaching danger. Its defense is to drop to the ground, where most bats cannot capture it.

The clouds barely move, picking up a tinge of pink, fusing to lavender toward the north. A cool breeze makes me snuggle down in my sleeping bag. A warbler spices the air with its singing. At six one last hungry bat is still out, executing a precise flight pattern right above my head. Suddenly it wheels, gains altitude, and goes straight north.

First sun paints the high rim at six-thirty and then disappears, blocked by low clouds on the horizon that can't be seen from here—how much the canyon confines your arc of view. The sky brightens. Down here it is a time of no shadows.

7

I often feel a certain reluctance at leaving a campsite in any one of these canyons. I wonder: will I ever come back, here, to this place? And, if not, then I want to remember it in infinite detail, to wedge it into my memory, to preserve it whole and complete with all its sights and sounds, smells and textures.

But often, in the melee of packing up, there is no time for looking around; better to get sleeping bag stuffed properly, fill water bottles, check to be sure no socks are left clothespinned to a tree. And then someone begins walking and is suddenly out of sight in a turning of the canyon, and at once everyone else is galvanized to get going and there's little time for anything except taking on that miserable pack and putting one foot in front of the other.

Halfway down the canyon, secreted in a sandstone overhang, visible if you know where to look and what to look for, a jacal structure still stands. I reflect that one walks here today under almost the same conditions existing eight centuries ago. Instead of turkey-quill and rabbit-fur robes, we have down jackets; instead of well-woven sandals, we have Vibram soles. Instead of parched corn, we have elaborate freeze-dried foods. But the means of locomotion is precisely the same: feet.

8

The U.S.G.S. topographical map shows an oil well nearby. The pipe, as high as my head, is now capped and filled with cement to prevent possible leakage of gas. On the ground another long pipe lies, rusted, and to it a cable is still attached. A big caterpillar of a cable, an inch thick, kinking around as if it means to burrow into the ground, lies near the drum of a huge cable spool. The two wooden disks of the cable spool, like some gigantic tiddlywinks, have rolled free. In this dry climate they have scarcely rotted at all. A mound of drill mud to the side is still bare and gray; in some seventy years nothing has sprouted on it: fine, compacted like cement, it discourages plant growth. A twenty-by-twenty-inch beam, ax marks on it still visible, must have been a beast to haul in here.

Two reconnaissance studies in this area were made by the U.S. Geological Survey, primarily to classify public land and its oil possibilities, one in 1912, another in 1936. Both describe the oil exploration that took place in southeastern Utah. The first oil claim was made in 1882 by E. L. Goodridge. Goodridge didn't begin to drill his first well until March, 1907, and on March 4, 1908, at 226 feet, it came in a gusher, spewing oil 70 feet into the air. Such promise of black gold engendered a modest oil boom and the drilling of nearly 100 wells, most between 1908 and 1912, activity that finally petered out in 1920. During this time the population of Bluff, Utah, was temporarily increased, and a small settlement was established at Goodridge, now called Mexican Hat after a distinctive local landmark of Halgaito Shale. There were small flurries of drilling between 1922 and 1928, and from 1943 to 1948. Some wells went down deeper, but essentially produced the same: nothing or not enough to justify the expense of major drilling programs. Production reached 25 to 50 gallons a day in the better wells; the common price of oil in the field in those days was $1.25 a barrel.

After accrued costs of more than $2 million, the value of the petroleum was estimated at but a few thousand dollars. In modern economic parlance, the cost/benefit ratio was definitely negative. For two reasons: not enough oil and the remoteness of the area. In 1938 all production was still consumed locally. Not only was production modest, but the rigors of the locale itself discouraged continued investment. The nearest railheads are still at Thompson, Utah; Albuquerque, New Mexico; or Flagstaff, Arizona. There were few inhabitants, thus most labor had to be imported, and from historical accounts they did not like it much after they got here. Water for drilling was as scarce as water for drinking or water for agriculture or water for anything else here, and generally had to be trucked in. Most of the oil is found in nine levels of oil-bearing sands that lie in quixotic isolated patches, so that finding it was largely a matter of accident or sheer luck.

The well here in Johns was drilled by a man named Galloway. It eventually went down to 1,900 feet, the deepest drilled in the area. On the first drilling, a strong flow of gas was encountered in the "Goodridge" oil sands with a trace of oil in other sand layers. No water was found below 100 feet. Then drilling was "abandoned because of lost tools." (I'm told "lost tools" is a euphemism for tools dropped down the well; their extraction is a difficult, expensive, and time-consuming business.) Drilling resumed in March, 1910, and operations were still in progress in 1912 although the well was capped soon after. Only a tiny amount of oil was ever bottled out of this well, and most of it was used to run the pumps. To come into this country, to build a road at God knows what physical and monetary expense, to drill a well here beyond nowhere: what dreams of wealth did men have when they looked at this harsh, unrewarding landscape?

Perhaps those dreams were based on an observation that this is a classic oil-situation landscape. The well at Johns was drilled into the crest of the Monument Upwarp, a huge gentle updoming of the earth, like those in which oil is often found. It is thought that the impetus for the tremendous lifting of the present-day Rocky Mountains, between 70 and 45 million years ago, came from pressures generated by movement of the Pacific and American continental plates. Compression pulses spread eastward. Along with the rising of the major mountain ranges, minor pulses caused local upwarps and doming on the Colorado Plateau, such as the Monument Upwarp. The doming of these large upwarps goes deep and may reach clear down to the Precambrian basement rock. Like most of the upwarps on the Colorado Plateau, the Monument Upwarp is asymmetrical, sloping up gently from the west, breaking off abruptly on the east.

Across the surface of the Monument Upwarp are the humps of smaller anticlines and their corresponding synclines, or depressions, lying, as one geologist aptly put it, like wrinkles on the surface of a prune. Oil, trapped underground, migrates to form pools from which it can be pumped, rising upward to fill interstices left between rock strata because of the doming. Oil may also accumulate in synclines under certain circumstances. If there is ample ground water, oil is more likely to be found in anticlines, floating on top of the water. If there is inadequate water, oil may occur in the trough of a syncline.

However, the reservoirs here have been breached. The San Juan River ruptured the pool of oil that might otherwise have been sealed in the synclines and anticlines for centuries. The oil seeps visible along the river near Mexican Hat and Slickhorn Gulch are likely the remnants of the oil that once might have been extensive in the area.

In spite of the small return and the difficulties involved, drillers kept at it here, off and on, for nearly sixty years. One comes to suspect that if they came here for wealth and fortune they stayed for other reasons, perhaps because they were loners in this tailor-made-for-loners country.

9

We plan by walking down the Halgaito Shale slope just below the drill hole to bypass a dry waterfall (which in good years has water sheeting over it), a sheer drop of eighty feet or so. We will camp where we find water, and tomorrow walk on downcanyon to the cliff overlooking the San Juan and peer down on the river more than a thousand feet below.

Thwarted by the resistant limestones in the lower half of Johns Canyon, water has not been able to erode a channel to the level of the river.

The only way down to the lower canyon is a zigzag course across a talus slope of slippery loose shale which only an insane skier would attempt, a drop of some five hundred feet. Granted, boots are somewhat more stable than skis, but on the loose shale there is little purchase anyway.

Let me go on record as saying that I find walking *up* anything—draw, canyon wall, cliff—*much* easier than walking down. When you are going down, if the slope is steep at all, there is constant strain on quadriceps muscles, engendered by having to hold your weight back from making a jarring landing. Going up is simply a matter of breath and endurance, leaning into the slope. Going down is pain, agony, and misery.

No one talks on this descent that Frank leads, just puts foot down, tests, shifts weight, puts other foot farther down, digging in at the side —continually testing, slipping, stiffening, slipping again, tensing thigh muscles until they quiver, testing and holding, never looking downslope to the side, just following the placement of the footsteps in front. One loosened rock on someone below, one unbalanced downside step, and the results are unpleasant to contemplate: there is no obstacle to keep you from going all the way to the bottom in a descent more swift than ceremonious. A friend of mine who did that got two broken wrists and had to be helicoptered out. For some reason, obscure to me but having something to do with gravity and lack of good sense, we all reach the bottom safely. I would not say it was a graceful descent, but it was a *very* careful one.

When we are finally down on the limestone-paved floor of the canyon, the first order of business is to find adequate water. A small spring seeps out of the wall about ten feet off the ground, filling a basin with clear water that is, of all marvels in this ninety-degree heat, cool and relatively uninhabited. But bitter. Bitter, but drinkable. Beyond, a couple of shallow pools, woven with algae and debris, are good enough for cleaning up.

Most of the spring water in these canyons comes from more or less saturated porous rock strata that lie in thin layers between zones of thicker impervious dry rock—limestone, shale, or mudstone. When a canyon cuts through these layers, an outlet is provided for the water that is stored within, often only enough to wet the rock face down which it dribbles. High up on the east wall, a spring, dripping like a leaky faucet, issues out of the Halgaito Shale; usually a non-water-bearing stratum, it is connected by joint cracks to a water-bearing bed above. On each side of the dark damp mark made by the water is the ubiquitous crinkly white line of evaporated alkali.

The salts that streak the walls and encrust the dirt were concentrated in the Halgaito Shale when the seas that covered this area evaporated. In shallow, more or less landlocked, fringes of the sea, circulation was low and evaporation high. As muds and silts filled in over the dried salt, it became incorporated into the shales and mudstones of eons to come. Such conditions were somewhat like the climate here today: arid, little rainfall, and rapid evaporation. Lime, gypsum, calcium sulfate, sodium chloride are given up by these shales, and now appear in the intermittent streams, seeps, and springs, commemorated in this country by names like Lime Creek, Alkali Ridge, and Sugar Creek.

By taking jugfuls out of the tiny pool into which the lower spring discharges, we nearly deplete the water supply. But it is replenished overnight. Some springs are so subject to evaporation that they are nearly useless during the day, taking half an hour to fill a cup; but at night they fill up and provide a sufficiency, a life-saving observation made by many travelers in this country.

After slogging some five miles or more through sand and sagebrush and walking a tense quarter mile down treacherous talus when my pocket thermometer reports ninety-eight degrees in the shade, even a small spring means refreshment and cooling comfort. One becomes sharply aware of how precious water is when you haven't got it. As the tag on my herb tea bag read this morning: "When the well is dry, we know the worth of water." Amen.

10

In damper climates limestone disintegrates easily, but in dry regions it becomes one of the most resistant of rocks. Where the finer sediments have been removed by repeated flooding, ledges of more resistant limestone are revealed. Water has a tendency to shoot off these ledges or "knickpoints" during flood, its force scouring out a depression at the foot, which sometimes retains the water for a while.

One such charming pool lies just a quarter mile upcanyon, shaped like the winged samara of a boxelder. Gentling down to a soft bottom studded with rocks, the deepest part is maybe five feet. The convex side lies against a rock ledge, reflecting it in dark perfection. A chute cuts the ledge, and moisture, outlined with white as always, drizzles down the slope beneath, a film of moisture that remains and works away at the rock. The walls of the chute bind a narrow slot of blue sky.

In the shallows of the concave edge of the pool, the silt is as slippery as pure grease, giving way to a velvety softness in the water, blossoming up deliciously between my toes. About six dozen tadpoles, one-inch bodies with inch-and-a-quarter tails, snorkle along the bottom, bodies slightly canted, siphoning up desmids and diatoms—minute algae— while their tails undulate above them. They have fat, bulbous bodies, some already with rudimentary legs. Their bodies are mostly filled with intestines, of necessary length to digest vegetative food. When they become adults in July or August, they will be carnivorous with much smaller intestines, an adjustment of physiology accomplished in the transformation from tadpole to frog or toad.

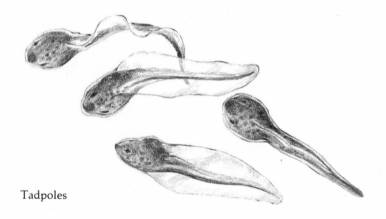

Tadpoles

As they bustle about feeding, they send up minute clouds of silt, so fine is the bottom material. Occasionally one rotates and reaches up to the surface, almost standing on its tail, smacking the air. They move in a rather dignified and leisurely quadrille. Against their clustered movement tiny water beetles dash frenetically through the water, dis- appear into the bottom silt, then pop out again, like minuscule Mexican jumping beans.

Standing ankle deep in the water, concentrating on the tiny beetles, I nearly jump out of my skin when a tadpole comes and nibbles on the side of my foot, a gentle but very unexpected tickle. I reach down to pick it up—they move so slowly that it's simple to scoop one into my palm. It wriggles there, its top the color of onyx shot with gold, underneath gilt and bronze, encased in a crystalline coating—lovely and soft to behold and to hold, a small Cellini creation. In the water, when the sun catches the whole fleet of them, they glint rosy gold. As I stand still, several, like miniature vacuum cleaners, clean off the thin layer of silt settled across my instep.

Red-spotted toad
(Bufo punctatus)

Up on the shelf above the pool hunches a small red-spotted toad. This silver-dollar-sized creature seems made of dull jade embossed with enameled dots the color of garnets. These toads are most likely to be found on rocks or in rock crevices, taking to water only when disturbed. During breeding season brown "nuptial pads" appear on the thumb and inner fingers of the male which helps them to adhere to the slippery body of the female during mating; eggs are laid singly or in strings on the bottom of these shallow basins. From April to September, during or after rains and in the evenings, their trilling adds to the quiet music along the pools and puddles of the canyons.

11

A place to spread my ground cloth and sleeping bag has to fulfill several prerequisites, especially if we are to remain more than one night. And in the interests of a good night's sleep I am quite willing to scour the countryside. Tonight I find what I consider perfection. Away from camp. Sand. Soft, warm, clean sand. Level surface. A tree with low branches for hanging laundry on. In addition to these necessities, this sand bar has another amenity: glorious clumps of Wyethia in full bloom. Sometimes called mule-ears, the big daisylike flowers have rich sunshine-yellow centers and petals, and grow in clumps well past my knee in height and sometimes four feet across, making a glorious show.

Drawing on backpacking trips, unfortunately, has proved difficult. The pressure of straps across the shoulders as well as arms hanging down for hours while walking tends to cut off circulation, and even though I am careful to walk with one or the other of my hands up, thumb hooked into a shoulder strap, my hands often swell. But this time, knowing it was going to be a more leisurely trip, I've packed drawing pad and pencils and now sit down to draw the Wyethia, which was named after Nathaniel J. Wyeth, an explorer and traveler across the northern territory in the nineteenth century. Wyeth collected plants in 1833, and sent them to his friend, the famous botanist from Harvard, Thomas Nuttall; the following year Nuttall described some fifty-five new species from Wyeth's collection. As I sit and draw the Wyethia, a feeling of deep serenity seeps into my consciousness, such total absorption in the task, such pure pleasure.

Nearby is an exotic green gentian, its stalk of blooms rising from a rosette of leaves strikingly rimmed with white, a plant looking more suited to a botanical garden than to this sand bar. As I draw it, a lesser earless lizard arrives and begins to feast on the ants swarming around the rosette; the lizard is called "earless" because ear openings are absent in this genus. Whenever it rises up on its forelegs, it reveals the salmon stain under its chin. It lets itself down, does a few pushups, and then resumes feeding again.

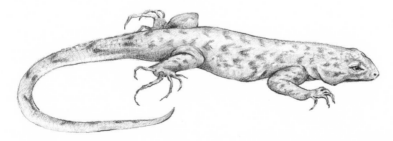

Lesser earless lizard *(Holbrookia maculata)*

Wyethia or Mule-ears *(Wyethia scabra)*

Its back, pearly-gray scales with clusters of darker scales that form sooty spots, appears dappled; it would indeed be nearly invisible among the speckled shadows cast by the small leaves of desert plants. Minute as they are, scales form consistent countable scale-by-scale color patterns usable for species identification. Coloration gives both camouflage protection and heat control. Its gleaming white belly, which I can see when it stands up on its hind legs, provides high reflectance, protecting against heat radiation from a hot sand or rock substrate; lizards whose habitat includes a soil base have much darker ventral sides. In addition, many desert lizards can darken and lighten their skin color, depending upon whether they need to absorb or reflect heat.

I move my arm very carefully but the lizard evaporates, its keen eyesight catching even a slight movement from above. A lens-squeezing device that rounds the lizard's eye enables it to change focus quickly from close-up to distant objects. Most lizards also have a nictating membrane, a semi-transparent membrane that sweeps across the eye and cleanses it. Not as speedy a long-distance runner as other small desert species, this one dashes between shelters, from one bush to another, and I fear it is gone for good. But in a few moments I notice an infinitesimal movement out of the corner of my eye. It's back.

Being such a tiny creature, this earless lizard has a relatively high ratio of surface area to volume, and therefore both absorbs and loses heat quickly. Although it's hot for me, air temperature this evening must be lizard perfect; most diurnal desert lizards operate best in an average temperature range of 78 to 90 degrees Fahrenheit. Were the sun out, it could not endure straight radiation; devoid of sweat glands, a lizard, depending upon species, must rely upon shadow or cool burrow in order to stay below the danger zone, which begins around 110 degrees. Were it cooler out, my confrère would become torpid, slipping away to a safe shelter where slowed metabolism would not render it vulnerable to predators—hawks, bats, snakes, and larger lizards.

I watch the lizard's tongue constantly flick in and out and wonder how many ants disappear down its gullet. Since a lizard has neither movable lips nor the capacity to use its front feet to push food into its mouth, it depends on jaw action, sometimes assisted by its tongue. Once an ant is in its mouth, it thrusts its head forward in a quick series of snaps, which works the ant far enough back to be swallowed.

Between gulps, its threadlike tongue, in characteristic lizard fashion, samples the smells nearby. Lizards have organs of smell located in the roof of the mouth that are probably of more importance than those located in the nose. The nose perceives odors at a distance, but then the tongue helps in more precise location. It picks up scent particles and carries them to the top of the mouth.

As I enjoy watching the lizard, a picture flashes across my mind of me as a bride when Herman was stationed in southern Florida. Hanging out laundry was a time of trauma for me because the sandy ground was frequented by little green chameleons, which could send me screaming inside. Fascination and a little research *do* give one a different perspective.

Even though gnats feast in my hair and a mosquito lands on my ear, I will not move and chance disturbing my companion again. I appreciate being allowed to share the same *Lebensraum.* Up on its back legs, front legs on the sturdy leaf, feet as fine as a spider web, it dines, I would like to think, happily.

12

The green gentian that I draw was described by the doughty Alice Eastwood, who came to southeastern Utah in 1895 under the auspices of the California Academy of Sciences, as "growing to a height of four or five feet, with thick hollow stems; flowering branches widely spreading above." (Of the Wyethia she noted that "both sides of the leaf are alike, and the tendency to assume the upright meridional position is marked.")

Although she did not ride as far as Johns Canyon, working in the canyons to the east of Comb Ridge, she still found many of the species that are widespread in this arid region of Utah. What's more, she did it at the hottest time of the year, starting out in July "with the knowledge of the isolation of some species discovered there and the hope of finding more by going farther, that I gladly accepted Mr. Alfred Wetherill's invitation to take this trip, full of hardships, through an uninhabited and unexplored desert country." She returned to California, "having collected about 475 specimens, representing 162 species and varieties, of which 19 are new and almost all are rare. It was a hard trip, about 300 miles altogether, through a desert country where springs are few and far between and good feed for the animals very scarce."

But hardship was nothing new to Miss Eastwood. While in California she traveled old cattle trails, collecting plants across the mountains and along the forbidding paths on the coast, hitching rides with rural

Whitemargin gentian
(Frasera albomarginata)

postmen, getting the loan of a horse from a remote rancher, and occasionally getting herself lost. She was the only woman ever invited to
join the men-only Cross Country Club, a group of strenuous hikers. She
had the longest tenure of any member of the California Academy of
Sciences, retiring in 1950 at the age of ninety. In the fires after the
earthquake of 1906 she managed to save nearly 1,500 valuable speci-

mens; of personal possessions, only her hand lens that was in her pocket was saved. She wrote about her loss, "my own destroyed work I do not lament, for it was a joy to me while I did it, and I can have the same joy in starting it again." She was, in short, an incredible woman.

It gives me great pleasure to think of Miss Eastwood, eighty-two years ago, noting these same plants, eating the same sand in her food, sweltering under the same sun, but with it all finding reward, as I do, in these handsome plants that simply grow out of dry sand.

The sense of utter harmony with the world about me persists, and when the light dies and I can no longer see either to write or to draw, I stretch out on top of my sleeping bag and watch the stars turn on. Wide awake, yet deeply relaxed, I think I would lie here all night and count stars. In this heightened state of awareness, it seems perfectly possible.

13

I should know better. I awake at midnight to a blue screamer. The wind rasps off the canyon walls. Fortunately, my toes point in the direction from which the wind comes so that it slides up my bag. At first the wind is merely annoying; I hear it coming, weasel down in my bag, wait for it to shriek past, then slip back out for air.

Then the wind changes direction and intensifies. Sand picks up. It sounds as if someone is throwing fine gravel on my sleeping bag. I have lotion on my sunburned face, which acts like glue to which the sand sticks. The wind comes across the unzipped side of my bag, drifting sand in by the handful, so that I lie on lumps when I turn over. I try to get the zipper up. It sticks. More sand streams in. I hear the pages of my notebook riffle open. I drop a boot on top. Hearing the gusts come I try to draw myself down into the bag far enough to be completely covered, and the bag becomes unbearably hot. Obstructing any concentration on going back to sleep is the unsettling knowledge that we have a fifteen-mile hike tomorrow.

Wind is a constant in the canyons but I have yet to get used to it at night. Upcanyon winds during the day, especially in warm weather, are welcome. They result from the intensive heating of sand and ground and rock, all of which can become, by mid-afternoon, too hot to step on with bare feet. As the air at the surface becomes heated, it rises and expands. Rising, it cools about 5½ degrees for every 1,000 feet in altitude in what is termed adiabatic cooling. Herbert Gregory, the pioneer geologist of the San Juan area, noted that "for the most of the region the winds are highly variable in direction, strength, and continuity. They blow in and out of canyons, up canyons, down canyons, and around buttes and mesas. They blow up over the box heads of canyons during the day, only to return down canyon at night. During the hot summer days they seem to head from all directions toward sand flats and stretches of naked rocks."

In the canyons this exchange of air tends to swirl and spin between the walls, making it seem as if the wind comes from every direction. Caught in the narrows formed by canyon walls, the wind, as it gains in velocity, picks up everything not battened down: sand, twigs, notebooks, unanchored ground cloths. I catch a glimpse of my white socks, clothespinned to a tree; they stand straight out with each good gust, the original windsocks.

As long as cold air is supplied from above, the wind burrows down the canyon. It comes in pulses. As soon as I stick my head out of the stifling sleeping bag and breathe comfortably again, I hear the wind ricocheting off the rocks, a warning to slither down inside again. The gusts come closer together. The strength of the wind increases. I feel buffeted and beaten, exhausted, as if it's never going to stop. I think of trying to walk in this wind tomorrow and know it will be impossible. Its strength, gathering off the walls and focusing around a corner, can literally stagger you.

Then, almost as suddenly as it began, the wind stops. I realize it only as I wait, stiff with dread, for the next blast . . . and it doesn't come. I discipline myself to unwind, to relax my muscles one by one, to fall asleep. I do so secure in the knowledge that tomorrow is likely to be a bummer.

I awake ill-humored. My ground cloth is totally submerged in sand and my sleeping bag is ten pounds heavier. When I brush my teeth there's sand in my cup of water, sand in my toothpaste, sand in my toothbrush. There's even sand in my lip ice and when I put it on it feels like sandpaper.

14

In the morning we set off downcanyon toward the San Juan River. The canyon below the waterfall is floored with hard limestone ledges, alter-

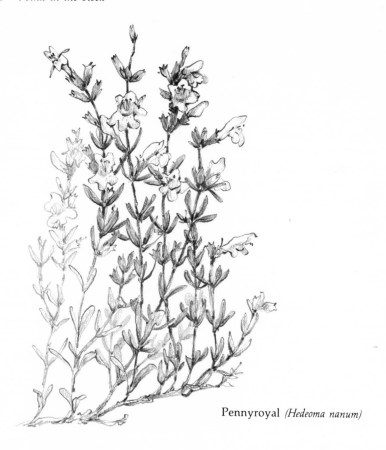

Pennyroyal *(Hedeoma nanum)*

nately exposed and covered with sand, that form the treads of giant stairs. The canyon marches toward the river, alternating flat stretches with breakneck drops. The combination of falls and near-level reaches are characteristic of a "young" profile, in contrast to a "mature" graded streambed in which the descent has been evened out. Not enough water has flowed here for enough centuries to level out the channel, and the dry bed remains a chart of fluvial processes at work. These dry washes and arroyos provide an understanding of what water does and how it flows almost better than the rivers and streams themselves, where water obscures the bed forms. The empty meanders, the ripple-marked beds, the fluted limestone record the water's passage as clearly as a diagram.

We continue down a limestone shelf that for a while is blown clean, pale gray rock embedded with hundreds of crinoid stems, recording the shallow water shelves of a Pennsylvanian Age sea 300 million years ago.

Along the channel sides, on blown sandy banks, bushes of pennyroyal are in full bloom, delicate lavender blossoms and pungent leaves that smell like a cross between rosemary and mint. The walking is easy, pleasant, with only a light daypack and the cooling of a light breeze.

We have crossed the boundary between the Halgaito Shale and the Hermosa Formation, a boundary not only of rock type but of different environments. While the shales were formed out of the silts and muds that lay on the border of the continental sea, the limestones were formed of the underwater silts and the calcium carbonate of billions of sea animals that flourished in the shallow warm waters near shore.

In many of the limestone slabs are fossils, most frequently of crinoid stems. These belong to the "sea lilies," animals of the same family as sea urchins and starfish. Anchored in the mud, the stem grew upward and supported a five-parted head that somewhat resembled a lily, hence the common name. The stems have survived, in bits and segments, just weathering out of the limestone matrix, telling of the shallow, quiet sea in which these swaying, long-stemmed animals grew and fed without being torn and damaged by harsh currents. Most of them are now coral-colored, the original shell transformed by time into a fine close-grained quartz called chert or jasper.

After an hour or so of walking we enter a narrow limestone chute, six feet across, fifteen feet high, all in cool shadow, scoured clean by water and sand, so much paler than the surrounding rock. At the foot of the chute is a tranquil pool some fifty feet or so across, absolutely still, reflecting the high walls of the canyon. Water must pound and bore through here during flash floods, for the pool is quite deep. But now it retreats, leaving the feathery patterns of succeeding hot, dry days on its edge.

We have to backtrack up the chute; there is a fifty-foot drop just below the pool. To avoid it we climb far up on the talus slope and contour above the streambed. Huge boulders of dolomitic limestone lie on this shelf, with solution patterns like sunbursts etched on the horizontal surfaces. Every small depression has fine wrinkled lines that feed it, and each of the fine wrinkles between is exceedingly sharp to the touch.

I have become acquainted with dolomite not by geological definition and chemical analysis but by sad experience. It is a fearfully abrasive rock, painful when used as a handhold, and it can skin shins right through heavy jeans. Named for certain carbonate rocks of the Tyrolean Alps, it is more than half magnesium carbonate. Dolomitic rocks are often characteristic of back-reef areas of ancient seas; limestone is more commonly formed in deeper water. Dolomite indicates times when the seas were shallowing out here. The magnesium comes from the surrounding sea water and replaces some of the calcium in the original limestone. Although dolomite looks similar to limestone, it tends to have a brown cast and a granular texture. And, once you have skinned your hands on it, you don't forget.

Just around the corner—"just around corners" being one of the special delights of walking in these canyons—the slope is thick with brachiopod fossils and chunks of crinoid stems. Handfuls of stems and shells, each more perfect, more exquisite than the last. The brachiopods are all small, none much over an inch across. At first glance one is reminiscent of a scallop or pecten shell, except that it is not symmetrical. Although the two valves are separately symmetrical, one is larger than the other, fitting over the smaller with a beak on the back that makes it look like a Phrygian cap. The shell is heavy for its size, of a deep coral color with a slight translucence, transformed, like the sea lilies, into jasper.

The two valves are locked in permanent closure. Since death usually causes relaxation of the inner muscles that keep the shell open, fossil brachiopods are typically found firmly closed (just the opposite of oysters, which are usually found open when dead). The joining of the shells forms a curvilinear **W**. Growth lines ripple across the plicate ribs, each year's growth extending out from beneath the line of last year's.

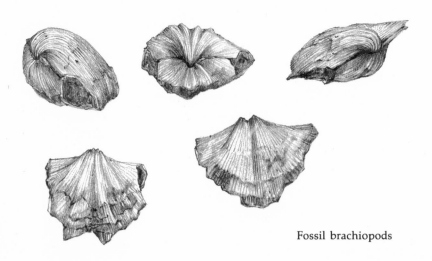

Fossil brachiopods

Brachiopods were plentiful, exclusively marine animals that grew attached to the bottom rocks or nestled in the mud. Their environmental habitat was limited, mostly confined to warm shallow seas. The evolution of siphons in present-day bivalves made possible a more flexible and protected life than that of the brachiopods. Brachiopods needed to be fully exposed in order to filter food-carrying water through the narrow crack between their shells, an opening that extended very nearly the whole circumference of the shell. The siphon of modern clams can be extended from the shell or retracted, allowing today's clam to burrow in the silt or mud and remain hidden while still circulating water and nutrients, or withdraw the siphon altogether and close completely. Brachiopods, with no siphons, had no such advantage, and out of a wealth of some 3,200 species identified in fossils, only a few species remain.

15

Another hour and the canyon makes a sharp U, putting the streambed in shadow. Rounding the corner is like walking into another world: knee-high rushes are stuffed thickly against the right bank. Maidenhair ferns cascade in close layers of small green, fan-shaped fronds on wiry black stems; giant hellebore orchids cling to the wall. Columbines spring from cracks in the rock, tiny pale flowers suspended like doves in flight. Above, a dripping spring wets the whole wall, nourishing this greenhouse. The air is cool and damp and soothing to the throat.

Again I think of Alice Eastwood on her journey:

> Late in the afternoon we reached the head of Willow Creek, a paradise in this awful desert. For some distance from the big spring the water flows in a continuous stream, finally settling in deep pools in the rocky basin of the wash. Several species of grass grew tall in this oasis, and here a greater variety of plants was found than in any other locality. *Aquilegia micrantha* was seen under the shadow of moist rocks.

I settle down to draw the columbine, minding not at all that I'm sitting in an exceedingly damp spot. Difficult intricate flowers to draw, for I soon realize to my consternation that there are no two blossoms alike. According to Alice Eastwood,

> There is considerable variation in the size and color of the flowers, length and uniformity of the spurs and the character of the

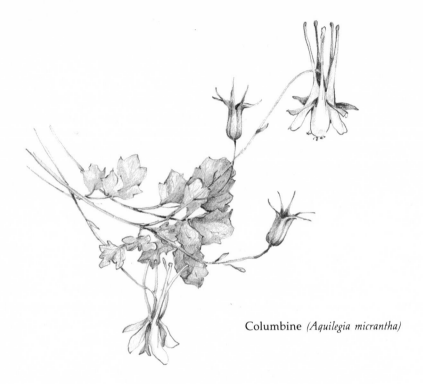

Columbine *(Aquilegia micrantha)*

foliage. The variations are due to the amount of moisture, which is not uniformly distributed under the cliffs, but oozes out more in one place and less in another, perhaps not a yard away. . . . The sepals vary from cream-white to rose color; spurs are sometimes all uniform in one flower and diverse in another on the same plant.

It takes an effort of will to leave this quiet, cool place and walk out into a glare of sunlight that turns the sand white. Opportunistic reed grass runners stretch across the dry streambed. The stout culms, which the Anasazi used for arrow shafts, form a palisade that extends well above my head. The rustling shafts were also used for prayer sticks and pipestems and loom rods, for making mats, screens, thatching—a useful and well-used plant to the economical Indian.

A cicada sounds off like an unoiled chainsaw. Blue-gray limestone protrudes through red sand. I stop at a debris-laden pool where cotton-wood leaves, soaked to thin translucent parchment, lie layered on the bottom, take my shirt off, dip it into the pool, and put it back on wet. As I walk the cooling water drips off the cuffs onto my wrists. But not for long. The shirt is dry within ten minutes except where my daypack glues it to my back.

16

By eleven o'clock my feet feel too heavy to lift, my arms hang like lead weights, my eyes throb with the strain of focusing in this reverberating white light. The eighties have long since passed and it's well into the nineties and I think we are in a class with mad dogs and Englishmen who go out in the midday sun. We find a large overhang and spread out a meager lunch, which is more than Susan or I want, but Frank insists. Heat destroys my appetite and I would be happy just gulping down a gallon of alkali-tainted lemonade, but I know the salted nuts and raisins are necessary. I've carried three oranges in my backpack for the last two days, saving them for today's walk. Although a little on the warm side, they are just what's needed, juicy, with the magnesium and potassium that are two of the salts lost rapidly with perspiration.

I look at the thermometer. The air temperature is now above that of body temperature. There is no more conductive cooling of blood as it circulates through the skin. One of the body's first reactions to heat is that the heart pumps more blood and blood vessels dilate at the surface of the skin, allowing the skin to shed its heat into a cooler atmosphere outside, but only so long as the ambient air temperature is below that of the body.

Sweat evaporating on the skin is an efficient cooling process that here, unfortunately, is largely nullified by the excessive dryness of the air and the heat. One simply cannot sweat enough in this pervasive high temperature. But the body loses salts through perspiration, upsetting the electrolyte balance, which brings on symptoms of headache, nausea, and general shakiness. Drinking large amounts of water only makes things worse, for water replaces only water, none of the salts, further upsetting the balance. Yet without water dehydration is an even more lethal danger. If one stops sweating, then body temperature rises, leading to heat stroke.

Frank passes out salt tablets; mine goes down hard. I'm convinced that the alkalinity of the water I'm slugging down, while replacing some needed salts, is making me more thirsty, for it's like drinking tepid ocean water. I start to put more sunburn cream on my flushed face and realize that it simply blocks pores and prevents perspiration, so opt for the sunburn.

Being aware of the symptoms helps one to take the necessary precautions, but their onslaught is not comforting. I know I need the energy, but have to force myself to eat. Susan, who feels the heat more than I do, decides to go back to the big pool upcanyon. That makes infinitely good sense to me, but I have obligated myself to see the remainder of the canyon, whether I feel particularly energetic about it or not.

We divide water and leave Susan sitting under the shaded overhang, like some dislocated gnome. We work across the talus, along an old threadbare trail part of the way, weaving carefully through blocks of dolomite. While the path maintains a more or less constant level, the canyon below drops sharply, and drops again in giant stairsteps that occasionally hold small pools. It takes forever for a rock thrown down into one of them to make a white pinpoint of a splash, and for the sound to travel back up again. If one were out of water, those pools would be of little help, for there is no way up or down.

At the crest of a small rise there is the first glimpse of the San Juan River and I look at it for several moments before I realize what it is: running water! Olive green, V'd with riffles, the river's susurration reaches clear up here, pulses audible over the wind in the canyon below. I walk near to the end of the promontory and sit down, rather more abruptly than I mean to, and look down at the river. I feel thick-headed, stultified. I notice that there is much more beach down there than usual but it makes no sense. The heat coming up from the dark ground is suffocating. The sun bears down on my shoulders like hot iron. I dig out my thermometer and put it in my shade, where it registers 102 degrees. Actually, it doesn't feel that hot, but my body tells me it is so: the lethargy, the heaviness. My face is so flushed it radiates its own heat.

Since I cannot see the final drop to the river, I get up and walk another hundred feet out to the farthest point of the cliff. Very little more cliff rises above me; most of it just drops off below and below and below, a sheer unredeemable thousand feet. I can see half a mile up, half a mile down river. Below all looks cool, fresh, the river sliding easily downstream in a silken hissing.

Up here the rock is hot, abrasive. Everything seems to adhere. My hand sticks to my notebook paper. My shirt sticks to my back. My hair sticks to my forehead. I stick to the rock on which I sit. After all the wind last night, there is scarcely a breeze up here now. I sit so close to the edge that I feel as if the slightest air current could pull me over. Yet I feel locked into a heat and a landscape out of which I cannot move, like a beetle pinned to an eternal display board, motionless, immobilized. A violet-green swallow wheels and turns below me, white rump dot like a white eye reeling through space. In the midst of this immobility, when it seems as if the rocks themselves begin to swirl as the river swirls, as the relationship with a level horizontal and a sturdy vertical begins to blur, a sense of elation floods through me. Elation? Exultation!

This brutal, dry, thorny, tearing landscape with the minimal river below is beautiful! It's beautiful because it's beautiful and because I earned it—the sound of the river slipping upward, the leaden descent of heat on my shoulders, the sharp reminder of rock beneath my hand —not what one usually would aspire to, not one of the usual sensible goals of life. I have even earned the uneasy euphoria of edging closer and closer to the drop of the cliff until I sit with my feet part way over, peering down only into time and water.

This stretching of self beyond stretchable boundaries, this glory of being where few have stood, of listening and seeing, of feeling the sun and the rock, somehow matters very much. The exhilaration is worth every bit of the discomfort and the duress. I have pushed through that discomfort to another level of being. I *like* being here, shot through with sunlight, incandescing it outward as I receive it inward. I feel an outer glory like an aura or a nimbus—not tainted in the least by the knowledge that there is an uphill eight-mile walk back. It will be as nothing.

Perhaps once in a while everyone needs a little glory after lunch.

The stream draining Slickhorn Gulch was observed on August 6 and 7, 1921, when it was flowing a fraction of a second-foot of pure, clear water. The last half mile of the stream was mapped by K. W. Trimble, and was found to have a fall of 150 feet.

H. D. MISER, *The San Juan Canyon, Southeastern Utah,* 1924

Unlike the graceful outlines of mountains and valleys in humid climates, the landscape is bold and rugged; curves are replaced by angles. In further contrast the protecting cover of vegetation is largely lacking; the dominant grays and greens of humid regions give way to whites, reds, and browns—the colors of the rocks themselves.

HERBERT E. GREGORY, *The San Juan Country, A Geologic and Geographic Reconnaissance of Southeastern Utah,* 1938

Slickhorn Canyon

1

Slickhorn Canyon is, as far as I'm concerned, the most elegant and gracious of these five canyons: the top miles cut into sandstone, the last miles incised into sleek pale limestone studded with coral-colored fossils, drifted with salmon-colored sand. Ten miles west of Johns Canyon, via the river, Slickhorn rises in an ascending series of limestone ledges for almost a mile, nearly every tread cradling a serene spring-fed pool reflecting the sinuous curves of the canyon walls and their subtle colors. Slickhorn is a joy to the eye, to the foot, intimate yet spacious, but most of all: elegant.

Yet my first view of Slickhorn several years ago, on a boat trip down the San Juan, was anything but. The campsite at the mouth of the canyon was as filthy as any I've ever seen. We spent half an hour burning toilet paper, burying feces, picking up metallic papers and assorted trash.

In addition, the mouth of Slickhorn reeks of hydrogen sulfide from oil seeps leaking into the San Juan out of the Hermosa Formation. The oil seeps begin about a mile upstream from the canyon's mouth and bubble up through the water, creating iridescent swirls near the shore, seeps that actually engendered the "oil boom" along the San Juan River. The first runner of the river, E. L. Goodridge, discovered small streams of oil emanating from boulders at the bottom of the canyon above the mouth of Slickhorn in 1879. Although he filed his first claim upriver at Mexican Hat, he later returned and attempted to put a well down here. All that's left of his ambitions is twisted cables and undecipherable pieces of rigging, all rusted to dark brown, high on the cliffside. Goodridge brought an engine all the way from Gallup, New Mexico, some 175 miles. That took a month. Then he wheedled it out onto the shelf that skirts the edge of the plateau above the river and cut a primitive road that snakes all the tortuous way to Slickhorn Gulch, coaxed it down the canyon wall to within sight of his well area, at which point, "owing to an unfortunate accident, the engine tumbled from the road and over the cliffs to the bottom of the canyon and was thus broken beyond repair."

In 1952–53 Don Danvers neatened up the road, brought in new equipment, and drilled two wells. The first went to 700 feet and produced 24 barrels of oil a day. The second well, only 50 feet away, went down 1,810 feet and was dry. As far as is known, no oil was transported out, the road being so difficult to traverse. Both wells were drilled in a small anticline, one of the "wrinkles" on the broad Monument Upwarp.

The rusted impedimenta of the old oil rig remain, as if in the throes of some last agony, clutched into the hillside, historically interesting, aesthetically unappetizing. In those days nobody carried out what they brought in.

2

One of my preferred times for walking the canyons is early spring. Walking is usually comfortable. There are likely to be few people in the canyon then. Early-blooming plants are just getting started. There's a real feel of greening-up in the air. So it is with much anticipation that I look forward to another spring vacation trip with Sara, and Dave and Frank Nordstrom. But when the time comes I have a sore throat that makes me less than totally enthusiastic about backpacking; I am sullen that a trip to which I've looked forward so much seems blighted before it ever begins. Somehow, no matter how I get my pack together, it weighs too much. My head aches too much, my throat hurts too much, and the thought of being anywhere but home in bed with the electric blanket turned up high seems totally ridiculous.

I question the wisdom of my going and rationalize it thus: trips are not all that easy to arrange, especially one like this. If my schedule is not flexible, neither is that of a doctor. Sara has but a few days home from college. Once a trip is scheduled, I incline not to cancel come hell or high water.

Standing on Cedar Mesa, I snug a scarf around my throat, blow my nose, and wait for everyone to pack up. I scan the landscape, trying to focus on something outside my own ills. The surface appears flat and wooded, but I've seen it from the air: I know little shoestring gullies worm their way all across the plateau, pale sand threading through the piñon-juniper woodland or the sagebrush-covered flats. But on the ground one comes on them quite unexpectedly, sometimes no more than a trowel-depth beginning behind a screen of piñon. We walk down just such a narrow gully to enter a side canyon of Slickhorn, a gully that quickly entrenches from inches to feet.

Even when the raw walls rise up to the top of my head at five feet, openings provided by the entrance of other watercourses give glimpses of evergreens in an endless progression of dark olive green. The gully walls fall away in dry chunks, exposing shrub roots that loop in and out of the soil like grotesque handles of buried teapots.

In Western usage, a gully is considered to be small, not over a few feet wide or deep, while an arroyo is the channel of an intermittent or ephemeral stream with banks of "unconsolidated material"—loose sandy debris which has not compacted into anything firmer or weathered into soil. Some of these gullies on Cedar Mesa may be at least 2,000 years old, since Basketmaker II hearths have been found on their sloping banks.

Here gullies and arroyos run only during a heavy rain. A light rain simply disappears into the sand. Water flow does not begin until a good downpour, lasting a while, contributes enough water to momentarily saturate the sand base. These gullies tend to have few branches, probably because most of the rainwater percolates down into the sand rather than running off to form new rills.

Gullies are normally thought of as V-shaped, but in the arid Southwest, both gullies and arroyos tend to be flat-bottomed. When a torrential rain does come and the arroyos run red with silt from the surrounding mesas, the bottoms often fill wall to wall, undercutting the loose material of the sides, removing blocks and chunks, widening the channel. The fact that lateral wall cutting is so prevalent is one of the reasons why arroyo cutting is so devastating; not only does it remove large amounts of useful acreage from use, but it makes the remaining terrain very difficult to traverse. The large amount of sediment dumped into the temporary stream is more than can be moved by such a brief rain, and most of it simply remains on the arroyo floor. In the long intervals between rains, the wind—the omnipresent canyon wind—cleans the floor of raindrop patterns. As we continue down the gully, the floor looks freshly swept. Within half an hour, sand disappears and we walk on bare rock.

As John Wesley Powell observed a hundred years ago, the materials of the walls determine the shape of a channel: when they are soft, the channel tends to be wider and shallower, like an arroyo. If hard rock, as they are now, the channel is narrower and deeper. Soon we are working our way down rock ledges, three-foot, four-foot steps, until finally, as they become larger and sharper, we are forced to walk a talus slope around the sides.

We come to the twelve-foot drop of a dry waterfall and walk down alongside to reach the slickrock floor beneath. It has been scoured clean by flash floods, and only a dusting of pink sand covers it now, sprinkled with a few blue-gray juniper berries and piñon needles. There is a constant variety of detail in color and bedding of the rock. Gray skeleton piñon cones scribble across the pavement with a sharp breeze. An early yellow parsley is tucked down like a pincushion among last year's dried leaves. Parsley and bladderpod, two of the earliest-blooming plants in the canyon, are both growing close to the ground for any residual warmth in the rocks, down below the wind.

Built under a narrow overhang in the opposite wall is a small dwelling. Above it, the cliff wall reaches up sheer, fifty feet. The ruin, tucked under its protective shelter, I pace off to be about eighteen feet long. The back wall is well blackened by the soot of long-quenched fires. The stones are well laid together, and the two door openings mark two rooms. A piñon stands sentry on the left, a juniper on the right. The structure is far enough off the floor of the canyon to be safe from flash flooding; nevertheless I would suspect that the residents often found a more ample water supply than they needed on their doorstep.

3

In another hour of walking the gully has grown to a small canyon, and we are nearly rimrocked by a fifty-foot limestone face which requires another detour around and another contouring down. These limestone shelves have a disconcerting way of dropping off, literally under your feet, not the place to walk and daydream. At the bottom, on small pools still in shadow, are heavy crusts of snow.

High above, four jet condensation trails, straight and smooth, limn the sky. The canyons lie beneath the Los Angeles–Chicago airway, and several flights go over every day, beginning around noon. With horizon visibility as limited as it is in the canyons, one often does not see

Bladderpod *(Lesquerella intermedia)*

approaching weather until it arrives. Jet condensation trails give an idea of upper air conditions and therefore of coming weather. If broad and fraying, there are high winds aloft and moisture and unstable air. If short and fading quickly, the upper air is very dry. If thin and undistorted, little wind and a sign of good weather. Or at least it's reassuring to say so. Otherwise I find the white streaks across *my* blue sky very annoying, and the sound intrudes on consciousness, reminding me of other places, other obligations.

I suspect that I am the object of subtle pity, for we have more rest stops than usual. I hate holding everyone up but I say nothing. In fact, if they would just like to leave me here, pounding head, sore throat, and all, I'd have no complaints. This time we stop by another small pool, secreted under the overhang of a large boulder. The pool remains half covered with ice, which is now two or three inches above the level of the water, on whose surface dance reflections of the ice sheet's white underside. Single drops coming off the filagree edge quiver the surface. Out in the sunshine, cozy in a rock niche, a bladderpod blooms, brilliant chrome yellow. I even feel a little chlorophyll in my veins. There's an intensely spring-on-its-way feeling, a turn of the season toward warmth, a pivot point, winter retreating drop by drop, visually, aurally, into spring.

By noon we reach the joining of this side canyon with Slickhorn proper. Often at these junctions there are small ruins, and a scanning of the cliffs shows a jacal structure on a ledge about one-third of the way up off the canyon floor. Rock falls and splits in various ledges provide access. I huddle against a warm rock, watching my companions working their way up. Ordinarily my curiosity would take me with any exploration; today I am quite content to sit and wait. The three figures, like three starfish plastered against the wall, become astonishingly smaller; it's much farther up than it looks!

On the ground around me handfuls of nodules have weathered out of the granular sandstone, although some remain embedded in the rocks, creating a warty surface. Some of the sand patches between rocks are laid so closely with nodules that they look paved. Others roll free, like tan peas, lined up neatly in little patches of sand or caught in small cushions of plants that grow tucked in cracks in the rock floor.

A call from above alerts me that something special has been found. I drag myself up the slope, hoping it's worth it. Indeed it is. Completely screened from view below is a perfect granary wedged against the cliff. Built in a sharp, narrow overhang on one side of a small alcove in the cliff, it is hidden by a huge juniper. It is constructed of large flagstones, the interstices neatly mud-packed and studded with small rocks between the larger ones. The granary must be about five feet tall. The real delight is that the door, a trapezoidal flagstone about two feet high, is intact. It falls into place against the mud coping with a soft thunk. Most granaries have the doors broken or missing; to see one in place, even to its impression in the mud mortar that calked it shut, is a treat. To prehistoric people accustomed to the fluctuations of wild plant production and the vagaries of hunting, the soft, hollow sound of this door falling into place, such promise of another year of food must have been particularly reassuring.

4

I pick my way downslope while the rest continue exploring. Part way down I rest. It feels good to sit here in the sun, not moving, just part of the landscape, waiting for summer. A slow-moving lizard trundles along the warm sandstone. I am surprised to see one out so early—it seems to me to move with the misery of winter still in its veins.

Scarcely as long as my hand, tail and all, it is one of the most common lizards of the semi-arid Southwest, a side-blotched lizard, so called because of the darkish blue blotch on each side just behind the front legs. It ranges over a wide variety of habitats although it has a small home range, and is one of the few lizards active most of the year. It has a catholic appetite, consuming everything from spiders, mites, ticks, and sowbugs, to scorpions, mosquitoes, wasps, indeed almost anything small enough to snap up. Its scientific name, *Uta stansburiana,* honors Captain Howard Stansbury, who led the government exploration and survey of the Great Salt Lake in 1850; the naming was done by two zoologists at the then newly created Smithsonian Institution.

The lizard's small size enables it to warm quickly, and I note that it lines up to the sun as I have: it receives the sun's warmth along its whole body length. Its color is darker, more intense, than that of most lizards I'm accustomed to seeing, of considerable benefit when it's necessary to absorb every bit of heat possible. It flattens its body to the rock, soaking up radiant heat from the ground as well as from the sun; desert lizards are naturally curved on their upper sides, flattened on their bellies, for efficient heat absorption. Unlike us, able to generate heat within our own bodies, this small creature depends upon the warmth of its environment; nor does it have the insulators against temperature change of a furry mammal or a feathered bird. It takes full advantage not only of heat from the sun and the ground, but of any reflected heat from other rock faces or pale sand.

Unlike other Southwestern lizards, this one matures within the same season that it hatches, at least in the more southern part of its range. After battering its way out of its shell by means of an eggtooth on the snout, sometime between June and August, it will be mature in time for the mating season during August. A female produces an average of twelve young; of these usually only two survive. The adults are short-lived, so there is close to an annual turnover of a population that survives on high reproductive capacity.

The sun on my shoulder blades and the back of my neck is mustard-plaster hot. I feel it go all the way through, swathing my throat in warmth. At almost the same time that I become aware of the heat, the lizard raises its body off the sandstone, stretching its neck, tongue darting, and trips off, insinuating itself among the pebbles and plant stems, warmed to stalking temperature. Not a trembled leaf marks its passage, and had I not followed it, I would not see that wary black bead of an eye among the ocellated shadows.

Wallflower *(Erysimum capitatum)*

The rock outcrops below me resemble the backs of ancient monstrous lizards that may have once stalked here. Every so often on the slope a yucca grows, or a rabbitbrush, or a broken-off stem or stalk where something bloomed last year. A single wallflower bears a head of molten sunshine. It seems a waiting land, more connected to the past than the present. Soil lichens castellate a patch of soil; they look like sandcastles built by children using Jello molds. The charcoal-gray lichen is darker than the soil, the difference in color emphasizing the one or two inches of relief.

A jay squawks. The call caroms off the cliff. The following quiet rings in my ears. Someplace another bird whispers, blending into the sound of the wind. Threads on the edge of the yucca leaves curl into circles. Black lichen graph crusts of islands and isthmuses on a boulder. Sara's distinctive laughter drifts down the slope. It takes me a moment to realize where I am.

5

After four o'clock, when we make camp, the canyon is all in shadow. The evening fire mutters and hisses, as if reluctant to heat up. Dave comes back with a bucketful of ice he's found somewhere, a little gritty but very refreshing to a sore throat nevertheless.

I find a good spot to sleep, on a narrow ledge above the streambed, protected by a four-foot rise to the main terrace, a place just large enough for my ground cloth. At the head end a big old cottonwood has split. One part of the trunk extends horizontally just off the ground, supported by a tripod of thick branches. The main trunk rises straight. The ground is cushioned with a layer of cottonwood leaves. I lie on my sleeping bag, listening to the sounds of supper getting ready, glad I don't have to fix it.

In a lunette of sand against the ledge are a dozen ant lion pits, mostly an inch or so across, little inverted cone traps. Ant lions are the larvae of an unassuming frail dragonfly-like creature that prefers walking to flying, flies with hesitant wing beats, and bears no resemblance to this carnivorous little consumer of ants. From eggs laid directly in the sand and hatched there, the larvae develop underground, plump bodies coated with spinelike hairs that help them remain anchored in the sand. They dig new pits by throwing sand with rapid snaps of the head and jaws, all the while rotating at the bottom of the pit. I drop a few grains of sand to see if these pits are occupied. In three nothing happens, but in the fourth the bottom seethes as the ant lion pulls down sand so that its nonexistent victim can find no purchase.

On the lower shelves of the canyon Mormon tea and buffaloberry grow among the loose rock. I can tell the plants apart by their outline even at this distance: buffaloberry is round, Mormon tea like a big whiskbroom stuck on end. Close by, a buffaloberry bush is not quite in bloom, knotted with little yellow buds. Silver scales make the round curled-under leaves look as if they had been sprayed with metallic paint. On the underside they look like matted wool.

Nor is the Mormon tea ready to bloom with its tiny papery conelike flowers. A family of one genus, *Ephedra,* it is characteristic of arid regions

Buffaloberry *(Shepherdia rotundifolia)*

and is one of the bizarre growth forms often found in desert plants, leaves reduced to scales, stems resistant to evaporation, a stalky moon-scape kind of a plant. Three species grow in this area and from a distance can be told apart by their color—olive green, blue green, or bright green. The last, *Ephedra viridis,* the most common in Utah, bears two leaf scales at each joint or node.

The Mormon tea stems brew up into a decent tea, slightly astringent from the high amount of tannin, but rather pleasant withal. It was used for tea by the Indians and early settlers (hence the common name) but its utilization goes back much further. The Chinese have used a species of *Ephedra* for over five thousand years, from the whole plant obtaining the drug ephedrine, a familiar ingredient of nose drops and old cold remedies. (Our species contain tannin, pseudoephedrin, and other alkalis, but not the medicinal ephedrine.)

I take my handful of stems with me for tea with dinner. After dinner I stretch out on the slickrock, head pillowed on a soft boulder, and listen to the conversation around me. Half asleep, my eyes follow the perforation pattern in a layer of rock close by, from quarter-sized to handhold-sized to melon-sized, beautiful patterns. The cold seeps into my right side. Oddly, it feels good. The fire flutters. Sara asks what it sounds like. Dave says, "Like junco wings."

6

Reluctantly I arise to walk the canyon before I simply become part of the rock. Two canyon wrens call in the dusk, a shimmering, silver trill, one on each side of the canyon—to the right a regular descending trill, to the left, the same liquid song but embellished with a lilting "dearie, dearie, dearie" and a little burr at the end, an absolutely delightful and distinctive song.

The day seems empty when I don't hear a canyon wren here. But not if I don't see one, for I have only caught sight of one once or twice. They are elusive and small, hard to find in the myriad crosshatched shadows on a sandstone wall. They prefer inaccessible crevices or ledges, high out of reach, where they build nests the size of small soup bowls, padded with moss and spider webbing and perhaps some soft catkins or feathers. There are laid five or six small white eggs tinted with just a salting of reddish brown.

I remember vividly a canyon wren I watched one afternoon, strutting up and down a cliff wall as if it were horizontal instead of near vertical, stopping now and then to poke for an insect in a crack, throat and breast bright white, slipping out of sight into a narrow, shadowed slot and appearing again, constantly in motion, tail bobbing, a "tireless bundle of feathered energy" as one ornithologist put it. I sat enchanted, feeling then as I feel now: the day seems empty when I don't hear a canyon wren's pellucid, descending arpeggio shimmer in the air.

An old piñon tree is running with pitch and I stop to collect some for starting the morning fire. It is as if the tree bleeds to death. Pitch flows down stripped panels on the trunk, runs down the rock against which the tree grows, and makes sticky puddles on the ground, the result of porcupine damage. During spring and summer porcupines seem quite content to feed on the leaves and twigs of undergrowth, but in winter, when such food is scarce, they often go after tree bark, doing greater or lesser damage depending on how much they strip from the tree. Since they do not hibernate they need quantities of food all winter long, which they obtain by cutting out the rough outer bark of conifers with their chisel-like front teeth, and then feasting on the tender inner bark. The food value seems to be quite low, and enormous amounts are required to satiate a hungry porcupine; up to a quart of masticated bark fiber has been found in the stomach of a single animal. If the porcupine, gnawing in haphazard fashion, girdles the tree, the tree dies; at best it is injured and opened to disease.

I feel a surprising and irrational anger: damned porcupines! I try to find something good about this plodding prickled beast, but given all the intellectual admissions of their place in nature, tonight I'm totally on the side of the tree.

Two tiny bats flicker over a little pool, swooping down to skim the surface. With impeccable control, mouths open, they dip a drop at a time off the water, and when they have imbibed enough, begin the evening's hunt. Although I never fail to see them in the morning or evening in the canyons, I've never seen one resting during the day, although overhangs and dwellings usually have as much bat guano as mouse droppings. I always look for the little body, hanging upside down, hind limbs attached backward at the hip so the bottom of the foot faces forward. It could be that bats use these particular shelters at night only and spend the day in dark crevices, where they're seldom seen. I admit to a vast curiosity: having grown up with the old wives' tale about them getting entangled in ladies' hair and now knowing it to be untrue, I have enough courage and curiosity so that I'd like to see one of those wizened little faces up close and have a good look. Besides, in the Far East bats are a symbol of happiness and longevity, and bringers of good fortune. The Chinese word for "bat" is also the name of the character for happiness.

Vespertine bats tend to have feeding times according to species; the tiniest of all, pipistrelles, come out the earliest. Most bats are small, usually weighing less than an ounce, but a pipistrelle is so tiny that it has been described as looking like a big beetle in the hand. Preferring desert and canyons, they appear where there are rock outcrops for daytime retreat. As is true of most bats, little is known about their migration or hibernation. Pipistrelles are rarely out after nine-thirty, which strikes me as an excellent time to retire too.

Yet, reluctant to sleep, to miss a nuance of this lovely canyon, I listen to the reed grasses nearby rattle softly as the night wind pushes against them. I look up at the curving cottonwood twigs, always curving upward, knobby, one branch with buds just ready to burst, swelled to the utmost. The repeated arcs of the branches are like basket ribs, cradling a sky full of stars. I fall asleep watching the stars tangle in the branches and a splinter of a moon.

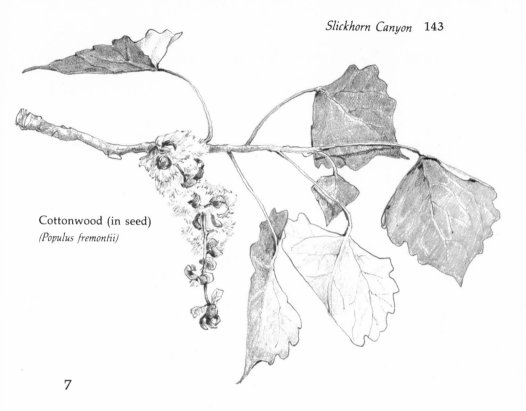

Cottonwood (in seed)
(Populus fremontii)

7

I awake at six in time to watch the slow light pick up the canyon colors. Although I heard the wind once or twice last night, here there was only a faint resettling of dry leaves. I think this little cul de sac with its mat of cottonwood leaves and filagree of branches is one of the most beautiful places I've slept, and what's more, my head is clear, my throat is comfortable, as if this spot contained some miraculous cure.

But at breakfast all I hear about is the wind. Frank complains that his tent rattled like a Model A. Sara says she fought her ground cloth, which threatened to take off like a hang glider, and claims she left fingernail prints in the rock trying to keep from being blown away. Dave swears he lashed himself to a piñon tree to keep from being blown out to sea. I claim only peace, respite, and healing.

All packed up, I sit on the terrace where I slept, reluctant to leave, and wait for the others. The sun burgeons up over the sandstone wall to the east, backlighting dry rabbitbrush seed heads and grasses on the other side of the streambed, turning cottonwood twigs white. Everything moves with the fresh breeze, as if some small animal just walked through, invisible and unheard, leaving wavering grass as the only trace of its passage.

A gray ghost did walk through last night, coming close to where I slept, its footprints making a short detour where it stood and sampled the smell and decided I wasn't something it cared about. Preferring the rough country of these canyons because it is less fleet than other foxes, the gray fox takes refuge in all the innumerable cracks and crannies.

It is a night wanderer, often following rabbit tracks. Almost as omnivorous as raccoons, both parents hunt to feed the three or four young born each spring. The kits remain in the protection of their crevice den until they are old enough to do their own hunting. Because of their acceptance of plant as well as animal food, these small hunters can thrive where more particular feeders might find slim pickings. A gray fox pounces on its prey, catlike, preferring to stalk rather than to chase, as it can usually be outrun.

I've seen only one in these canyons, a mere gray shadowy streak that left me wondering what had passed by. But I see the tracks often, threading down a sandy wash or, with curiosity scalloping the usually straight trail, exploring around camp.

Other smaller feet were abroad here last night, perhaps a tiny canyon mouse, whose body would fit in a teacup, nosing around for any seed it might find, certainly one of the mice that would have cleaned out an Anasazi granary had it not been well built. The range of this mouse corresponds closely with that of the Indian sites in the Southwest.

About six feet below me is a pool, circled with rocks, shimmering with the slate gray blue of the sky, thatched and cross-hatched with straw-colored grasses. As early in the year as it is, the surface is webbed with water striders that change position each time a breeze wrinkles the surface. I think of Loren Eisley's lines:

> I tread most gently in this season; I
> > feel all the tension that the striders feel
> > and sense the gamesters in the molecule.
> Knowing how suddenly a world can fall,
> > I always watch the striders in the spring.

8

We wend down a streambed still partially shelved with snow, crusted on top, studded with tan cottonwood leaves, whose darker color has caught the furtive spring warmth and melted them in half an inch, and stalked with cattails whose seeds catch in everything—snow, soil, jeans, hair, eyelashes.

After an hour of walking, we divest ourselves of packs, propping them upright against a big boulder, and proceed to explore a small side canyon. The floor shelves steeply upward, laid with loose rocks that clank hollow with our footsteps. Debris lies entangled four feet above the streambed; a big boulder has a log balanced on top. A tremendous flash flood must have torn through here—not a place to pitch one's tent during the rainy season.

I push through an oak thicket that reminds me of a Massachusetts woods where I walked only a week before; there the oak leaves were as big as my two hands together. Here they are but a couple of inches long, dwarfed as are the trees—Gambel oak, one of the two species able to grow in these dry canyons. Gambel oak is poisonous to cattle; the oak sends out new shoots earlier than other plants, and is most toxic in the budding and leafing-out stages. Oddly enough, it is not poisonous for deer and is an important browse for them.

The oaks here are farther along than others we've seen; this small canyon runs east-west and undoubtedly gets more sun earlier. Small magenta locoweeds stud the pavement, and there are numerous yellow parsleys, and some of the shrubs are twined with vines, perhaps wild sweet pea. Compared with Slickhorn's main canyon, the air here is perceptibly balmier. A huge beetle, flying close to the ground, latches onto a grass stem. At least three-quarters of an inch long, its elytra, the hard-shelled wing covers, are redwood color with a black border, its head and thorax dark green, but most notable are the hairs on its back and the wool on its underside, a beetle in a fur coat! I do not know its name. This is, after all is said and done, the most frustrating aspect of a backpack trip to me: the inability to carry a fully-stocked library for reference and not being able to identify insects when I finally do have the book in hand at home.

Against the skyline is a handsome bridge cut out of the Cedar Mesa Sandstone when water ran through here two hundred feet higher, before these canyons in which we now walk were even cut. A multitude of rivers must have looped across the plateau at different times, wandering, changing channels, carving intricate serpentine patterns that are characteristic of gently sloping terrain with an easily-eroded soil mantle. As always in a meander pattern, the water ate away at the outside of the curve and deposited on the inside. The meanders that created the bridge above, rather than sweeping in big curves, coiled as tightly as ribbon candy, leaving a narrow fin of rock between curves. At the base of this fin the water worked slowly from either side, until it finally cut through the sandstone. Because Cedar Mesa Sandstone is well cemented and strong, the upper part of the wall remained in place, leaving a splendid span which frames now not tan water but blue sky.

The warmth of the canyon and the natural bridge, in which the Anasazi may have found some magical quality (why not? I certainly do, geological explanations to the contrary), suggest the possibility of finding an Indian ruin. As we walk on we stop frequently to look up and scan the walls.

And then there it is, perched on a ledge, high up and seemingly inaccessible, a small dwelling. But patience and a walk farther upcanyon soon reveal a series of interconnected ledges which lead upward. However, we can approach only as far as the ledge beneath; the dwelling is twenty feet above. There is no way to reach it short of making a ladder. There are some shallow handholds in the rock which an agile Anasazi could have used, or perhaps even chipped out, and a ladder might have been in place originally. With such a controlled approach, the dwelling is nearly impregnable.

The overhang opening is not very high, and evidently the floor had a considerable downward slope because juniper logs have been laid at the front edge to make a level floor inside. The wall is built of good-sized rocks with some smaller ones in between, and appears dry-laid. The wall paces out to about twenty feet, ending where the overhang ledges out. Another dwelling around the corner is totally unreachable without ropes.

Much of the rock underfoot is unstable, with many sandstone nodules that roll like marbles and make footing treacherous, especially when the first step is 150 feet down. Nevertheless we venture into the next alcove for a surprise. The back wall is fire-blackened. On the ground are tiny ears of corn, not more than three inches long, and a full set of ram's horns. Deer grow and shed antlers yearly; sheep horns are permanent, each ridge indicating a year's growth: it takes around ten years to complete a full curl. The arc of these is handsome, a beveled curl nearly two feet across.

What a magnificent ram these must have belonged to, whose cloven hooves were adapted for just this precipitous terrain, edged like a razor to cut into snow and ice and lock onto the slightest projection on the canyon wall, hoof interior as tough as hard rubber, able to absorb the shock of two hundred pounds coming down at the end of a twenty-

Wild sweetpea *(Lathyrus zionis)*

Gilia or Skyrocket *(Gilia arizonica)*

foot leap. Was this one a sentinel for his band, amber eyes scanning the cliffs for the surreptitious shadow, giving the alarm and bounding away, white rump patch a clear signal to follow? Or did he stand, wary but curious, and did that curiosity hold him within range of an arrow strike, the sudden painful flash, the sickening loss of light? And did the Anasazi clever enough to kill him celebrate his success and in eating assume some of the attitudes of this animal he could not help but admire —its strength, fleetness, wisdom, and beauty?

As we leave, Sara looks up and spots the third treasure of the morning, wheeling above in lazy open spirals: a bald eagle. Catching the thermals and soaring, it is able, with its superb eyesight, to focus on any movement below that might mean food, and woe to the unwary jackrabbit that strays too far from cover. Hit from above and behind by talons that cut, scimitar-like, through muscle and bone alike, it will never know what happened, never profit from its experience to be more wary next time. Quite likely at this time of year there may be eggs in the eagle's nest, and it hunts more efficiently and more desperately, needing to return and brood. On this overcast day, there will be no shadows when it dives, wind streaming through the primaries, only a swift silence and death for one and life for the other.

9

The cottonwoods along the streambed in Slickhorn grow outward, trunks dividing, branches arching to the ground, rather than upright as they do along stream courses on the mesa top.

Other things are different down here in the canyons. Life is more limited, more selective, the changes smaller, more subtle. As we walk downcanyon it would not seem that the altitude change is sufficient to bring more flowers into bloom, but there they are, opening at my feet —a brilliant gilia, a prickly phlox. I remember a trip down upper Grand Gulch at the end of April one year that began with cottonwoods barely leafed out and ended, thirty miles later, with trees in full splendid summer leaf. It makes me aware of how closely plant life is adjusted in this marginal environment, how a few hundred feet of altitude bring the extra fraction of warmth that is the equivalent of a day, two days, a week more in plant development, a nicety of adjustment that the Anasazi were certainly aware of when they planted corn on the small alluvial terraces in the canyons. Now in late March the cottonwoods are just coming into bloom, the bud scales lying shiny and red on the ground, like the elytras of an exotic beetle species; on some trees the flowers hang like little dark red mulberries.

As we round a corner a flock of piñon jays unbird a tree, taking flight and wheeling, sounding just as Alfred V. Kidder, the famous Southwestern archaeologist, described them—"the far-off mewing of a flock of Pinyon Jays." Quail tracks pattern the sand and thousands of crisp cottonwood leaves have lodged vertically between the streambed cobbles, as if inserted by hand, making neat pleated fans.

In a side canyon are ample amounts of "road apples" and finally we come upon the horses, six in all. Owned by a local rancher who has had grazing rights here for many years, the horses wander freely in this natural corral. (Slickhorn's name came from a herd of longhorns with unusually shiny smooth horns that were grazed here at the turn of the century.)

Now backpackers are beginning to object to horse droppings bobbing in their water supply, and are pressuring the BLM to rescind all

Prickly phlox *(Leptodactylon pungens)*

grazing rights in the canyons. Slickhorn is often used by hikers as an ingress/egress in tandem with Grand Gulch, just a few miles farther west, and as a consequence, these two canyons probably get more use than Johns, Steer Gulch, or Whirlwind Draw.

The conflict between traditional grazing use and people who come into the canyons for a couple of days at a time is a difficult one to resolve, and many ranchers tend to resent the closing-off of traditional range. In many of the local restaurants of nearby towns, a sign is posted that reads simply: SIERRA GO HOME.

10

Poking around side canyons is one of the pleasures of walking a big canyon. You can leave your pack, and every time I take mine off I think of the ancient answer of the man who was asked why he pounded his head against the wall: "Because it feels so good when I stop!" Divesting oneself of thirty pounds and leaving them up against a tree is a psychological as well as physical event. I feel as if my arms float upward—I rise a foot off the ground with every step—I levitate up the canyon.

The mouth of this particular canyon rises about eight feet from the bed of Slickhorn. Once up, the floor is like fresh-scrubbed stairsteps, immaculately clean. Bootsteps echo softly against the canyon walls. The canyon is short, less than a mile perhaps, and has a swift rise, nearly seven hundred feet, to take it up to the Cedar Mesa Plateau.

We veer to the left, walking across sandstone ledges that become progressively more canted. By contouring back and forth we rise higher and higher above the canyon floor. The sandstone, bedded in long sweeping curves, provides good traction. "Rock walking" is like downhill skiing in that on a traverse one should lean out from the slope rather than in, which is the natural protective reaction. The latter tends to change the angle of boot contact with the slope, leaving less sole in touch, moving one's center of gravity outward, making it much easier to lose footing. There is never anything to grab on to—no well-rooted tree or shrub, no firm outcrop—and nothing below but a great deal of space.

A lovely fawn-colored spider stretches out under a large flat rock. I discover her when I try to use for support the slab under which she lies; it teeters and hangs there in sheer defiance of gravity. The spider's legs are black-tipped, head squarish, eyes in a line, a faint curving V marked on her back. She does not move when uncovered, but stays securely splayed out on the rock. I envy her her eight legs and secure traction.

We come to a chimney in the rock, a slot about two and a half feet wide between the wall and a house-sized boulder. Dave patiently shows me how to place feet and back in position and move up the slot. I press my back hard enough against the sandstone to leave vertebra prints, press my feet in front of me, half sitting in the crack, and inch my way up. When I am nearly to the top, Dave leans over to grab my wrist for a last hoist up and says, "When you have a minute, whistle Dixie!" and I have to laugh, mostly from relief.

A last push-pull brings us out on the rim, miles of slickrock with a stupendous 360-degree panorama. The perfect dome of Navajo Mountain rises in the distance, milky blue. The Clay Hills catch a shaft of sunlight, like some grandiose operatic stage set that will be rolled up and stowed away as soon as we leave.

After looking down at my feet for so long, the optical illusion when I look up is vertiginous: the clouds seem to seethe and coalesce in strange patterns. A jet drones over, obscured, the sound humming off the rock pavement. The undersides of the clouds, heavy with moisture look like globular cauliflowers, hollows as blue-gray as the juniper berries.

At my feet the Cedar Mesa Sandstone undulates like a calm ocean. Cracked mud patterns fill its oval and round depressions. A few scrubby junipers grow here, bonsai trees, pruned by wind. Soil and rock lichens cluster in profusion, but otherwise the rock pavement is innocent of detritus. The sandstone weathers to gray-brown and exfoliates in large plates that clank when walked upon, and lift up to reveal the delicate cream of the unweathered rock beneath.

There is no sun and I chill quickly. The wind cuts through my shirt. In the canyon it was warm and protected; up here it's freezing. And the weather prognostication, to judge by the clouds, is unpleasant: cold, windy, and wet. The first raindrops freckle the sandstone. Then the freckles become leopard spots and begin to overlap. But, as soon as the rock begins to shine, the rain stops, and the sandstone dries in a second. Nevertheless, we start down immediately. Slickrock, where a human is the tallest object in the landscape, is not a place to be in a lightning storm.

11

When we reach our proposed campsite, it's well past lunchtime. Lunches are not my favorite meal backpacking, perhaps because I seldom eat lunch at home, and because of what they contain. Usually they consist of some kind of easily portable, nonspoilable, hard sausage, a chunk of cheese, and a bag of "gorp"—that amorphous combination of nuts, raisins, cereal, salt, and heaven know what that is supposed to add quick energy, lighten one's pack, and put a sparkle in one's eye. I am not especially fond of handfuls of things no matter what their highly touted nutritional value. My cheese has reached the consistency of putty, and the salami tastes like grout.

All of this boosts my popularity to a new high: I am a source of extras for those who are still hungry, who dig the last pulverized bits out of the corners of their plastic bags, look around wistfully for any tidbits dropped on the rock, and make clutching sounds of unsatisfied hunger. When they get my leftovers there's even an extra bonus: they didn't have to carry them.

After lunch I want to walk as far down Slickhorn toward the river as possible in the time that's left of the day. I have walked up Slickhorn from the river, as far as the first main branch of the canyon, and after lunch I would like to walk down to that junction, but *not* farther, for that "farther" takes me back to an early agonizing hiking trip into Slickhorn. After fairly easy going, coming up from the river, the canyon becomes choked with brush and boulders that have to be circumnavigated. One of these walk-arounds is a thread of a path, one human footprint wide, hung on a precipitous unstable slope. The view below takes a strong stomach: back-breaking boulders and a long, long way down. Above there is no consolation either: simply loose soil and scree at an appalling angle of repose. Nothing to grab on to, no place to stop and reconsider, and, above all, no place to chicken out and turn around.

Sara sashayed across as if practicing for the human-fly job in the circus and there were nets strung below to catch her in case of misstep. If she could do it, I was determined to do so too. But once is enough. When we finally got back to camp at the end of the day, two ravens had raided it and gotten into everything available, including gorp and powdered milk and dried cereal. Furious at our return, they sat on the rim directly above us like two bad omens, squawking deprecations.

Between camp today and that junction is a gamut of boulders and some slow talus walking. Frank demurs about accompanying us, saying he's done it enough times already. Somehow other people's descriptions are not deterrents, and as a wan sun comes out, we set off walking down the dry streambed as if on a city sidewalk, which the canyon turns out to resemble. First we pass four other hikers, then half an hour later, five more, and three students with a big dog. "Too many people," moans Dave. Sara and I agree. We like it best when we see no one else.

We have set ourselves a time limit at which point we must turn around and go back. Reaching that limit, we are still not to the junction, but from a vantage point high on the east side of the canyon, I can see where the canyon splits, the intersecting walls paling in the late thin sunlight.

We start back, weaving up and down the slope between rough blocks strewn across it, and occasionally walking down in the streambed itself, something not easily done except in a dry year like this. The walking is rough-slipping, unstabilized ankle-turning and ankle-knocking. We make a rest stop at a frozen pool, the water nearly gone from underneath. But three inches of ice remain, looking like frozen champagne. Chipping off large cooling plates, we discuss how to get it back to camp. None of us has a daypack and there are no volunteers for hand carrying. The ice stays where it is.

12

When we get back, Frank is there, fuming. He has gone downcanyon to say hello to the group we had passed earlier in the afternoon and with whom he had spoken earlier. They had passed our campsite and turned back because of no water upcanyon, and are now camped below us, an outdoor-education class from a western state university. Instead of adhering to some of the more conservative practices of experienced backpackers, they have constructed a four-foot-diameter fire circle, rimmed it with rocks, and have built a fire suitable for a funeral pyre or a rescue signal from a remote Pacific island.

The mystique of a big fire is part of the camper's heritage: the leaping flame, the hissing log, the tale told at midnight. Surely it dates back to the desire to hold back the darkness of primeval forests. But such fires (without a large fire pan beneath) leave an unmistakable scar: blackened sand or dirt, charcoal and half-burned logs, fire-smudged rocks left for the next camper, to say nothing of wildfire danger in a canyon often choked with brush and dry grass, where the closest water is a difficult mile away. Old fire circles invite new fires in the same place, and soon the peripheral area is worn and trampled beyond recovery, and the sense of wilderness, the feeling that "I am the first person here and I am alone," is destroyed.

A small narrow trench, dug with a trowel, no more than four by fifteen inches, fueled with small twigs and branches, can produce enough heat to cook for a dozen people. Charcoal can be kept to a minimum by allowing the fire to burn to ash that blows away. The remainder can be buried (which is no longer such a good idea with so many fires in the area and the limited number of level campsites) or pulverized and dispersed to the winds. Or carried out. A tiny stove, which involves toting a small amount of fuel, can solve the whole problem.

Piñon cones *(pinus edulis)*

What has annoyed Frank about the group with the monstrous fire circle is that an outdoor-education teacher, who should well know the fragility of these canyons, is teaching by example how to muck up the wilderness to the very young people who will teach the same to even younger students. Frank is sullen for the rest of the evening. I don't blame him. He has walked this canyon for twenty years and found only peace and solitude. Tonight he finds too many people.

13

After dinner we decide to climb up the talus slope above camp, about four hundred feet straight up, to get a look at the pinnacle that rises right above our heads. We scramble up as the light grows dim, the sky darkening early because of another bank of clouds coming in from the west. A freshening wind flickers the Mormon tea and buffets anything three feet above the ground. I think wistfully of the long, long days of summer and the leisurely after-dinner walks, when the sand is warm and the air just cooling, which seem to have a way of tying up the day for me.

The pinnacle must be at least fifty or sixty feet high, a narrow pillar of rock with a narrow saddle between it and the remainder of the ridge. Such pinnacles are formed by vertical joints in the rock and are fairly common in these canyons. Toward the end of a narrow ridge some of the blocks have fallen away, leaving a single stack still vertical at the end of the ridge.

Although the pinnacle has stood for thousands of years and is more than likely good for a few thousand more, standing at the bottom, the perspective is overpowering and it looks as if it could topple any minute, as if the clouds are standing still and the pinnacle is swinging. It's scary somehow, in the semi-darkness, and I feel as if I have stumbled, forbidden, onto the edge of Valhalla.

I sit, taking notes as long as I can see, and then go up to the saddle. The wind is fierce across this twenty-foot gap, this hiatus in the rock, but somehow it's the right wind. Up here it is fitting that there is wind, keeping open the slot in the wall, charging through, honing the air, taking voices away. The moon sharpens and brightens, bringing Saturn with it, rising in an open quadrant of sky. I absorb the strength of the earth through feet rooted in the rock. If I could raise my arms high enough I could garner thunderbolts and grasp them like a bouquet of crackling light. Did an Anasazi once stand here, pulling strength out of the earth as I do, making obeisance to the gods of the winds?

We work down the slope in the darkness, a declivity of mind and feeling. Looking up at it the next morning I don't know how anyone could have descended it in the dark. Perhaps when one scratches the underside of heaven one is granted a special grace. But the euphoria remains, and I can still call back that feeling of being astride the world and what it was like to be charged with the energy of the universe. Perhaps one true gift of these canyons is that they become so deeply imprinted on the psyche that they can be invoked at will, bringing back their particular charge of serene energy whenever needed.

The flora of San Juan Canyon and the adjacent country is so sparse that the widely scattered patches of green constitute only a small part of any landscape view, whether the view is taken from the canyon floor or across the adjacent plateau. The predominant colors in such a view are the browns and reds of bare rocks.

H. D. MISER, *The San Juan Canyon, Southeastern Utah,* 1924

The desert down there has a peculiar horror; I do not mean thirst, nor Indian massacres, which are frequent. The very floor of the world is cracked open into countless canyons and arroyos, fissures in the earth which are sometimes ten feet deep, sometimes a thousand. Up and down these stony chasms the traveller and his mules clamber as best they can. It is impossible to go far in any direction without crossing them.

WILLA CATHER, *Death Comes for the Archbishop,* 1927

Steer Gulch and Whirlwind Draw

1

The last two of the five canyons descending to the San Juan, Steer Gulch and Whirlwind Draw, are the farthest west, seven and nine river miles respectively from Grand Gulch. Two more Western-sounding names I cannot imagine.

Both begin in the most barren reaches of the country and drain a formidable wilderness before they reach the San Juan River. Both are lower in altitude and drier than the other three canyons. Without tree cover, the land is ruthless and rough, close to pure desert, of a baking, unshaded harshness in summer, a bitter, sinking cold in winter. Both are small canyons; each could be covered in a long day's walk if one could keep from exploring all the tempting side drainages.

Although it's October, purple asters and rabbitbrush are still in bloom, bright against the pinkness of the sand. Where I hoist on my pack Mormon tea is plentiful, casting spiky shadows; a single stunted and gnarled juniper stretches grotesque fingers across the sky. In the distance a horned lark sings. Lenticular clouds are suspended near Navajo Mountain to the southwest, formed by sheering winds at that altitude; they look like lenses of ivory mounted on a blue background.

A small group of us will walk and explore Steer Gulch, and then cut off cross country to Whirlwind Draw. There are no reliable springs in either, and no sure source of water. Water in potholes will be the only source, and until that water is found, we carry enough for one day's needs; that means five quarts, which translates to ten pounds. I stuff the water bottles in my backpack and barely manage to get it up and on.

It would be hard to say where Steer Gulch actually begins. Unlike the sharp drops at the heads of the other canyons, where the contour lines on the map are repetitive and clustered, the contour lines delineating Steer and Whirlwind both are far-spaced, open and loose. Although

Steer Gulch probably drains a larger area than Slickhorn Canyon, Slickhorn is much steeper from the start, bounded by sheer sandstone walls. Steer Gulch is more open and gradual. I am scarcely conscious of walking downhill. The streambed is merely smoother sand than the terrain alongside, fed by little channels a sand grain wide and a sand grain deep.

2

Occasionally fine pebbles pave the streambed and the ground is firm to walk on. Sometimes the sand is so deep it seems bottomless and I alter my stride to accommodate it. Every so often a fan of fresh sand, like a ten-foot feather, splays out where water dropped it, gave up its rush, and soaked in, a pulse of flood that went no farther.

At first I don't notice the weight of the water bottles so much. All in all, walking is fairly easy and there are no abrupt ups and downs. But gradually I become aware that my thigh bones grind against the pelvic socket. Walking becomes uncomfortable. The bones in my feet feel suddenly unreliable. Each step is an admission that too much rides on my hips and that to do this for any length of time would probably be injurious. I am exceeding my personal critical load.

The ten- and twelve-foot slides of silt are treacherously slippery still, glistening with a recent rain, which is one reason we decide to hazard this canyon, hoping the potholes will be filled with water. The silt is rippled and shines in the sunlight like patent leather. However, stepping in one of these patches is taking your life in your hands. They are worse than walking on greased ice. The edges of each patch have begun to curl and crack with drying. Cigar-sized rolls, shiny side in, are gritty with coarse sand and silt on the outside. Every indentation in the bedrock that occasionally floors the wash has its own little silt pool with curls springing up around the edge, deep rosy tan at the center where still moist, pale beige at the drying edges, ringed with curls like gigantic chrysanthemum petals.

Mud curls need a homogenous, cohesive material, such as mud or silt, in which to form, and deep drying; hence they can't form on, for instance, tidal flats, which never dry out completely. At the beginning the silt cracks into rough polygonal patterns. As drying deepens, the cracks widen at the top. The layers begin to separate into plates, resembling pieces of melon rind. The silt continues to shrink with drying, like an untempered pot, and as air replaces the moisture in the pores, the silt becomes paler. As the edges of the plate are exposed, new stresses cause the plate to lift up at the edges. Here on this pavement are all the stages of curls from just beginning to bow to tight cylinders. Although they seem to be scattered without order, like chocolate curls on a torte, they tend to orient to certain edges of the polygons, and the large rolls which form first, often coil parallel to the banks, the way the water ran. Underfoot they crunch like cornflakes.

I am intensely aware of the water signs. There must have been a good flow of water to leave ripple patterns several inches deep. All the ways in which water writes are here: lunette-shaped depressions scooped out alongside boulders, deep-cut ripples, cleaned slickrock. Tiny pools begin to appear, trapped in the slickrock. Opaque with silt they have a certain beauty of their own, rock made liquid, gleaming and shining like polished copper. Yet the silt around their edges dries and pales almost as I watch.

At the first rest stop I clean off the lug soles of my boots. I'm not being fastidious—it's just that the damp silt clings in enlarging layers and I don't need any extra weight. As I lower myself carefully onto a handy boulder, a blacktail jackrabbit flushes, sunlight shining through its long black-tipped ears.

Blacktailed jackrabbit
(Lepus californicus)

Although called "rabbit" a jackrabbit is really a hare; unlike rabbits, newborn hares have fur and relatively well-developed eyesight, and the adults are longer-legged and larger. A blacktail is well suited to a life in desert country. It gets sufficient moisture from the food it eats, preferring succulent plants with a high moisture content, and feeding mostly at night when temperatures are lower and humidity higher. In the spring and after rains there are fresh grasses; at other times there are leaves and cactus pads and other greenery.

By the sheltered ledge where I sit is good brush cover and I undoubtedly startled the hare into action with my boot cleaning, awakening it from its daytime rest. It cleared out slowly enough for me to see its coloring and large luminous yellow eyes, well adapted for nighttime vision. Set far on the sides of the skull, they give almost full-circle vision. Ears always at the alert, each turning like a radar antenna, it must have heard the vibration of my boots on the ground before it saw what blocked out its horizon. I remember Walter de la Mare's poem about Master Rabbit that ends:

> And—*stamp, stamp, stamp*
> Through dim labyrinths clear—
> The whole world darkened:
> A human near!

3

The signs of recent water continue encouraging. A little bullsnake slithers down the wash, so rattlesnakes, too, can still be out. Thick crusts of salt crunch underfoot. Puffy and white and spiny, the salt leached out of shales in the Halgaito Formation to the north. Rocks are coated, ground encrusted with it; even the drainage lines on the sand are crystalline white. Often there is wet silt hidden beneath, which makes one very wary of walking on it.

The channel deepens imperceptibly and begins to narrow. The banks become high enough to obscure the countryside. Five mule deer bound off ahead in stiff-legged jumps. When I reach their hoofprints, the impress is slurred in the silt, deeply impressed and elongated with their hurry. One of them is a buck with a beautiful wide set of antlers, rising high and handsome from his forehead.

Mule deer were an important food source for the Anasazi, and were relatively plentiful in this area, being able to utilize a wide number of plant species. Although they are fleet of foot and spend most of the day, except early morning and evening, undercover, they also follow the same trails day after day through a small home range, rendering themselves vulnerable to the observant hunter who waited in ambush.

Puddles and pools become more frequent: graininess of sand gives way to shine of silt and glint of water. On exposed bedrock long continuous pools gleam, a foot or so wide and up to thirty feet long, opulent parabolas and sinuous ellipses, an interplay of convexity and concavity, of sandstone and water.

Two monstrous boulders, fifteen feet high, shaped like two vertebrae, are so set together that they relate to each other, curve and hollow, bellied and bowed, like a Henry Moore sculpture. Arches cut through each and a narrow alleyway winds through the middle so that I can stand inside. One bears a scapula-like thin ledge. So bonelike in contour are these rocks that one immediately envisions the beast from which they came: a huge ponderous creature, not ill-hearted, lumbering across the desert, leaving a canyon for a footprint.

Large rocks ahead mark the confluence of the main channel of Steer Gulch with a side drainage. When we finally reach them they flank large potholes, filled with water so slightly settled out that it looks like liquid sandpaper. When water charges down this canyon during flash flood it carries with it a considerable amount of sand. Flowing down a bedrock channel, the water slides across the flatter reaches with slowed current; then, because of jointing or crossbedding in the rock that forms a step or dropoff, it picks up speed and abrasive capacity, swirling its sand load into every depression, enlarging and rounding it out to a pothole basin. The size and the shape vary: some are circular bowls, others elongated basins, some scalloped ovals, commonly not deeper than a few feet.

We take the water bottles out of our packs, drink, then hold the bottles upside down and listen to the water gurgle and glug out. I have a momentary panic when I think that there may be no more pothole water, but weigh the evidence of these pools against carrying that much extra weight and trust in the logic of knowing at least there is water here and available.

Strangely enough, even though the water in my cup looks like bleached tomato soup, it isn't bad drinking. All the water for the cattle that were run here came from potholes. The name Steer Gulch refers to the cowboy practice of storing steers here. Two roundups were made yearly, the major one in June, when the cattle were drifted up to higher country for the summer, and a second one in October, when cattle were brought down. Because of the paucity of plant cover, cattle raising in this area depends upon the use of massive acreages and shifting cattle about according to the season. In the fall, calves were weaned and branded, and marketable stock was culled out to be sold. An old cowboy camp still remains under an overhang at the junction of a tributary canyon with Steer Gulch proper, with enough artifacts inside to indicate long habitation—even a mattress.

4

Camp is set in a curve of the canyon, rock wall on the outer side, sand bar on the inner. A stunted cottonwood draped with debris documents the height of the last flash flood through here. Its big thick leaves rattle in the breeze. Rabbitbrush, so named because it is favored cover for these animals, flowers in huge tangles. A wide-ranging species, its bloom is familiar throughout the West. Because it is common on over-grazed lands and where other cover is sparse, its great masses often make a splendid show of color. A yellow dye is made by the Indians from the flowers, and the stems are occasionally used in wickerwork and as a kiva fuel—why I cannot imagine, for rabbitbrush gives off a viscous sooty smoke that I find quite unpleasant. Perhaps this is due to the rubber content of the plant; it has been estimated that, if recoverable, there are 300 million pounds of good-grade rubber blooming in the arid West.

Golden asters and a single rich deep-lavender tansy aster are flow-ering in warm protected crevices; even the tumbleweed seems to be in bloom, its papery bracts resembling thin parchment flowers with pink centers. Summer still seems to persist into October although the wind is more restless, as in fall. But between gusts there is a deep, warm honey stillness that holds the waning afternoon close and warm. Out here I feel keenly the pivoting of the seasons, all the plants that betoken fall, the sun warmth reminiscent of summer, the looping, buzzing fly not yet stilled, the snow not yet fallen. Each day, each place is a fulcrum of passage, a moment held for a few hours before tumbling forward with a cruel gust of wind and a crushing frost.

That night a full moon balloons over the canyon wall. I count: eighty seconds from the first chink of light on the rock horizon to the appearance of a full round globe, cold and white. Cold light and cold night, with a steely stillness. Not a breeze stirs to mix the air. No cloud cover holds in residual heat and reduces nocturnal radiation. The reality

Rabbitbrush *(Chrysothamnus nauseosus)*

Tansy-aster *(Machaeranthera linearis)*

of autumn sinks in, as the cold air just flows in and lays itself down and mantles everything. A cricket sings for a moment, but it's more a pulsation than a singing, so slow and reluctant. And all night long the whole canyon gleams, as if dipped in silver.

5

In the morning a tentative dawn breeze doesn't even nudge the cottonwood leaves but sends a sharp chill down the canyon. The sky is a pale lavender gray with no hint of the warmth to come. Getting out of the sleeping bag before the sun is out takes an act of courage. When it finally blasts over the sandstone wall I feel warmed and alive and energized and agree with Nels Nelson, the archaeologist who traveled down Grand Gulch in 1920: "Wonderful stillness of a sunny morning following a cold night—no bird or insect making a sound."

Around my ground cloth the sand is untracked; the night was too cold for lizards to go foraging. But a kangaroo rat was here—while packing up I discover its little corpse, front feet drawn up much as they are in life, tail with a minute shaving-brush tuft of fur at the end. I have no idea why it died. Having only seen them on the run at night, I take the opportunity to look at this little creature with care. Its back legs are long and well-muscled for jumping, and the long tail with its brave banner provides balance. By swinging its tail it can make rapid plunges in either direction, and up to ten-foot leaps.

Its ear openings are large, gathering in subtle sounds that presage danger. More than half of its skull is an air chamber, thought to catch and magnify sound vibrations in much the same way as an ear trumpet. The ears are protected from dirt by hooded tips. There is also a small lobe that closes over the ear opening when the kangaroo rat digs.

I poke around to see if I can discover an open den nearby, since they are usually noticeable if one knows where to look, often a mound of excavated earth topping a many-tunneled burrow beneath ground, containing nests and storerooms and feeding places. During the hot summer days the many entrances are closed to prevent loss of humidity; all food gathering is done at night. The doorways are usually quite large, as befits an owner who often escapes being someone else's dinner by getting home on a dead run.

Because a kangaroo rat is so vulnerable to the other hunters of the night—the horned owl's silent approach on velvet-barbed wings, the coyote's quick pounce and snap—it only gathers its seeds, not eating until safe in its nest. It carries the seeds in fur-lined cheek pouches (the kangaroo rat is like the pocket gopher in this respect) that open along the line of the lower jaw and hold about a teaspoonful each. It stuffs the pouches with quick movements, cramming in seeds, chaff, husks, and all, and empties them with a single paw push from the back.

Kangaroo rats are exquisitely fitted to living in dry areas because of a complicated chemical process that creates free water from the metabolic breakdown of food. Consequently they do not need to drink, securing all the moisture they need from their diet. Breeding is probably keyed to the amount of food available and occurs erratically. After breeding the male is expected to depart; if not he is more than likely killed by the female.

Three or four young are usually born in the spring, when food plants are at their most succulent, and so I would guess the tiny creature alongside my boot could be five or so months old. The newborn are helpless: hairless, eye and ear openings covered, no teeth, soft claws, but at two and a half months they are apparently full grown, although they retain their juvenile coats; by four months they are adult. Such rapid maturing is a necessity in a desert environment in which future survival often depends upon the quick gathering and storing of sufficient food that appears briefly after a good rain.

Kangaroo rats avoid water. To keep clean they take sand baths. A small gland on top of the shoulders secretes an oily substance that soon mats the hair; a good sand bath returns gloss and shine. They are fastidious creatures, and even in death the little fellow has a clean white vest and a neat tail brush.

6

Walking up a side channel, we find it necessary to traverse a steep wall in order to miss an eighty-foot dry waterfall around the corner. As I climb up through rock and rubble, half scrambling, half walking, a big horned owl flares out of some brush and scares the daylights out of me. In a quarter mile the waterfall is visible far below.

The whole canyon floor up here is a still life. When it is dry, it's a clean palette, but when damp, a sampling of desert life appears: spidery seed heads and single yellow blossoms from rabbitbrush; a tumbleweed sprig standing on one barb; deer hoofprints deep with scattered sand at the margins; coyote tracks in a wandering casual line; a minute blackbrush leaf; a gnarled cottonwood twig; a yellow cottonwood leaf, caught at the tip, browning at the veins.

Ahead a spotted ground squirrel scampers across the shiny pavement. It seems to fly, scarcely touching the ground. When I get there, the tiny footprints just tick the crest of the silt ripples. Slightly bigger than a chipmunk, the spotted ground squirrel is seldom seen except in motion. It feeds on the myriad desert seeds, and often lives in overgrazed areas invaded by tumbleweeds. (The only other ground squirrel in this area is a whitetail antelope squirrel, but it runs with its tail curled up over its back, showing the white underside.)

Dark holes at the base of some of the shrubs along the channel side catch my eye, regular shapes against the irregularity of the shadows, likely ground-squirrel diggings. They are nearly all on the shaded north side, burrowed into hummocks of sand that have blown up around the base of the shrubs, the cool side chosen for protection against the heat of summer. I try to peer inside or to listen, but there are no sounds of residence, and I lack the courage to poke a finger in. Were it an inhabited kangaroo-rat or pocket-mouse burrow, the door would most likely be plugged with dirt. If an abandoned burrow, it could house a snake, a scorpion, or poisonous spider, with none of which do I care to shake hands.

Animal life here is characterized by swiftness, like the fleet lizard or bounding kangaroo rat or scampering ground squirrel. Jumping or leaping gaits are common among small animals. Predator and prey alike have highly developed powers of hearing, perhaps because tracks are constantly covered with blown sand, smells mixed and lost by the wind

Kangaroo rat *(Dipodomys spectabilis)*

and the constant shifting of the ground. Many desert animals are nocturnal, lizards and ground squirrels being two of the exceptions. And
many burrow, as do the mice and many spiders and other insects. Most
are closely adapted to the hues of the landscape—the lizard and the
rattler patterned like the weathered, shadow-splotched sandstone, the
ground squirrel speckled, even the coyote the buffy color of the country
rock.

At times like this I feel my clumsy humanness, clomping along on
feet that are not my own, unable to survive on the land for long, an
interloper, an interrupter, a frightening shadow caster and ground
shaker.

7

As I walk up this wing of the canyon, the walls come closer and closer,
reaching up higher and higher without break, and then the canyon ends
against a box wall, blocked by a dry waterfall with no passage to the
rim above. While someone looks for a route, I choose to sit here, facing
a monolithic curved wall hollowed out with niches and depressions in
which the water once spun, subtle convolutions that cradle soft-edged
shadows.

The back wall flutters with reflections from the plunge pool that
fills the last twenty twisty feet. The back of the pool rests in shadow,
the front in sun, breathing without wind, bedecked with a few water
striders that punctuate the warm cinnamon brown of the water. The
reflection of the walls in the water is perfect, curve opening below to
curve closing above, even reflections of the reflections, so that I cannot
tell which is mirror, which is image, which is real, which is dream. But
in all its beauty is a certain stubbornness, a place that resists passage,
that forces you to go back in order to go on, a small inviolate ending.

Yet here after hiking eight miles with a heavy pack, in this stubborn
stillness is one of the reasons for which I come to the canyons—these
few minutes of quiet, of solitude, of absolute solace. No cricket chirrs,
no water pounds, no stone falls. Time stands still and then expands. I
feel my breathing become timed to that of the pool.

8

It turns out that getting up from here means walking back an eighth of
a mile or so, roping my pack up, climbing huge on-end boulders, step-

ping across a crevice with a thirty-foot drop below, and then traversing a sloping rock surface that would brook no slip.

We stop in the afternoon at a possible campsite, leave packs, and go exploring, coming across, in the middle of nowhere, half a dozen rusted-out cans and a cairn placed by the U.S. General Land Office Survey in 1927. A high butte a quarter mile away presents an incredible horizon-to-horizon view, low continuous horizons, so far away that they are beyond reaching, and if one walked a thousand years one would never get there.

A quarter mile away the streambed is lined with cottonwoods, and so perhaps has more water and is a better campsite than where the packs were left. But once there, the campsite is not propitious. The continual search for the perfect place to set up camp is a variation of "the grass is always greener" theme.

After some hot, dusty miles of walking hither, thither, and lots of yon, pothole bathing and privacy are worth selling one's soul for. The pothole that is my lot is not much bigger than a bathtub and in it I am submerged up to the chin. The depression is one of several in a rock chute, showing the lines of sandstone crossbedding in short repeated curves, moiré in stone. The water is at least sun-warmed on the surface. I upset the water striders, which flee up the sides with the sloshing; in deference to their delicate sensibilities I soap up and rinse off outside.

After dinner I walk up a nearby rock knoll. Wearing sneakers after boots makes my feet feel practically weightless. Last light washes the land. To the southwest Navajo Mountain glows, paler at the base, incandescent. No wonder the Navajos consider it a magic mountain. It has a symmetry, a serenity, that contrasts with the more fanciful landmarks like the Bears Ears or the markers of Monument Valley to the south. The realization of this tremendous emptiness closes in, of being miles from what is already nowhere, with a view that seems to reach farther than one can perceive. Perhaps the world *does* drop off beyond the rim.

Rock and more rock as far as I can see. And sand. And desolation. And mosquitoes. Fierce mosquitoes—I wish we'd have a good frost to put them under. But not even they can dim this time of peacefulness. In other canyons there are other concentrations: the fascination of ruins in Grand Gulch, the presence of more recent past in Johns and Slickhorn. But here there is nothing. Nothingness. And I find myself responding through every pore to this serenity, to the purity of this landscape.

I crawl into my sleeping bag, with a pale yellow blazing star, just open, blooming at my head, and a pale yellow blazing star blooming over the cliff rim. Far and away a coyote warbles.

9

From Steer Gulch one can walk cross country to intercept the head of a small drainage that leads into Whirlwind Draw. The divide between the two is desert. One or two plants stand here or there, but certainly not enough to be called "cover." Often the sand is tessellated with irregular pebbles, sometimes evenly laid with little cubes, each casting a geometric shadow. Most beautiful are those pale pavements laid with irregular sandstone cobbles and pebbles, the contours matching, each convex contour fitting neatly next to a concave one, the smallest stone a quarter inch, the largest not over an inch. Wind, blowing across the surface, removes the fine sand but cannot move the heavier pebbles and rocks, leaving these concentrations of gravel and small stones on the surface, pavements that look like mosaics, laid tessera by tessera.

Ahead a huge knob of rock is the eternal temptation: what's there to see from the top? There's always a way up if you just poke around enough, and this one is no exception, this hump of sandstone wound like an elaborate turban, swirled with crossbedding. On the knob itself, small rocks make lacy shadows. In the crevices tiny bushes grow within a protective micro-environment nourished by extra water that collects in the cracks, an island in the sky gardened by the wind.

Again, the view from the summit is a wide-open one, a view that makes me resolve to climb every promontory I may ever come upon. In deep shadow is the notch of Steer Gulch; Whirlwind Draw is still hidden and out of sight. The terrain on either side of the canyons in this country tends to be so identical, and the dropoff so sharp, that a canyon is often invisible until one walks right up to the edge and discovers the canyon is *there.*

To the north is a flatness of desert interrupted by bedrock outcrops that look like surfacing white whales—sometimes with scrub—but always rock, lumped and heaped and rolling, and beyond it, more rock. House-sized mushrooms of sandstone have white caps and red shale stems.

Ahead to the south is the San Juan River, a slight shimmer on its surface. Upstream the canyon weaves back and forth until it disappears

Blazing-star *(Mentzelia multiflora)*

in a welter of cliffs which are cut with so many shadows that to the eye there is total confusion of terrain. The Clay Hills to the west, a lavender band, and the blue cone of Navajo Mountain to the southwest anchor those horizons. The horizon binds the earth to the sky, a heavy untainted blue that has, for days, been confined by canyon walls, now released, expanded, opened out, holding down the rock and the mesa and the mountain.

Back down, tracking across the sand, I think perhaps I walk here as an Anasazi once did. There are no cow pats, no jeep tracks, no other footprints where I walk. The area has probably never been grazed; there's not enough here to graze. There are no uranium adits, no oil pipes. What the *Deseret News* wrote in September, 1861, is still essentially true. The reporter described southeastern Utah as "measurably value-

Yellow flax *(Linum aristatum)*

less, excepting for nomadic purposes, hunting grounds for Indians, and to hold the world together."

Occasionally a spidery pattern in the sand traces a small wash. Sometimes bushes and herbs grow here, nourished by the furtive run of water. Sometimes the wash is absolutely clean, the water tumbling out anything that's rooted so that no plants get established. Where there are plants, there is much space between; each stands isolated, distinct.

In this whole drainage area of nearly 26,000 square miles, only 20 percent of the land has cover. Walking here you have to believe it.

It strikes me that there are about as many rock outcrops as there is sand. The outcrops lie low and horizontal, with a slight sparkle of quartz, pale sandstone that becomes pitted, uneven, sometimes scaly, sometimes peppered with tiny black lichens or scabbed with gray or chrome-yellow ones. On some, sandstone nodules are attached like pebbles growing out of the rock, not yet weathered off. And sometimes the stone forms a pavement. But most of the ground is sand-drifted and sand streams off the ground with the wind. Within my vision is only one plant, and an unexpected one to me: yellow flax. Yellow flax blooms with flowers lined with red, a desert counterpart to the familiar blue flax of the mountains. The basal leaves are clustered in a rosette, and the stem leaves are reduced in size, grouped vertically on the stem, not opening out flat to receive what might be too-intense solar radiation.

Where I sit to write the sun is warm and there is an absolute stillness; the loudest sound in the air is that of my pen on paper. I notice that my footprints are sunk more than an inch deep in the sand over which I've come, which is probably why my calf muscles hurt. In another hour we reach the lip of a side drainage that leads into Whirlwind Draw, and angle down eighty feet to the damp sandy floor, moistened by two dripping springs. Two dunes lie parallel to the axis of the drainage, one eight feet long, the other double that.

Walking above, in all the loose sand, one wonders why dunes do not form there, where one would expect them to. In spite of the aridity there are no large sand dunes in the area. There are few places where the wind has a long enough reach. Only small dunes form and these tend to pile up in the lee of canyon walls or on the floor of protected washes. Big bushes and a few cottonwoods grow here, a charming green after all the empty rock above, and a wiry clematis, full of tousled seed heads, scrambles over some of the shrubs. There is only this one entrance from above, but it is too small to be indicated on the map. Down here the stillness combines with the coolness, to produce a protected dampness, in sharp contrast to the shadowless desiccation above.

A big datura, huge and luminous in the shadow, grows in a crack in the wall, bearing the last flowers of the season. Beautiful, but somehow evil, cloying flowers, sticky and clinging to the touch, like some exotic white petunia, leaves rough and coarse and unpleasant on the fingers. One of the main drug plants of the Southwest, it was used ceremonially by the Indians, who made a decoction of the leaves and stems. All parts of the plant are potentially poisonous, containing alkaloids, principally scopolamine, atropine, and hyoscyamine. Datura belongs to the potato family, which contains a number of plants known for their narcotic properties: belladonna, tobacco, henbane, nightshade. Generally used to induce visions and for divination, or simply like a prehistoric marijuana, it was also used as an anesthetic for setting bones or during surgery, or, of all things, to prevent miscarriage! But taken too frequently or copiously, serious disorders result. Oddly, the larvae of the striped datura beetle (a first cousin to the old-fashioned potato bug), which chew on both stems and leaves, are not immune to the plant and sometimes die of it.

The walnut-sized husks hang stiffly from the branches. When they break open in four parts they reveal plentiful seeds. The observant Alice Eastwood noted that in every cliff-dweller site she visited she found an abundance of datura seed pods and seeds.

A few grasses grow on the outstretched paw of the dune, locked with rhizomes into the shifting sandy substrate, sharp green growth tenacious against the imperious onslaught of the sand. The leaves may dry during drought but the plants remain in place, protecting the growing buds that lie at the surface. The leaves arch in that grace of form that a Japanese artist achieves with brush and ink. The longer leaves bend down to the sand and when the wind blows inscribe their own tachygraphy of arcs and segments on the dune's surface. One scribes a near circle. The leaves draw and draw again with each nudge of the wind, always those same lines, always the same perfection. What the human hand achieves compared to these grasses seems gross and awkward. But neither will they ever draw anything else. I admire their perfection but cast my lot with human frailty and inconsistency.

The cool quiet of this small canyon lasts only as long as it takes me to reach the main channel of Whirlwind Draw. Here the wind streams up the draw, whirling dust devils into the air. Whirlwind Draw was named for just this phenomenon by the cowboys who watched the towering spinning sand march up the slot of the canyon.

There is an incessant blowing. The sand flows toward me like ectoplasm. I cross a beetle's track and trace it to find the beetle, lumbering across the sand. I follow it for about fifty feet, timing my own steps to its silent progress. Its track is a double scallop with dots on the outside where the legs push, six legs being the most efficient number for insect walking. An insect walks with the two outer legs on one side coordinated with the middle leg on the other, proceeding in the three-point stability of triangles.

Datura *(Datura metaloides)*

Another large black beetle, hour-glass-shaped, plods by, leaving half an inch between tiny backward-pointing trident footprints. These larger beetles have a smaller ratio of surface to body bulk, important in conserving water. Both these beetles are darkling beetles, common to the Southwestern deserts, identified by heads that are as wide as the thorax, the next body segment.

10

In this driest of all autumns, when we have husbanded water like an Anasazi, carrying extra poundage to assure cooking water until being sure of a new supply each evening, it is a surprise and pleasure to find a small round pool—an extra-large pothole really—in the shadows at the base of a dry waterfall. Water streaming off the ledge thirty feet above hollowed out a round basin, some twelve feet in diameter. The only source of water is rain since there are no permanent springs to feed it, nor is it in the line of the major drainage. Even though a two-foot band of concentric alkaline circles marks its slow retreat, it is well populated.

Just when it might have been filled or how long it has been filled is difficult to pinpoint. Meteorological data for this remote area are nearly nonexistent. Weather comes in from the west or southwest, and in that direction the nearest weather station is Tuba City, Arizona, or Las Vegas, Nevada, both a good piece away. Even were there rain recorded at either of these stations, it would still be of little help in locating a storm here, since most simply float overhead as virga, never touching the ground, or leaving only a trace of rain, or else the storm will dump on a single isolated drainage that may or may not reach down into a particular canyon.

One could conjecture, from the life cycles of some of the creatures contained in the pool just how long it might have been filled, how long for encysted eggs to dissolve out of the bottom silt and hatch, how long for all the mosquito wrigglers to go through their life stages—the pothole mosquito can do so in six days. Subject to total desiccation, sometimes no more than a darker slick spot in an otherwise bone-dry streambed, there is more life per ounce in these pools than anywhere else in the canyon.

There are certain invertebrates well adapted to this intermittent ephemeral existence. They are not tied to a seasonal life cycle, but have special morphological or physiological peculiarities which enable them to survive a dry season of uncertain length: they may have very short life cycles and not require water at every stage, like mosquitoes. They can withstand a wide environmental range, from cool rainwater to sun-warmed shallow water, and the changes in mineral concentration as the water evaporates. They have methods of surviving when the pool is dry: burrowing in the silt as the toads can do, laying eggs that will survive even if the parent does not. Some species may burrow as much as twenty inches underground; other species, especially winged ones, may fly in immediately when water returns. Just as migration permits verte-brates to withstand less amiable seasons, so these devices, singly or in combination, allow these minute creatures to endure in sufficient num-bers to populate the ephemeral pools.

The bright red bloodworms look like pieces of red thread, made brilliant by the erythrocruorin in their blood, a hemoglobin-like chemi-cal that acts as a respiratory pigment. It may be of some help in survival where oxygen concentrations are low, since this chemical seems to have a higher affinity for oxygen than vertebrate blood hemoglobin. The bloodworms snap and loop in frenetic undulations in order to maintain the flow of water through their bodies.

No less active are the mosquito larvae. I watch them rise to the surface, tail up, to breathe, and then sink downward, only to flex them-selves up again. Larvae in the early stages (a mosquito has four) are less dense than water, so the larvae rise when they stop positive movement; those in the last stage may be slightly denser, so inclined to sink, and must actively propel themselves to the surface to breathe. There they hang upside down from the surface film, fans of dense hairs on their tail ends spreading out to break the water tension, allowing air to diffuse through their entire bodies.

Every cupful of water is a soup of daphnia. They have always had a special appeal for me, appearing to have such expressiveness: the large eye gives them a baleful look, as if they loathed being subjected to scrutiny but put up with it because their manners are better than mine. As they are confined momentarily in my cup, the two minute transpar-ent valves that house each one like minuscule clam shells are just visible, hinged at the top and open at the bottom, where tiny swimming feet are in constant motion. These produce a continual current of water between the valves, bringing in food particles to the mouth as well as oxygen. These daphnia are darker and larger than most I'm familiar with, and are largely females since most reproduction is parthenogenetic

—reproduction without fertilization, common in many lower plants and invertebrate animals. Males are usually produced toward the end of the breeding season or when conditions become less than favorable.

A forecast of the pool's desiccation would become apparent to the daphnia through a change in mineral concentration and a rise in water temperature. Crowding of females and a concentration of excretory products, a decline in food supply, and other factors evidently alter the daphnia's metabolism and cause male eggs to be produced. "Resting eggs" are the product of mating of males and females. These eggs are tougher than those produced parthenogenetically; they can endure drying out, freezing, or excessive heat, and may be transported on birds' feet or wind. As a consequence, daphnia are exceedingly widespread and plentiful.

I delight in watching them, ticking along like tiny watches, nudging up against the side of the cup in a constant restless motion. If there were sound magnification, what would they sound like? Great thumpings as they bump against the side, gratings as the shells rub against each other, whirrings of the spinning feet, but no voice sounds, no communications, no passing on of collected knowledge, and yet they know a thousand things I don't.

11

The floor of Whirlwind Draw is laid with much more colorful rocks than that of Steer Gulch—lavender, green, red, mauve, a mosaic of many colors including chunks of petrified wood that glitter in the sunshine. These varicolored rocks come from the Clay Hills to the west, where Whirlwind Draw begins, specifically from the Chinle Formation, which forms the base of the hills.

After the seas that laid part of the Cedar Mesa Sandstone in this area retreated, continental conditions persisted for millions of years. Large amounts of red sediments were washed down by streams from the Ancestral Rockies to the northeast. Laid down first, on top of the white Cedar Mesa Sandstone, were the chocolate-brown strata named Moenkopi after the Indian settlement to the south where they are handsomely exposed. These shales and mudstones bear the cracks of tidal-flat conditions in symmetrical ripple marks and mud cracks.

On top of these muds and mucks, sometimes eating channels many feet deep into them, sometimes slithering across the surface, were the deposits that formed the basal layers of the Chinle Formation. The stream channels that carried these sediments flowed in haphazard manner across a flood plain, meandering down to a distant sea, looping and eroding and piling up sand bars, sometimes flooding over, leaving a complex pattern of gravels, sands, and silts. In some of the point-bar deposits on the inside of meanders, large amounts of debris collected, from twigs and branches to logs. This organic material concentrated uranium minerals carried by ground waters, or became a nucleus around which the ores clustered, and much uranium prospecting goes on in these strata.

The upper part of the Chinle Formation is composed of a rich variety of vividly colored shales, fine-grained sediments that sifted down into rivers and lakes, often containing logs and chunks of wood. The Clay Hills consist predominantly of these two formations, Moenkopi and Chinli which give them their bright striped façade.

As I walk on downstream, I overtake a small red-spotted toad that leaves tracks like two parentheses in the sand. I walk on, enticed by that pull that must lure explorers to the ends of the earth: what's ahead? The sunshine is warm and pleasant. I disturb a sunning lizard or two—in a way, such an alien world, but the quiet is home. A marsh hawk hunts, beating low over the ground. I see or hear no other birds.

The channel banks, which have been quite low, suddenly rise and the draw narrows swiftly. I walk on bedrock which shelves down in rounded steps alternating with small sloping sand pockets, but mostly rock, full of holes and handholds, sometimes streaked with crossbedding, sometimes swirled like taffy, sometimes thin lenses, layer on layer, sometimes rock pillows whose contours are so emphasized by the bedding that they actually look soft and plump.

The rock squeezes down to a passageway but one foot wide, shelving up on either side, about two feet deep, continuing for at least thirty feet. As I walk, one foot precisely in front of the other, suddenly the slot ends and I'm looking down to nothing, standing on the slanting lip of the ultimate overhang.

Between my toes, forty feet below, is a clear, gleaming plunge pool, and another, and another, set in bedrock, collared with big boulders, and beyond, pebbled sand with greenery, an oasis of sunlight and shadow and *clear* water. I gingerly back up and hunt to find a way down. The right wall rises up another thirty feet, sheer rock curving over into an underhang with the top ledge at least twenty feet deep; no access there without ropes. The same is true of the left side, but the rock is more jointed and I walk along the upper edge looking for access.

There is no place, no where, no how to get down. In a way I feel it appropriate. There should be places that are inaccessible, untouchable (although one might be able to reach this Eden from the river). I return and sit on the lip, watching the beadlike sparkles around the edge as water striders ply the surface; hear the breeze take a small dry leaf and scratch it across the bare rock, float it off the edge, and spin it down to land on the pool below. Some gray juncos flit in the shadows. Dragonflies patrol the pool's perimeters. It's all right with me that there should be places that only dragonflies and small gray birds can go.

12

To get to the cliff overlooking the river is a half-mile easy walk on a whale's back of slickrock. The variety of weathering covers the whole vocabulary: perforations, exfoliations, knobs, mushrooms, balanced rocks. The sandstone is always curved and the interplay of convex and concave as I move among the sigmoid shapes makes me feel as if I walk in a magnificent sculpture garden. In little pockets of sand there are Japanese gardens with bonzai piñon or bitterbrush, or perhaps a few stately grasses.

Some shallow depressions with pools contain dozens of tadpole shrimp that look for all the world like miniature horseshoe crabs, with a shield-shaped carapace that covers the head and thorax, and at the ends of each tail two thin spiny projections. There are all sizes, from creatures the size of my little fingernail to those the size of a man's thumbnail. They breathe through delicate paddlelike appendages attached to the abdomen; these also aid in swimming. The rhythmic fluttering of these legs is constant, sometimes stirring up the silt in the bottom upon which they are feeding—algae, bacteria, protozoa, whatever is small enough to ingest.

Tadpole shrimp in the United States occur west of the Mississippi, most often in the Great Plains, although one species is a pest in the rice fields of California. Their constant agitation of the silt prevents rice plants from rooting. They are typical of temporary pools that completely dry up, and are totally absent from running water and salt water and large lakes, and are seldom abundant where there are predacious fish or insects.

Populations are maintained by means of thick-shelled resting eggs, produced, as those of daphnia are, by sexual mating; most of the time eggs are nonfertilized, produced by parthenogenesis. Indeed, males are rare and in some species have never been found. The appearance of tadpole shrimp is sporadic; in some years there are many, in other years, none.

After an egg hatches, the shrimp goes through a series of molts, progressively adding, each time, more abdominal segments and append-ages. A complete growth cycle may take as little as fifteen days, and indeed such swift growth is a necessity in these quickly evaporating pools. There are so many unanswered questions about these primitive creatures, which nevertheless are capable of such incredibly sophis-ticated adjustments to their very tenuous environment, so many inge-nious studies that might be done to find the whys and wherefores—at this moment, if I had my education to do over again, I'd be tempted to become a research biologist just to answer some of the questions rattling around in my head.

As I walk on, I anticipate the river—the white ruffles on the water, the delicate whisperings, animated and evocative.

It's a disappointment to reach the cliff overlooking the river five hundred feet below and gaze down, not at a running river, but the dead back waters of Lake Powell.

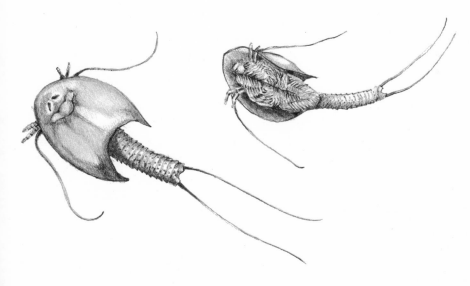

Tadpole shrimp *(Apus longicaudatus)*

13

When a whole glorious afternoon stretches ahead, I determine to see as much of Whirlwind Draw as possible, to discover why the ambience of this canyon is so different from that of the others. A lone bedraggled cottonwood spreads shade upcanyon, but the rest of the plants are desert adapted *par excellence*. All the branches of horsebrush end in spikes covered with velvet, a pubescence not on older plants; the leaves are tiny, falling off early, leaving just the spiny spikes. The sagebrush has threadlike leaves, a different species from the big sagebrush more familiar at higher altitudes. The Kiowa dried *Artemisia fillifolia* for winter use; they drank it in the form of a hot decoction for, as two anthropologists noted, "indigestion, flatulence, biliousness or used as a remedy for intestinal worms. It may also be steeped in hot water, wrapped in cloth, and applied to the stomach as a hot compress." It was also used for drying hands after using yucca soap and "as a very soft and convenient substitute for toilet paper."

The rigid twiggy branches of blackbrush and Mormon tea and the splayed spears of yucca cast spiny shadows. A scrub oak grows along the ground, rooting where it touches. Its round-lobed leaves are studded with spherical galls up to an inch across. A gallfly laid her eggs on the leaf and the larvae, by means not yet fully understood, caused an abnormal growth of leaf tissue that formed a nursery for itself as well as a food supply, and seemed to do the plant no damage.

In the sand a tiny spurge makes a hand-sized carpet. Petals wilt to pink on a white evening primrose. Sand drifts into buckwheat tussocks, plants which seem to grow just enough each year to keep up with the mounding; the leaves are fuzzy to the point of silveriness. Many of these plants have exposed roots, often wind-polished, looping across the ground.

The shrubs that utilize this desert rim are tough plants, furred and sealed against the climate. Their spiky silhouettes have a basic growth resemblance one to the other, the numerous branches ramifying upward, fanning out from a narrow center. The amount of growth belies the desperate growing conditions, but all the shrubs bear the scars of battle in shredded and dead wood. Sometimes only an eighth of the plant or less is actually green and growing. Plant productivity in the desert is the least of any plant community. It must look to me precisely as it did to Herbert Gregory when he did all his field work here: "Except in forested areas the vegetation is gray, and in places its color is less conspicuous than that of the rocks on which it grows; bright-green plants constitute but dots and short ribbons disposed here and there in the landscape."

Despite the lateness of the season, there are a number of plants still in bloom and still setting buds as if nights were not already pushing freezing. The individual pink flowers of a skeletonweed look like small single carnations on a spiky bush, but in truth the plant belongs to the composite family and each "petal" is a separate flower that opens in the morning and dies at sunset. Some are already in cottony seed heads that break loose with the wind; like many other desert plants, these have windborne seeds that skitter along the ground or rise and float in the wind like dandelion seeds.

A yellow beeplant has a cluster of green buds at the top, pale pods developing below. The stalk is filled with small flies and moths, hanging on the stem, both pollinators of this plant. I wonder: how many plants did the Anasazi potter try until she found that this one would produce the right kind of pigment for painting her pots?

A globemallow blooms still, bright orange. A small milkvetch like one I remember drawing early one spring sprawls along the ground, furry leaves and stems almost pure gray, the fat curled pods spotted with red, the seeds inside already beginning to dry and rattle. Its generic name, *Astragalus,* comes from the Greek name for a small bone in the foot that the seed pods of some species supposedly resembled. Yellow cryptantha, through blooming, has small nutlet seeds still confined in

Fendler carpetweed *(Euphorbia fendleri)*

the furry heads; the leaves are covered with loosely laced hairs that under my hand lens show liquid inside.

A bladderstem, with its peculiar inflated stalks, is one of the plants collected by John C. Fremont in the Mohave Desert in 1844. Now dried and bleached, their hollow stems whisper in the wind. These provide living space for a genus of wasp larva. First the female drills a hole in the top of the stem and drops in some tiny pebbles. On top of these she dumps in insect larvae, upon which she lays her eggs, and covers them with sand, assuring them both food and shelter.

Every one of these plants, each in its own way, is beautifully and efficiently atuned to this arid climate. Since a plant may lose, by evaporation through the leaves, between 97 and 99.9 percent of the water it takes in, adaptations to stop water loss are most obvious, and the leaves show the most striking alterations: Mormon tea leaves have been reduced to scales on spiky stems (photosynthesis is performed by the stems); skeletonweed looks just like its name; cactus spines are the extreme. Like the tumbleweeds, other plants have many extremely small leaves, often less than one-half square inch in area. The part of the plant most remote from the water supply is that which is damaged and dies first, and the leaf tip is the most vulnerable. Small leaves have less area that has to be reached by veins, and the smaller the leaf blade, the less likely it is to become overheated when exposed to strong solar radiation.

Many leaves have coatings that help to slow evaporation, such as the "varnish" on the leaves of a creosote bush. More common in the hotter deserts farther south, there are still a few this far north, tufted with white furry seed balls stuck on the stem. Some plants have leaves that are succulent, with a mucilaginous sap; others, like sand verbena, have secretions that make them sticky to the touch, and the sand grains that cling to them may be helpful in shading tender tissues. Hairs keep air currents elevated above the stomata, the plant's breathing pores. Sagebrush is silver because of the thick layering of fine white hairs that protect the tender green beneath.

Leaf position is important; the flax leaves fit vertically against the stem. The leaves of mule-ears fold upward so that the inner half is in shadow and the outer surface receives glancing light rather than direct light, which is intense and potentially more damaging. The narrow leaves of a desert lily splay out on the soil surface like water troughs waiting to funnel to the stem whatever moisture is available. A foot and a half below ground lies the lily bulb, its flowering long since over.

There are some prickly-pear cactuses, the quintessential desert plant. The fruits are overripe and inedible; I reflect that no Anasazi would have permitted these to get to this stage and go to waste. I reach out to pull one off, being careful to avoid the huge, sturdy spines, but find that, despite my caution, I have garnered a fingerful of tiny reddish-brown hairs called glochnia. The big unbarbed spines are easy to avoid, but these tiny hairlike ones are not easy to see, and being barbed are difficult to remove. Glochnia were found in 90 percent of the human feces examined at Mesa Verde, indicating that prickly pear can be eaten with impunity. Most of the plant is edible in one way or another: the fruit raw or dried, the pads best cooked (very mucilaginous when fresh), and the seeds roasted.

It has been suggested that the reduction of the leaf to spine has preserved cactus not only from desiccation and heat, but from herbivorous animals such as thirsty desert rodents; they are so palatable to cattle that in dry years ranchers often burn off the spines to make fodder. The old stems are wrinkled and creased with broken-off spines; the spines on newer stems are laid in a neat diamond grid. Between rains these flat stems store water, swelling when inflated, wrinkling with drought. A cactus's wide, shallow root system quickly absorbs water over a large area after a storm, an advantage when rains are characteristically brief and tend to sheet off the ground.

But the spines do not protect the cactus against the small nibblers, and these prickly pears are infested with tiny crawling creatures. Beneath the picket of spines cochineal insects, like small red dots, suck out the plant juices. Before the discovery of aniline dyes, these were the source for scarlet hues, and lake and carmine pigments. Squashing one between the fingers leaves a strong stain. Only the female contains pigment (and the ratio of females to males is between 150 or 200 to one). A female lays several hundred eggs beneath the cover of her own body and then dies. The young hatch beneath this shield within hours, and remain in place or are scattered by the winds. Since there are several broods a season, numbers become astronomical but necessary for survival by chance landing on another prickly pear for which the insect seems to be host specific. Once a female inserts her beak into the cactus pad, she remains there for her short life; if the infestation is heavy, the plant is destroyed. Longhorn beetles tunnel into the stems, and cactus borers lay their eggs on the spines, the larvae chewing into the pads and opening the interior to desiccation. Like the other prickly inhabitant, the porcupine, the cactus too has its vulnerable side.

14

There is ample space to sit and draw, for all the plants are spaced far apart because of their spreading root systems. Each is a marker on an imperial chess board, each spaced just so far apart from the other in a territorial defense: rabbitbrush castles, sagebrush pawns, Mormon tea bishops, saltbush knights. Some of these plants have root secretions that discourage other plants from growing too close, but the sparseness of plant cover is largely the result of a paucity of resources—little water and almost no soil.

I dig down in the sand, marveling at its coolness just a few inches under the surface. But no humus particles darken the handful; there is too little precipitation and too sparse a vegetative cover and too much wind constantly worrying the surface for humus to form. This desert country has been formed so recently that there has been insufficient time for soil building, and the rocks from which these sands develop are high in resistant quartz that doesn't decompose easily. The top layer of desert commonly contains less than 1 percent organic matter. Pulverized debris may color the sands pale gray, but it is undecomposed debris, dried and not rotted.

The only sounds in the afternoon are small ones, and when they stop they leave a waiting silence. A grasshopper clacks, and then is silent. A light wind rustles a dried tumbleweed caught up against a rock; the sound is a death rattle. The whole plant has broken off near the ground and rolled, distributing its seeds in a whirling, bouncing progress across the sand.

Heat comes up through the soles of my sneakers. The wind pushes through the air, making a hollow sound across my ears, whistling across the sand, and then is gone. Silence again. A silence made of heat. Heated from below and above, heat radiating off all surfaces. I wonder that I was so chilled to the bone eight hours ago, wearing gloves because my hands were tingling and red, a scarf wrapped around my neck. I feel my flesh beginning to dry on the bone, and wonder, how many years for bone to bleach to calcium white in this climate?

I foolishly have not carried water; it was cool on the slickrock near the river, and I guess I assumed that it would be cool here. It's not. I keep looking for pools in the patches of slickrock. There is a big empty basin with the sand still damp in it, but no water. My mouth and throat are dry. I feel as if I'd swallowed a dead mouse. Evidently the shower that dumped on Steer Gulch did not leave equal water in upper Whirlwind Draw only a few miles away.

I start back to where I've left my gear and water, and where we'll camp. A chunk of jasper, split open, lies in the wash like a cloven heart, hemoglobin red. Ahead is a cairn, built on the south end of a rock island. Around it are more pieces of jasper and other non-country rocks washed in from the Clay Hills, but no reason for the marker—no Anasazi dwelling, no worked chips, no granary—so perhaps it was cowboy built to signal an entrance to Whirlwind Draw.

Since there is almost no wood at the campsite, it is incumbent upon me to carry some back. I tuck my notebook and sketchpad under my arm and try carrying the wood cradled in my arms, which makes walking exceedingly awkward. In the sand in front of me are large tracks, big pads that ambled across the draw. No claw marks show since bobcats walk with their claws retracted. The tracks are in a single line, typically cat. They are slightly blurred from today's wind and were undoubtedly made within the last few nights, since bobcats are nocturnal hunters, prowling after the other night feeders: kangaroo rats, mice, jackrabbits, a careless porcupine. Surprisingly short on endurance, a bobcat prefers to hunt by stealth, not to chase.

I detour to follow the tracks, wood banging on my chin, and they begin to look too large for bobcat; in my only encounter with one it surprised me by its smallness. But heat and fatigue outweigh my curiosity, and I'm too listless to drop my load of wood in order to measure the tracks with my hand. I wonder if any mountain lions still frequent this area.

Most of the big predators were trapped out years ago because of stockmen's losses; forty years ago trappers took 100 wildcats and 150 coyotes a year. A local historian says that by 1892 mountain lions, wolves, and coyotes were killing so much stock that trappers were hired for a $5 bounty on bear and mountain lions, $1 on bobcats, gray wolves, wildcats, and coyotes, and 5 cents on prairie dogs. At any rate, only the coyotes, bobcats, and prairie dogs have survived with any certainty, and in the wilds of the less-frequented canyons, perhaps an occasional mountain lion.

As for the coyotes, I see their tracks every time I come into the canyon, and occasionally catch a glimpse of one. Perhaps the most widespread mammal in the United States, it attains this by great speed and wariness and catholic eating habits, from fresh meat to carrion, insects and vegetation. As a predator, by culling out the weak and old animals, a coyote keeps other animal populations healthy, and is very important in rodent control.

Coyotes were chiefly animals of the plains when white men entered the West, participating in the kills made by other animals, such as bison remains left by wolves. When bison and wolves were nearly exterminated, coyotes spread to upper and lower country as well in search of food. Never a hunter of big game, a pair may nevertheless run a cow to ground, which makes them such an anathema to cattlemen. Canny and quick, the coyote survives in spite of attempts at extermination.

I stagger into camp, drop my wood in an unceremonious heap, and reach for a canteen.

15

I sit back against a comfortable rock and marvel, as always in these canyons, at the graceful sandstone patterns, swirled, stacked, knotholed rock, from palomino tan to weathered brown, perforated with tiny holes as if it had been peppered with buckshot, holes all in a line, thumb-sized and smaller; in other places the rock turns and the holes are elongated into minute tunnels, clusters that look like barn owl faces and skulls, a whole horizon of slickrock, curving, convoluted, smooth walls sloping upward, sensuous shapes washed in light—and what beautiful light! Pervasive, ubiquitous, the whole canyon glows, awash with light, poured with light.

The shadows take on a softness. Contrasts dim. Dawn light has a clarity; evening light has a reluctance, a gentleness, a lovely peacefulness. Light ebbs from the far mesas. A tentative cricket speaks, a hesitant breeze slips across the rock, and this small canyon, embedded in sandstone, has no yesterday, no tomorrow, just the granular sandstone present that circumscribes my horizons, rolling back and away.

There is no dramatic Turneresque sunset, nor has there been on any of these October nights. The atmosphere is too clear. There are no clouds to reflect off of, no moisture droplets to refract and create orange and apricot and glowing gold. The light simply dims, as if on a rheostat. The bright blue of the afternoon sky becomes paler. And still paler, until it's almost platinum. The lower band of sky bleaches and then flushes, a narrow strip of pale rose, tinged with peach, lies along the horizon, even to the east.

And slowly the earth darkens. The rocks, the cliffs, the mesas lose their interior modeling and turn to silhouette. The evening deepens. The sky falls into itself. Colors disappear, leaving only an infinite variety of grays. Dusk has come almost undetected, so slowly that my eyes adjust to a new shadowless world, perceiving only what is close by. Then into the darkening sky pops the first chip of a star. And one by one they punctuate the sky, Gerard Manley Hopkins' "fire-folk" and "elves' eyes" and "circle-citadels." And breath by breath the sky darkens to meet the rock and there is only one vast cocoon of night, pellucid, totally enveloping.

When I get home I find it hard to sleep indoors.

16

At 7 A.M. light seeps into the sleeping bag but I'd prefer to ignore it; it's too chilly, this time of year, with the sun still blocked by a high-rising cliff to the east. Last night the moonlight was again bright enough to show colors, certainly bright enough to write by. I felt like that enigmatic sleeping figure in Henri Rousseau's "Sleeping Gypsy," immobilized by the weight of the moonlight.

I get dressed by sliding my clothes inside the sleeping bag to warm up. But putting on my jacket is like donning a coat of mail that sat out in the frost all night. My hands are too chill to write and sting with the cold. My eyes and nose water with the first sharp breeze of the day. I button my wool sweater up to the neck and wish I had a cap with me.

During breakfast, the sun blasts over the rimrock and begins to warm, but only a modest warmth, barely enough to take the edge off. Its light is brilliant, harsh. The moon on the other side of the sky, not yet set, dims to pearliness. I sit between the two, sun warming my right shoulder, forearm, hand, thigh, calf, boot. The moon slips away, still firm in the sky but offering nothing in the way of life support, only a tidal pull in the blood.

Walking-out days always have a certain poignancy. No one talks. The quiet rings, punctuated only by the small whiffling flares of a tiny fire. No grass quivers, no bird calls, only the smoke, both its streaming shadow and its diaphanous self, moves in this terrible stillness. No sound, no sound at all. The softest of breezes touches my head but moves not a hair, not a tumbleweed sprig, and is gone with no mark of its passage. No day has ever begun so quietly. If I drop a sand grain surely it will fall like thunder.

The region last explored [the Colorado Plateau] is, of course, altogether valueless. It can be approached only from the south, and after entering it there is nothing to do but to leave. Ours has been the first, and will doubtless be the last, party of whites to visit this profitless locality . . . excepting when the melting snows send their annual torrents through the avenues to the Colorado, conveying with them sound and motion, these dismal abysses, and the arid table-lands that enclose them, are left, as they have been for ages, in unbroken solitude and silence.

LIEUTENANT JOSEPH C. IVES, *Report upon the Colorado River of the West,* 1861

Although the Southwest is littered with ruins, one of its greatest charms is its emptiness. There is a profound sense of peace in the great reaches of open country and the silence and solitude of its canyons. The sky and the weather are so important a part of the Southwest that it is easy to understand how the people who have lived there have been governed by the march of the seasons and the cycles of sun and moon and stars.

HAROLD GLADWIN, *Southwestern Archaeology,* 1957

Honaker Trail

1

I have wanted to make one last trip back to these canyons by myself, but in this drought year it is not wise to go alone. However, there's plenty of water at the foot of the Honaker Trail—the whole San Juan River—and the trail itself is just around the corner and upstream from the mouth of Johns Canyon. While I've walked the Honaker Trail several times during other explorations of the canyons, from plateau to river and river to plateau, this is the first time I've gone it alone to camp down by the river.

I've looked forward to this time, and yet, as I sit here at the top, I know a tinge of apprehension. I'm not quite sure what I expect, and now that my ride is long gone and it's too late and I'm committed, even why I wanted to do this. But here I am, quite alone, and I should start down before the sun bathes the whole slope and I have to cope with heat along with everything else. Yet I sit a moment longer because the view is so glorious.

Sitting at the top of the Honaker Trail is to be suspended in the middle of a rocky, sandy, sagebrushed nowhere. Cedar Mesa rises a thousand feet above me at my back; a thousand feet below me the San Juan River silts its way downstream. To the west, hidden in the turning of the earth, are the five canyons that I have walked. To the south, across the river, lies Monument Valley, looking just the way geologist J. S. Newbury described it in 1859:

> The distance between the mesa walls on the north and south is perhaps ten miles, and scattered over the interval are many castle-like buttes and slender towers, none of which can be less than 1,000 feet in height, their sides absolutely perpendicular, their forms wonderful

imitations of the structures of human art. Illuminated by the setting sun, the outlines of these singular objects came out sharp and distinct, with such exact similitude of art, and constrast with nature as usually displayed, that we could hardly resist the conviction that we beheld the walls and towers of some Cyclopean city hitherto undiscovered in this far-off region.

The Honaker Trail runs down the north cliff of the San Juan; the two inches' worth of river that I can glimpse from here are just about the proportion of water to land in this country. Across the river are tiered cliffs, mirror images of what I shall be walking down. Passage looks absolutely impossible.

In 1904 Henry Honaker bossed the building of this trail down to the river; he had gotten a permit from San Juan County to do so some eleven years previous, in 1893. Prior to that he and his brothers had run a daily stage between Cortez, Colorado, and Bluff, Utah, and before that he lived in the Mancos area and helped the Wetherills run their cattle. Gold fever was in full swing on the San Juan when Honaker envisioned an access road from river to canyon rim that would aid in transporting all that heavy placer gold that was going to be found.

The first horse taken down the trail fell off the narrow path, and after that supplies were lowered over impassable cliffs by rope. The anticipated gold boom came to naught; only some $3,000 was ever recovered, the flour gold that was more trouble to sift out than it was worth. The trail is a formidable piece of rough engineering and cuts through strata that are the "type section" for the Honaker Trail Formation, surely a kind of immortality undreamed-of by a hard-working businessman with his eye on the dollar.

The predominantly gray Honaker Trail Formation underlies the red Halgaito Shale. The Honaker Trail strata were laid down some 280 to 300 million years ago when a tropical sea flowed and ebbed here, leaving thin deposits of marine limestones, sandstones, and shales, some of which are oil producing in the Four Corners area. These strata have been eroded into a tiered, multi-layered cliff some 1,500 feet thick.

For the most part, in building the trail Honaker traversed the friable shale and siltstone talus slopes until he found a break in a wall of sandstone or limestone through which he could descend to the next step down, building dugways in only a couple of places to get through the thicker layers. In all, Honaker blazed a tortuous three-mile trail in order to make a quarter-mile descent.

2

I check my gear one last time, a useless gesture since what I don't have I don't have. And one thing I've forgotten is Halazone tablets, so I'll need to boil drinking water, but at least the river will provide plenty of that. I have full water bottles for going down, and I plan to eat lunch halfway down at Horn Point, a sharp promontory that juts out thirty or so feet toward the river with a precipitous drop on either side. The view there is unparalleled, the next best thing to hang-gliding, without the worry of landing. I have enough food to last a week if need be and the usual gear of sleeping bag, mattress, etc.—it strikes me as grossly unfair that no matter what *my* size I still have the same amount of basic gear as someone a foot taller and sixty pounds heavier.

I get out my note cards from various sources that give the layer-by-layer description of the Honaker Trail Formation to read as I go down. I take my glasses off. Since I am nearsighted, the bottom half of the lens is plain glass, and the bifocal line between makes a slight blur just where I'm about to put my foot. I've found I'm better off without them when navigating treacherous or littered slopes.

The trail is visible for only a few yards, then disappears behind boulders and a turn of slope. It's always a surprise that, in this vast and open country, one can be totally out of visual contact with familiar landmarks in a matter of minutes. I recheck all the fastenings on my pack. I retie my bootlaces. And finding nothing else that needs to be done I stop procrastinating and take the first steps down with combined eagerness and reluctance.

I'm down the trail ten minutes and I'm lost. The trail has simply ended, and having been here before I know that it doesn't *do* that. Not much of a path, true, but a path nevertheless. I turn around and look back. Nothing seems right. I can't even see where I went astray. At this moment the cliff above me appears undifferentiated talus and impassable ledges. I couldn't even get back up from here!

I sit down, ease off my pack, and a grasshopper, as rusty red as the soil, jumps onto it. I flick him off before he crawls inside. I put on my glasses and look around. I spot the trail threading down and stopping behind a pile of boulders. I've gone straight when I should have made a hairpin turn. I stow my glasses, pick the cheatgrass seeds off my jeans, struggle my pack on, and put a cairn of four stones on top of the boulder at the turning. And I continue placing one at every uncertain turn the rest of the way down. I will topple them off when I come back up. A beetle takes off with a soft burr that sounds like a rattler. My heart still stops at such a sound.

I continue slowly downhill, holding back my weight on the steep parts, trying to keep my toes from jamming aginst the boot toes. Having no one I have to keep up with, I pick up rocks to my heart's content—a tube of limestone with a black chert center, chunks of red jasper that gleam in the hand—all the while trying to keep track of the separate strata through which I walk. My note cards are becoming increasingly smeared with shuffling and being held so tightly because the wind is kicking up. No matter what direction I turn the wind catches me, from the front, the back, the side.

There are handsome fossils in the rock, a fat brachiopod just weathering out, another on the ground. I pick it up and it fits closely into my palm, convolutions of its shell shape matching pad and hollow. I close my fingers tightly over it and the perceptible pulse seems to belong to the shell rather than to me.

3

I reach Horn Point, where I intended to have lunch sitting out on the exposed promontory, but the wind is gusting so fiercely that I think perhaps wisdom is the better part of valor. I am suddenly *extremely* conservative about reaching the end of the promontory—to get there I must leap over a three-foot-wide crevice that looks as if it goes clear through to China. So instead, I move to the dugway on the north face of Horn Point, a formidable job of road building. Honaker constructed a ramp a precipitous hundred yards long by blasting out rock above and using it as fill material below. Near the top of the dugway, I sit on a limestone step near the top and without taking my pack off fish in the side pocket for a can of vegetable juice. Somehow I'm more thirsty than hungry but the warm juice isn't very good. Thinking to be protected here, I find it unpleasant to have the wind still whirling dust and sand, which unerringly stings me in the face. The wind seems to attack the very rock itself, pushing and shoving with intent to maim the cliffs, the slopes, to reduce them to particles small enough to be spun away to another continent.

A Shell Oil Company geological trip left large yellow letters marking the tops of various zones in the Honaker Trail Formation, along with yellow numbers of various stops and points of interest. I find it helpful to know I'm sitting on the top of the Ismay Cycle of the Honaker Trail Formation, a highly oil-productive unit in the Four Corners area. Within a shallow niche I pass below are unusual rounded shapes that look like stone heads of lettuce with the outer leaves peeling off, fossilized beds of calcareous algae. In the shallow edges of the Pennsylvanian-time seas, these algal reefs formed and the porous beds have proved to be excellent reservoirs for oil. Still the big yellow letters are graffiti and highly visible pollution. Fie on rock painters.

Below Horn Point is a near-mile-long traverse going due north, along a narrow, narrow ledge that drops off sharply, rimmed by a sheer cliff fifty feet below. I keep my eye on the path and ignore the drop to my left. Suddenly a wave of nausea makes me stop, jolted. I turn to face the wall, press my hands firmly on the rock and close my eyes until the nausea subsides.

When I open my eyes I get another shock: I can't believe *those* are *my* hands in front of my nose, splayed out, clawed into the rock, tendons rigid, fingernails broken to the quick, scraped, a fresh scratch beaded with tiny drops of blood, swollen from cut off circulation from the pack straps. I recognize the hand shape, but not the dirt under the nails and packed into the cuticle. I read them not from the palms, pressed so close against the rock upon which my life seems to depend at the moment, observing heart and life lines and stars of fate, but from the scruffy backs. Abraded, unladylike, rough as the rock they cling to, sunburned, callused, and in them I recognize a different reality. I can go home, clean up, buff the nails, repair the damage, put on lotion, make them look better. But these ill-used hands clutched into the abrasive wall belong to another place I live, where I am also at home, another way of life whose isolation and quiet have become a necessity. I lean here until I feel steadier.

I start out again with a sense of uneasiness. This is *not* the place to be nauseated. As soon as I walk on again, another wave hits, and another. Ridiculous, I tell myself, as the path blurs again. Ridiculous, I say, and discipline myself to continue walking carefully and slowly. I feel a wave of total despair: why did I come? I worked so hard to get here and now I'm ready to cry. Like a little kid, all I want to do is go home! I stop to look at no note cards, no rock formations, no interesting plants. I just want to get off this shelf. The nausea and dizziness do subside but my shoulders ache with tension. A sharp switchback finally brings me off the ledge and starts another traverse. I rest on a ledge labeled "Barker Creek Cycle," identifying another oil-bearing layer. I really don't much care.

4

When I get to the river beach at last, the wind blasts down the canyon. Great swirling gusts broadcast their arrival in a cloud of sand. I try to find some kind of windbreak; the best I can do is a cluster of willows and they're not much good. When the wind really gusts, the sand stings right through the leaves. Ordinarily the first priority of business would be to find a campsite but right now it's more important to find shelter from the wind and get myself together.

I wonder if part of my uneasiness is that I remember all too well a raft trip on the San Juan in a windstorm one April; if I thought I would have to endure that again I'd walk back up right now. It had been windy that spring morning, just the usual river wind, when far downstream the water changed sheen and a peculiar crinkled surface proceeded upstream. I watched, totally unprepared for the flat gust that caught me full face with a blast of sand. As the wind intensified, it pumped up the canyon with a locomotive roar, amplified against the walls, a great hurtling heavy sound as if it would uproot the cliffs themselves. Although there were no clouds, the light was so dimmed by blowing sand and silt that it looked dark enough to storm, the light an odd rosy tan. The canyon ahead was fogged in, the rimrock obscured, all outlines blurred. I felt in the middle of a caldron of wind. Even though everyone on the raft paddled to exhaustion, time and again we had to pull ashore, time and again we were beaten back, exhausted, until the wind quit at darkness.

I hope that with the setting of the sun today's wind will diminish, but that's a long time off, and until then there's no sense in trying to set up camp. I might as well stash my backpack, ignore the wind, and go walking. I remember a cobble beach upstream. To get there I cross a beach well used by boating parties, and although not dirty, certainly not pristine—chunks of burned logs, a few branches broken, rocks left in rectangular patterns where ground cloths were anchored.

At the cobble beach the variety of colors is fascinating, all stones smoothed to a size that just fits comfortably in the hand, rocks carried all the way down from the San Juan Mountains to the northeast. The beach is on the inside of a meander, a broad hard beach that's usually covered with water part way up. Now it's open and would be a great place to camp; the hard sand doesn't pick up and blow all over, but it's much too exposed and gets the full brunt of the wind charging around the corner, so I discard the idea. I also remember the description, written by Hugh Miser, the geologist who made the first geological reconnaissance of the San Juan River in 1921, of a flood in August at the foot of the Honaker Trail. The flood stage was six feet higher than normal and carried so much silt that Miser says it was brick-red in color, and hundreds of fish that could not get oxygen swam to the surface, exhausted.

I stoop down to examine the rocks, which are rendered jewel-like by a thin laving of water. Quartzite, agate, conglomerate, chalcedony, they all derive from mountains nearly three hundred miles away. Overhead two ravens patrol the canyon and make a second pass just over me, calling; doubtless they know that humans leave tidbits and are just checking.

On the underside of many of the cobbles caddisfly cases are cemented. On the tops of many of the dry ones spiders sun like eight-legged starfish, hurrying away at the sign of any crossing shadow. While I'm hunkered down a half-dozen chukar partridge fly low across the river; I just catch a glimpse of them out of the corner of my eye. The white faces outlined with a dark stripe, the stripes on the wing, their direct and sure flight, and their size are unmistakable. They thrive on the cheatgrass that grows all over the slopes. They would have made marvelous Anasazi food but are only a recent introduction to the United States.

I walk on until my equilibrium is restored, until I feel at peace with the river and myself, and then sit quietly facing the river: "The rush of the river soothes the mind," Richard Jeffries, an English naturalist, wrote a century ago. With my eyes closed I listen to the soothing peaceful murmuring.

As I return, paralleling my own footprints, I contemplate taking a bath, but the wind is still up enough to cause a chill, and I remember Miser's description of bathing in the San Juan when "the body of the bather on emerging from the river would be covered with red and dark stripes and splotches, depending on the color of the muddy water."

5

One's priorities become rearranged very quickly down here. The most important thing still is setting up camp and making certain that I have drinking and cooking water, things one rarely thinks about in the city. Since I have but one pot to cook in, the logistics of boiling water and cooking have to be worked out in orderly fashion. I fill the cooking pot with water for dinner; the contents look like coffee with too much cream in it. Still, I'm no worse off than the Mormon settlers who remained in Bluff in 1885; when they carried water from the river they had to settle the silt overnight with cottonwood ashes.

While I wait for the water to settle, I begin to sketch, even though sand occasionally drifts across the page. More than anything else drawing sets me at peace with the world; perhaps it is the intense focusing outside oneself. There are handsome things to draw here, such as salt-bush with interesting spine patterns and wide papery bracts ruffled around the seeds, and all the other things I never seem to have time to do on a long trip.

In an hour the river water has settled enough to be decanted into an empty water bottle. I look for sand damp enough to hold a trowel-dug slot, and two rocks to hold the pan. I grin as I collect wood to do it *my* way. Every guide has his own style of setting up a kitchen: one collects enough wood to build fires for an army until next May, dividing it into precise stacks of tinder, kindling, and firewood. Another garners just enough to start a fire and, when more wood is needed, goes out and scavenges what is necessary even if it's pitch black. Another one considers choosing the proper wood too important for anyone but himself to do and no one had better clutter up *his* woodpile with any extraneous debris. My way is a condensation of observation and my own proclivities, which haven't changed much during the years. I mostly want small wood, or at least wood broken into short lengths; by the time I'm finished my hands sting from the whacking I have to give bigger sticks to fragment them.

I pluck a handful of dried rice grass, which makes ideal fire start, lay a tiny fire and light it, a point of pride to see just how small a fire I can cook on. Water boils quickly; I dump in dried lentil soup, bring the pot back to a simmer, and feed the fire a twig or two at a time as needed.

Saltbush *(Atriplex canescens)*

Broom senecio *(Senecio spartioides)*

While dinner cooks I find a spot to spread my ground cloth, unroll my air mattress, and drop my sleeping bag, still rolled up, on top. No good. I turn to put wood on the fire and a gust of wind lifts the mattress with the intent to transport it to Colorado. I end up with seven rocks on the ground cloth and a cairn on the mattress. Even though the wind has died down considerably it still gusts with vivacity, shooting flames out from under the pot, first one side, then the other. I know I'll have to shake off the ground cloth later but there's a psychological something that says "home" when my ground cloth is spread out. Whether it's the orange cloth or my red plastic trowel, a black-chinned hummingbird buzzes in close and investigates.

Nearby is a big boulder just the right slant for a backrest, against which I lean. As I take notes a faint scribbling sound, just louder than my pen, makes me look around. A collared lizard, about ten inches long, appears at the top of the rock, head washed with orange, black and white and tan collar, brownish-gray back, tail about one fourth of its total length, a striking creature. It perches on the rock just above my head, remaining there as long as I write, lunging and grabbing tidbits out of the air, head gleaming as if gilded, red-lined mouth opening and snapping shut, showing formidable teeth. Collared lizards are pugnacious and have teeth big enough to inflict a painful bite if caught and handled incautiously. And those teeth are generally in good fighting trim, since new teeth are produced throughout its life. Old teeth are shed in sequence, in a complicated but discernible order, so that every other tooth is a strong new one.

Because it is a relatively large lizard it requires more time to warm up than tiny ones, and risks a longer period of vulnerability before it is completely agile. It likely had a period of feeding this morning, shuttled about to keep its body temperature at the optimum in the heat of the day, and now feeds again in the warm of the evening before going down for the night.

I put the second part of the lentil soup in to cook and in the fifteen minutes of time left walk a way downstream. I mark the supple willows and the occasional seep willow, which isn't a willow at all but a member of the Composite Family with willowlike leaves and growth. Indians used to chew some of the stems as a toothache remedy.

But where the shoreline is webbed with tamarisk roots, I do not enjoy the flora. When I am an old lady and have nothing else to do, I am going to walk every river in the Southwest and uproot all the upstart tamarisks and let them float down to Lake Powell. To get in practice I pull out seventy-two and cast them on the river, a useless gesture since they will be replaced by twenty times seventy-two. They are weedy, grasping trees that form ugly thickets and are fire hazards, an introduced pest that adds nothing to the beauty of the river. Eight species were brought in by the U.S. Department of Agriculture between 1899 and 1915, and now they choke small watercourses, and their greedy shallow roots and the dense shade of their thickets make it impossible for native plants to get started. They have vapid blooms that non-Westerners are always oohing and aahing about, blossoms that ripen into thousands of tufted seeds with a vicious viability, so that they quickly clutter up the landscape.

On the new shoots of some of the willow bushes are small beetles, most of them mating. They're about half an inch long, with pale green wings with a black edging and stripe. The wings fall open when they lift off to reveal a reddish-tan body, and they navigate about two feet through the air before plummeting into the sand. I watch several land on a willow stem and wonder how on earth they find each other. One bug makes a sustained six-second flight, and upon landing proceeds up a willow stem which is, alas, uninhabited. Two are on the sand, separated only by the crest of a ripple, each oblivious of the one on the other side.

The male is smaller than the female. A male clings tightly to a female's back as she ambles up to the end of a branch, turns, and starts back down again. Out of a hundred, how many make it to connubial bliss on a willow stem? (The next morning the insects are immobilized, some still coupled, some still fast to a green branch, some falling off as I brush by. One lies in the sand, feet up, as still as if dead. I put it in my hand and close my fingers over it. Within the minute it warms and revives and turns over, antennae waving, ready to set out mate hunting.)

I return and eat a solitary supper, enjoying the quiet of the evening. I scrub the pot with sandy silt and the smoke black comes off easily. I fill it full of water again and put it on to boil. It's so full of silt that it doesn't boil, it erupts. After it burps hard enough to rattle the pan, I take it off the fire to settle overnight, so that I can replenish my drinking water. Over the time I've spent in this slickrock canyon wilderness, the preciousness of water has been brought home to me. Although here, by the river, I have plenty, it is not drinkable without treatment. And most of the time there hasn't been plenty, just enough for a day's minimum comfort for a very few people. The water I so casually use in the city —to brush teeth, wash hands, cook, rinse dishes—I no longer take so much for granted. I know what it's like to be thirsty, *very* thirsty, to wonder where the next water is coming from, and to drink water that I would not only have disdained in the city but thrown out had I been offered a cup. Out here, the dryness sticks in your throat.

6

I let the fire burn to ash. When I hear a breeze coming I flick out whatever is totally burned and let it float away. The wind has diminished to an occasional gust so it at last seems safe to lay everything out for the night on my ground cloth. I arrange things where I can find them in the dark, a pattern of convenience I've worked out over the years. I carry no flashlight so have a precise place for everything I may need, including my tent, which is within reach in case of rain. I consider pitching it just for wind protection, but a nylon tent rattles enough to keep me awake and I'd rather sleep out.

While there's still light left I walk down to the river to brush my teeth, sending the water striders in a back eddy into paroxysms. The path, the apron of wet silt which clutches my boots, the rock I balance on to reach the water are all so familiar now. I experience a sense of comfort here that I had not expected, a sense of home. Of *home.* Obviously there is romance in knowing I will stay here for only a short time, that I do not have to cope with primitive living for weeks on end. Yet I would like to stay much longer, a week perhaps, have the time to walk farther, maybe up to the Goosenecks, maybe down to the mouth of Johns Canyon, and on to Slickhorn. Have time to draw and watch the river go by. In solitude.

When I come back up from the river the collared lizard is back at its sentry spot, snagging whatever unlucky moth flutters by; it also eats many other insects, including those that must fight all the way down like grasshoppers and crickets. And even other small lizards. It bounds off the rock, gets into the pile of cooking wood, and hightails it out, running on its back legs only, using its tail for balance, looking like a miniature megalosaurus. At full pace a collared lizard can make twelve to sixteen miles per hour on two legs alone. It leaves a track with a tail line down the middle and footprints alternating on either side, centers nearly three inches apart, a much bolder track than that of the little lizards who leave a dainty chain of imprints in the sand.

I sit against the lizard's rock and the residual heat seeps into my

Collared lizard *(Crotaphytus collaris)*

backbone. This is what wilderness is to me: being alone and knowing no one is within miles, and that although others may have passed here there is minimal, or no, trace of their passage. That the materialistic agenda of everyday life does not pertain here. That here I set my own priorities based upon the immediate necessities of survival. That my time is totally mine to use, to expend and extend as I see fit. That I am totally responsible for my own well-being.

Many of us need this wilderness as a place to listen to the quiet, to feel at home with ancient rhythms that are absent in city life, to know the pulse of a river, the riffle of the wind, the rataplan of rain on the slickrock. Romantics, perhaps, but realists too: here in the wilderness is a safety valve for our civilization, an environment which can absorb our pollution, and, given time, cleanse itself. It is a museum of complexities, a demonstration of how plant and animal communities coexist in their own beautiful order.

I wonder if the increasing pressures of civilization, of economic exploration, will encroach until the only wilderness we have is that left by default, land that has no value to anyone for anything else for the moment. And what of the pressures on the federal agencies administering wilderness lands—the Park Service, Forest Service, and Bureau of Land Management, beset by people who wish to use wilderness lands for purposes which *ipso facto* render them unwilderness: grazing, mining, development, roadways? The management problem for Grand Gulch is a microcosm of the one that faces all agencies administering these lands. Dr. William Lipe, an archaeologist who not only has worked in Grand Gulch many seasons, but has a feel and empathy for this land that is unmatched, writes:

> It is still a place where one can visit the ruins alone, and often walk for days without seeing someone else. But it is no longer "three days on the road from Bluff." More come every year, and there has been recent vandalism in some of the sites. The Bureau of Land Management, the federal agency responsible for protecting Grand Gulch, has stationed several rangers in the area, to contact visitors, and to patrol the area. Although they take care not to establish a "police" presence, it is clear that even in Grand Gulch, we are moving into an era of managed remoteness, of planned romance. I think that is probably how it has to be if we are to preserve the qualities of the area at all in an increasingly mobile and exploitive society. The challenge is to have effective management that does not itself overwhelm the values it is designed to protect.

I have seen the changes in the wilderness in the last decade, the hordes of backpackers and river runners, most of them solicitous of the environment, but some just out to beat the river with the help of a six-pack, or log as many miles as they can in one day, seeing nothing but the toes of their boots. Mountain trails where formerly one saw no one else now are trampled and widened by hundreds of hikers; mountain meadows that were once beautifully empty now look like tent cities. Is it wilderness when you share it with twenty other people? Even ten? Even one? The tenacity and fierce protectiveness I feel for this small segment of the West forces me to realize that I am a raging conservationist in pragmatist's clothes, knowing some land will be lost to the encroachment of civilization, determined that pristine country can still be preserved.

And what of the designated wilderness land that we still have: how does it remain wilderness? Idealistically I would like to hope that people could be educated to carry out their trash, leave no signs of their passage, disturb no prehistoric sites, knowing in this way they will come away richer. But even education and understanding will not check the wear and tear of too many people, no matter how well intentioned. The greatest danger may be in loving it to death.

Roderick Nash, in *Wilderness and the American Mind,* points out that it isn't dams or mines or roads that are

> the basic threat to the wilderness quality of an environment. People are, and whether they come with economic or recreational motives is, in a sense, beside the point. . . . Any definition of wilderness implies an absence of civilization, and wilderness values are so fragile that even appropriate kinds of recreational use detract from and, in suffi- cient quantity, destroy wilderness.

Nash believes that we will come to a quota system, just as people buy tickets for the theater, or wait until seats are available; they don't insist upon sitting on other people's laps:

> One hundred people might be physically able to squeeze onto a tennis court, but the game they then played would not be tennis. So they wait their turn, placing the integrity of the game ahead of per- sonal considerations. They realize, of course, that when they do get a chance to play, they will be accorded the same respect.

In other words, when your turn *does* come, the wilderness *is* there to enjoy. Intellectually, I somewhat agree; emotionally, I'm not sure I'm ready for the galloping bureaucracy that will accompany such regula- tion and intense supervision, or that wilderness and such rigidity are not mutually exclusive.

Sitting here in the darkening evening I feel a sadness, that perhaps the time I have walked here has been a golden time of wilderness enjoyment, before there were too many people, a time of freedom, joy in living in a simpler way that gives meaning to all living. Will those who come after me know what it's like to wake up in one of these canyons, hear the tentative murmurs and scratchings, feel the sixth singing sense of quickening heartbeat of hunted and hunting, of life that shuttles and scuttles and plods and leaps, leaving tracks to tell who went where and sometimes why, and the wind erasing them so that it is only the cool sand that one ever remembers?

7

Darkness comes so softly now. The cliffs seem to retain the last light of day as they retain the heat of the sun and give it back at night. The .

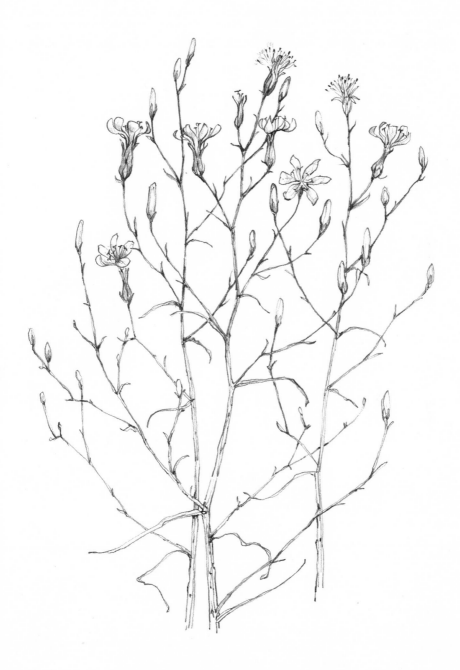

Skeletonweed or Milkpink *(Lygodesmia juncea)*

willows are in silhouette but rose and tan and gray still glow on the cliffs, silver still shimmers on the river. Stars appear slowly, only the bright ones, and then galaxies of lights flood this clamshell-horizoned sky.

I don't think I've ever sat and watched for so long, hypnotized with the splendor of this time, this place, this sense of being. It is enough to know why I came here: to breathe in the solitude and the silence. I simply accept what I've been learning in these canyons, finding resources I didn't know I had, stretching, accepting that there are times when one has no options, and I sit here in peace because of that. I know that I will never be content without risk and challenge and the opportunity to fail, to know pain, the chance to test my endurance, unwarp my horizons, know physical stress and the blinding satisfaction of coming through. If the cost is great, the rewards are greater. And I sit here in peace because of that.

And then, in the star-dark lightness, I shake open my sleeping bag and stretch out to watch the stars. A parure of ten stars lies in precise alignment against the eggshell curve of the canyon wall. They stand time still, in poised perfection, before wheeling on to other appointments.

In the quiet, the air is singing.

Notes
Acknowledgments
Index

Notes

U.S.G.S. topographical maps, 15-minute series, covering this area are: Grand Gulch, Cedar Mesa, Mexican Hat, Goulding, Natural Bridges, Bears Ears, and Clay Hills.

Plant identification books helpful here, other than those mentioned below are: Arthur Cronquist, Arthur H. Holmgren, Noel H. Holmgren, James L. Reveal, and Patricia K. Holmgren, *The Intermountain Flora, The Monocotyledons,* Vol. 6 (NY: Columbia University Press, 1977); N. Natt Dodge, *Flowers of the Southwest Deserts* (Globe, AZ: Southwestern Monuments Association, 1969); Frank W. Gould, *Grasses of Southwestern United States* (Tucson: University of Arizona Press, 1973); Ruth Nelson, *Plants of Zion National Park* (Springdale, UT: Zion Natural History Association, 1976); W. B. McDougall, *Grand Canyon Wild Flowers* (Flagstaff: Museum of Northern Arizona, 1965); Pauline M. Patraw, *Flowers of the Southwest Mesas,* Southwest Monuments Association, Popular Series No. 5 (Phoenix: McGrew Printing and Lithographic Co., 1953). Stanley I. Welsh and Glen Moore, *Utah Plants (Tracheophyta)* (Provo: Brigham Young University Press, 1973) is definitive but technical and sparsely illustrated; Harold W. Ricketts, *Wild Flowers of the United States,* Vol. 6 (New York: New York Botanical Gardens/McGraw-Hill Book Co., n.d.) is scarcely a field guide but is expansively illustrated. Herbert E. Gregory, *The San Juan Country, A Geographic and Geologic Reconnaissance of Southeastern Utah,* U.S.G.S. Professional Paper 188 (Washington, D.C.: U.S. Government Printing Office, 1938), pp. 25–26, lists area plants by their scientific names, some of which are out-of-date.

page LOWER GRAND GULCH

12   Herbert E. Bolton, "Pageant in the Wilderness. The Story of the Escalante Expedition to the Interior Basin, 1776, including the Diary and Itinerary of Father Escalante, Translated and Annotated," *Utah Historical Quarterly,* Vol. 18 (1950), is a full account of Escalante's journey. See also Leroy R. and Ann W. Hafen, *The Old Spanish Trail, Santa Fe to Los Angeles, with extracts from contemporary records and including diaries of Antonio Armijo and Orville Platte* (Glendale, CA: Arthur H. Clark Co., 1954), and Archer B. Hulbert, ed., *Southwest on the Turquoise Trail, the First Diaries of the Road to Santa Fe* (Denver: Steward Commission of Colorado College and Denver Public Library, 1933). Herbert E. Gregory, *The San Juan Country,,* p. 20: "As the Spanish priests and soldiers seem not to have visited the San Juan country, reliable knowledge of its Indian inhabitants dates only from the days of pioneer settlement—most of it within the last half century." Gregory's well-illustrated paper is the most germane to this area.

12   Joseph H. Hill, "Ewing Young in the Fur Trade of the Far Southwest, 1822–1834," *Oregon Historical Society Quarterly,* Vol. 24, No. 1:1–35 (March, 1923), and Kenneth L. Holmes, *Ewing Young, Master Trapper* (Portland, OR: Binford and Mort, 1967), p. 20:

Young "established a headquarters on the San Juan River, for more than a year later a Mexican official reported that measures had been taken to demolish fortifications built by this Anglo-American party on the San Juan." The location of Young's fort is not known.

13   Although many crossings of the upper reaches of the San Juan River in New Mexico and Colorado were recorded, I can find no documented evidence of crossings below Bluff or Mexican Hat before 1880. Antonio Armijo, going from New Mexico to California in 1829–30, crossed the San Juan near Aztec, New Mexico. Cornelia A. Perkins, Marian G. Nielson, and Leonora B. Jones, *Saga of San Juan* (San Juan County Daughters of Utah Pioneers, 1957), p. 21: the Coronado expedition that left Mexico in 1540 to search for the fabled "Seven Cities of Cibola" came up through Arizona, where a segment of the party encountered the gigantic gorges of the Colorado River with the San Juan leading into it; "Time and again, by various routes, the party tried to go down the impregnable chasms, but each time failed. Completely baffled, the men turned back. Some historians believe these explorers tried to descend the San Juan Canyon south wall, somewhere between Honaker Trail and John's Canyon." *Saga of San Juan* is an example of the fine work that can be done by local historians who have the heritage of the history they write about. Now unavailable, a copy was generously loaned by Jackie Steele of Monticello, Utah.

Albert R. Lyman, "First Whitemen in San Juan County, Utah, *Utah Historical Quarterly,* Vol. 2, No. 1:11–13 (1929): White men may have been on the lower San Juan in 1872 and 1873, searching for a mysterious mine, led by a Charley Jones who claimed he knew of one and would take anyone who would grubstake him to it; Jones plus nine greedy innocents probably crossed the San Juan River in the vicinity of Comb Wash and traveled westward toward lower Grand Gulch, then up through Clay Hills Pass, on what turned out to be a wild goose chase. David E. Miller, *Hole-in-the-Rock Expedition* (Salt Lake City: University of Utah Press, 1966), pp. 35 and 150: Peter Shirts (or Shurtz) had been living near the mouth of Montezuma Creek since 1877 and was there when the Mormons arrived; his route in getting there is unknown. Ives quote: Lieutenant Joseph C. Ives, Report on the Colorado River of the West (explored in 1857 and 1858) (Washington, D.C.: Government Printing Office, 1861), 36th Congress, 1st Session, House Exec. Doc. 90, p. 110. Captain John N. Macomb, *Report on the Exploring Expedition from Santa Fe, New Mexico, to the Junction of the Grand and Green Rivers of the Great Colorado of the West in 1859* (1976): although Macomb's exploration was made in 1859, printing was delayed by the Civil War. It is not likely that the Mormons had a copy, their relations with the U.S. Government being what they were; had they, it would still not have provided the specific information needed.

O. Dock Marston, river historian *par excellence,* kindly made available his 1976 typescript of "James White's Grand Canyon Cruise ????" from which I have quoted. See also Arthur Cronquist, Arthur H. Holmgren, Noel H. Holmgren, James L. Reveal, *Intermountain Flora, Vascular Plants of the Intermountain West, U.S.A.* (New York: New York Botanical Garden/Hafner Publishing Company, 1972) on the early explorations of the Southwest; also William H. Goetzmann, *Army Exploration of the American West, 1803–1863* (New Haven: Yale University Press, 1959). Goetzmann sees little practical contribution of these surveys but geologically they were important in establishing the drainage of the San Juan River and the intricate terrain of the canyon country. Perkins *et al., Saga of San Juan,* p. 21, list the military, railroad, and other government surveys in the Southwest between 1842 and 1875.

14   The definitive account of the two Mormon expeditions to the San Juan is David

Miller's *Hole-in-the-Rock Expedition,* which contains diaries and journals of participants, from which I have quoted.

Gregory, *San Juan Country,* p. 31, who had access to many church documents, remarks that unrealistic reports portrayed a "picturesque region rich in farm land and grazing land, supplied with timber and water, and occupied only by a few Indians awaited settlement." Herbert E. Gregory, *Geology and Geography of the Zion Park Region, Utah and Arizona,* U.S.G.S. Professional Paper 220 (Washington, D.C.: U.S. Government Printing Office, 1950), p. 24: the Mormons had "nothing to guide them except the little knowledge gleaned from the Piutes, old-time trappers, and prospectors. They had no usable information regarding soil, forage, timber, predatory animals, noxious plants, kind of winters, rainfall, length of growing season, or the size and regularity of streams available for irrigation."

15　　Kumen Jones, "First Settlement of San Juan County, Utah," *Utah Historical Quarterly,* Vol. 2, No. 1:8–11 (1929); Jones was a young man and served as a scout on the 1880 trip. Hobbs quote, p. 87, and Lyman quote, p. 168, both from Miller, *Hole-in-the-Rock Expedition.* In 1959 the fills and rock work of the old road where it crossed Clay Hills Pass were still plainly visible, with many portions of it too steep for a jeep. See Thomas E. Mullens, *Geology of the Clay Hills Area, San Juan County, Utah,* U.S.G.S. Bulletin 1087-H (Washington, D.C.: U.S. Government Printing Office, 1960), p. 267. Part of Salvation Knoll has been cut away by the realignment of Highway 95, which leads to the bridge crossing at Hite that replaces the old Halls Crossing. The Mormon trail exists now only in part; some of the trails that are evident today were bulldozed by overeager descendants who jeeped the trail in the 1950s and '60s.

18　　H. D. Miser, *The San Juan Canyon, Southeastern Utah,* U.S.G.S. Water-Supply Paper 538 (Washington, D.C.: U.S. Government Printing Office, 1924) was the first river survey (the first run of the river was made from Animas, New Mexico, to its junction with the Colorado by E. L. Goodridge in 1879–80). Miser, pp. 1–2: "This report, which describes the San Juan Canyon, San Juan River and the tributary streams, and the geography and to some extent the geology of the region, presents information obtained by me during the descent of the river with the Trimble party in 1921. The exploration of the canyon, which was financed jointly by the United States Geological Survey and the Southern California Edison Co., had as its primary object the mapping and study of the San Juan in connection with proposed power and storage projects along this and Colorado rivers." The first accurate maps were produced from this trip. Pp. 72–73: "Grand Gulch, which is a narrow and tortuous canyon, with red walls several hundred feet high, heads in the slopes south of Elk Ridge and runs in a southwesterly direction, joining San Juan Canyon at a point 3½ miles below the mouth of Slickhorn Gulch. According to earlier maps it joins the San Juan at a point some 10 miles farther west, near Clay Hill Crossing. At its mouth there is a waterfall 50 feet high. On August 8, 1921, a clear stream of pure water with a flow of a few second-feet was pouring over the fall. In the upper part of the gulch water is stated to be found at most places throughout the year."

19　　T. Mitchell Prudden, *On the Great American Plateau* (New York: G. P. Putnam's Sons, 1906), p. 10.

21　　Gregory, *San Juan Country,* p. 5: "Except under the direction of men acquainted with the topography of the plateau province and experienced in finding water holes, tourists are advised to limit their travels . . ." and Herbert E. Gregory, *The Navajo Country, a Geographic and Hydrographic Reconnaissance of Parts of Arizona, New Mexico, and Utah,* U.S.G.S. Water-Supply Paper 380, 1917; p. 132: "Safe traveling in this region involves a knowledge of the location of these springs, and exploration consists essentially in directing one's course from spring to spring."

23   The canyon country rattlesnake is the midget faded rattler, *Crotalus viridis concolor* (in some books called *"decolor"*). The comprehensive book on rattlesnakes is Laurence M. Klauber, *Rattlesnakes: Their Habits, Life Histories, and Influence on Mankind,* 2 vols. (Berkeley: University of California Press, 1963). Robert C. Stebbins, *Amphibians and Reptiles of Western North American* (New York: McGraw-Hill Book Company, 1954) and *A Field Guide to Western Reptiles and Amphibians* (Boston: Houghton Mifflin Co., 1966) are excellent identification guides; see also Albert H. Wright and Anna A. Wright, *Handbook of Snakes of the United States and Canada* (Ithaca, NY: Comstock Publishing Association, 1957), 2 vols., and Sherman A. Minton and Madge R. Minton, *Venomous Reptiles* (New York: Charles Scribner's Sons, 1969).

   Of the some 6,000 snakebites reported a year, about 12 are fatal, which means that if you get hit there is a good chance of survival although it will be a nightmarish experience. First of all, avoid places where snakes are likely to be: don't put your hand in a woodpile, check a ledge or log before stepping over, etc. Under optimal conditions a rattler can be heard 30 yards away, but there's the occasional rude specimen that strikes first and rattles after. An antivenom injection as quickly as possible is the safest antidote for snakebite; barring that, some doctors feel that snakebite kits can cause more damage than nontreatment. Instructions about cutting an incision across fang marks should be taken with a great deal of caution. The chances of slashing muscle and tendon are great (especially since the most frequent bites are on the foot, leg, and ankle), and the loss of blood simply adds another factor that the body has to deal with. The chances are, with the smaller rattlers of the canyon country, that you'll be excruciatingly sick for about three days, and that you'll survive. Immediately drink as much water as possible to counteract the dehydration that will come with continual vomiting. Be prepared for grotesque swelling and devastating pain; if the strike is on a leg there is no way you can walk out. The best cure for snakebite is to walk scared.

24   Gregory, *San Juan Country,* p. 105: "In Grand Gulch the elimination of meanders has left several abandoned horseshoe bends at different levels above the floor. In some places water is seeping through meander necks, and in others the stream passes through high-walled chutes that have not been long in use." The origin of Cedar Mesa Sandstone is at present controversial, some geologists adhering to underwater deposition, as near-shore marine deposits, and others to wind-deposited sand dunes. See also Donald L. Baars, *Red Rock Country, The Geologic History of the Colorado Plateau* (Garden City, NY: Doubleday/Natural History Press, 1972), an attractive, well-illustrated book for the general reader interested in the geology of southeastern Utah, and Lehi F. Hintze, *Geologic History of Utah,* Brigham Young University Geology Studies, Vol. 20, Part 3, Studies for Students No. 8 (Provo, UT: Department of Geology, Brigham Young University, 1973). Also, W. L. Stokes, *General Geology of Southeastern Utah,* Guide Book No. 9 (Utah Geologic Survey, 1954).

28   Useful field identification books are Anne Haven Morgan, *Field Book of Ponds and Streams* (New York: G. P. Putnam's Sons, 1930) and James G. Needham and Paul R. Needham, *A Guide to the Study of Fresh-water Biology* (San Francisco: Holden-Day, 1962). For more definitive reading, see Robert W. Pennak, *Fresh-water Invertebrates of the United States* (New York: Ronald Press Co., 1953); Mary Gardiner, *The Biology of Invertebrates* (New York: McGraw-Hill Book Co., 1972); James G. Needham and J. T. Lloyd, *The Life of Inland Waters* (Ithaca, NY: Comstock Publishing Co., 1930); and Robert E. Coker, *Streams, Lakes, Ponds* (Chapel Hill: University of North Carolina Press, 1954).

31   See Karl W. Butzer, *Environment and Archaeology* (Chicago: Aldine Atherton, 1971); Emil W. Haury, "Post-Pleistocene Human Occupation of the Southwest," pp. 69–75, and John P. Miller, "Problems of the Pleistocene in Cordilleran North America,

as Related to Reconstruction of Environmental Changes that Affected Early Man,"
pp. 19–41, both in Terah L. Smiley, ed., *Climate and Man in the Southwest* (Tucson:
University of Arizona Press, 1957); and C. Vance Haynes, "Carbon-14 Dates and
Early Man in the New World," in Paul S. Martin and H. E. Wright, Jr., *Pleistocene
Extinctions: The Search for a Cause,* Vol. 6 of the Proceedings of the VII Congress of the
International Association for Quaternary Research (New Haven and London: Yale
University Press, 1967), pp. 267–86; Haynes (p. 267) finds no carbon dates earlier
than 12,000 B.P. for man in the New World and thinks that 13,000–11,000 B.C. is the
critical time of entrance. See also Robert F. Spencer, Jesse D. Jennings *et al., The Native
Americans* (New York: Harper & Row, 1965) and Jesse D. Jennings, *Prehistory of North
America* (New York: McGraw-Hill Book Co., 1968). For population estimates, see
Henry F. Dobyns, "An Appraisal of Techniques with a New Hemispheric Estimate,"
Current Anthropology, Vol. 7, No. 4:395–416 (October, 1966), and Gordon V. Childe,
"The Urban Revolution," in Mark P. Leone, ed., *Contemporary Archaeology, A Guide to
Theory and Contributions* (Carbondale and Edwardsville: Southern Illinois University
Press, 1972), pp. 43–51.

32   Paul Martin is the sturdiest proponent of the fascinating theory that the disappearance of 30% of North American megafauna at the end of the Pleistocene is due to
man. Martin and Wright, *Pleistocene Extinctions,* give a thorough presentation of opin-
ions on this score. Also pertinent is Karl W. Butzer, *Environment and Archaeology*
(Chicago and NY: Aldine Atherton, Inc., 1971). See also Emil Haury, "The Greater
American Southwest," in Robert J. Braidwood and Gordon V. Willey, eds., *Courses
Toward Urban Life: Archeological Considerations of Some Cultural Alternates* (Chicago: Aldine
Publishing Co., 1962), and Paul S. Martin and Fred Plog, *The Archaeology of Arizona*
(Garden City, NY: The American Museum of Natural History and Doubleday
Natural History Press, 1973).

32   Paul S. Martin, *The Last 10,000 Years: A Fossil Pollen Record of the American Southwest*
(Tucson: University of Arizona Press, 1963), p. 70: "Following extinction of the large
mammals the early hunters probably suffered economic depressions and a population crash. Under a climate similar to the present and with the existing biotic zones
in place, the early hunters were obliged to begin their 7,000-year experiment with
native plants, leading in the altithermal to increasingly skillful techniques of har-
vesting and gathering, to the domestication of certain weedy camp-followers, and,
within the last 1,000 years, to the widespread adoption of flood plain agriculture."

Kent V. Flannery, "Archaeological Systems Theory and Early Mesoamerica,"
in Leone, *Contemporary Archaeology,* pp. 222–34; p. 222: As "we learn more about the
food-collectors and early food-producers of that region, our mental image of these
ancient peoples has been greatly modified. We no longer think of the preceramic
plant-collectors as a ragged and scruffy band of nomads; instead, they appear as a
practiced and ingenious team of lay botanists who know how to wring the most out
of a superficially bleak environment." The modern eye is not attuned to the considerable and available supply of native plant foods, and a good variety and amount
was available to an omnivorous and skillful gatherer; see Richard G. Matson and
William D. Lipe, "Regional Sampling: A Case Study of Cedar Mesa, Utah," in James
W. Mueller, ed., *Sampling in Archaeology* (Tucson: University of Arizona Press, n.d.),
pp. 124–43, and Euell Gibbons, "Stalking the West's Wild Foods," *National Geographic,* Vol. 144, No. 2:186–99 (August, 1973), who found ample food.

33   Elman R. Service, *Primitive Social Organization* (New York: Random House, 1962), p.
100, defines a band as a more or less residential association of nuclear families,
numbering 25 to 100; p. 47: "All societies at the band level of integration are foragers
of wild food . . . the band level of integration is by far the most frequent among

known hunters and gatherers and must have been the characteristic, though perhaps not universal, form of social organization during the paleolithic era." D. E. Dumond, "Population Growth and Cultural Change," *Southwestern Journal of Anthropology,* Vol. 21: 302–24 (1965); p. 313, Dumond estimates that in a preindustrial agricultural society, only 5 to 10% of the population could be employed outside of food production.

33   Dating of this site is uncertain; unverified information is that it dates between A.D. 450 and 525 and is early Basketmaker II (my thanks to Mr. Robert Delareuelle for this information). However, Dr. William D. Lipe, an archaeologist with extensive experience in the Cedar Mesa/Grand Gulch area, has some doubts. It is much more elaborate than the simple windbreak shelters positively dated to Basketmaker times and may well belong to later Pueblo times, when there was an influx into the canyons.

34   Gregory, *San Juan Country,* p. 106: "Both the flat-roofed and arch-roofed rock shelters of all sizes and shapes are essentially the work of ground water. . . . In the thick, massive sandstone beds the first stage in the development of cavities is the seepage of water along the surface of some locally impervious lens, with consequent removal of the cement, then the grains from the base of porous, saturated rock. This slight undermining permits grains and thin laminae to fall in response to gravity. As the process continues, shell after shell is detached from the roof and, because the cement has been largely removed by percolating water, reaches the floor as a disintegrated mass that is borne to the mouth of the cave by intermittent run-off. The back walls of many rock shelters are moist and thinly coated with water-loving plants. Some give rise to springs; others are coated with alkali or salt 'bloom'; still others, especially those above the local water table, are dry. No field evidence supports the popular notion that the cavities in the walls of canyons have been produced by sand blasts. On the contrary, little wind enters them. Most of the small ones contain leaves, wings of insects, and dust that even a slight breeze would remove. Birds, bats, and rodents live in them, and during severe windstorms the large ones serve as refuges for beasts and men."

35   Frank McNitt, *Richard Wetherill: Anasazi* (Albuquerque: University of New Mexico Press, 1957) is the definitive biography of Wetherill. Wetherill's "Letters, 1893–1901, to B. T. B. Hyde, F. E. Hyde, Jr., and George H. Pepper, in connection with the work of the Hyde Exploring Expedition," are on file in the Department of Anthropology of the American Museum of Natural History in New York. Wetherill's Field Notes, also there, are handwritten in pencil; a typescript has been made, corrected as to punctuation and capitalization, that somehow lacks the immediacy and flavor of Wetherill's style. I am very grateful to Dr. David Thomas and Barbara Conklin of the Anthropology Department for access to the catalogues, letters, inventories and other papers pertaining to Wetherill. Frances Gillmore and Louisa Wade Wetherill, *Traders to the Navajos, The Story of the Wetherills of Kayenta* (Boston and New York: Houghton Mifflin Co., 1934). Louisa was John Wetherill's wife.

  The Antiquities Act and National Monuments Act, Public Law 59–902, 34 STAT, 225; 16 USC 431–433, was passed June 8, 1906. See Charles McGimsey, *Archeology and Archeological Resources, A Guide for Those Planning to Use, Affect or Alter the Land's Surface* (Washington, D.C.: Society for American Archaeology, n.d. but post-1971), and *Public Archeology* (New York: Seminar Press, 1972), which give state requirements for obtaining permission to dig. In Utah, archaeological excavation or exploration is prohibited on state or federal land without a permit from the Division of Parks and Recreation.

  Nels C. Nelson, *The Cartier Grand Gulch Expedition, Archaeological Field Notes, Recon-*

naissance of the Southwest, New Mexico, Arizona, Nevada, Utah, California, Various Museums, "Grand Gulch Region, Utah, 1920" (American Museum of Natural History, Department of Anthropology, 1920), pp. 1–4, lists the early workers in Grand Gulch. Donald R. Keller, Richard V. Ahlstrom, and Dana Hartman, *Final Report for Surface Cleanup of Cultural Sites in Grand Gulch* (Bureau of Land Management, Monticello District, San Juan County, Utah, Contract #53500–CT4–558, 1974) is a detailed examination of some of the larger Anasazi sites in the Gulch; pp. 14–16, the first removal of archaeological material from Grand Gulch was apparently before 1890, although little is known of what was taken. Larger-scale activities began with McLoyd and Graham, whose work appears "to have been motivated in part by the strong nineteenth-century spirit of relic hunting and in part by the profit that could be realized by the sale of prehistoric artifacts and relics to collectors, exhibitors, and museums." McNitt, *Richard Wetherill,* p. 36: that such an august magazine as *Archaeologist* ran a "Collector's Department" was virtually an invitation to vandalism; the column indicated where objects might be bought and said that "single specimens" could be sold without conscience.

35 John O. Brew, *Archaeology of Alkali Ridge, Southeastern Utah,* Vol. 21, Peabody Museum Papers (Cambridge: Harvard University Press, 1946), p. 22: "In 1894 McLoyd and Graham of Durango, Colorado, published a catalogue of a collection of 'relics' offered for sale. The collection had been made in southeastern Utah, mostly in Grand Gulch, and it is now in the Museum of the American Indian, Heye Foundation, in New York City." See also Helen Sloane Daniels, "Adventures with the Anasazi of Fall Creek," *Occasional Papers of the Center of Southwest Studies* (Durango, CO: Ft. Lewis College, 1976), pp. 9–15, which contains a copy of Graham's diary of the 1891 exploration; and William W. Adams, *Ninety Years of Glen Canyon Archaeology, 1869–1959, A Brief Historical Sketch and Bibliography of Archaeological Investigations from J. W. Powell to the Glen Canyon Project,* Museum of Northern Arizona Bulletin 33, Glen Canyon Series No. 2 (Flagstaff: Northern Arizona Society of Science and Art, 1960). Quote: Richard Wetherill, Field Notes, typescript, p. 8.

36 *Ibid.,* undated but "early 1893"; Wetherill was in Brooklyn at the time. One of the problems with Wetherill's collection from the 1893–94 trip, which was shipped to Talbot Hyde in New York in 1895 and thence to the American Museum of Natural History, according to H Catalogue, Vol. VI, p. 58: "It was numbered and catalogued, presumably by Mr. George Pepper (Mr. Hyde's personal secretary), who, instead of following the original field catalogue chose to separate the items, at least in part, into type groups. The result was the present mix-up of the original field numbers and also of the more or less definitely given localities of origin. The Museum catalogue thus produced indicated some of the localities correctly, others incorrectly, and still others not at all. . . ." Some of the items represented by field numbers apparently did not reach the Museum. Other specimens, especially pottery, catalogued here as part of the collection, have also disappeared. In a 1936 examination and overhaul, the present Catalogue H was compiled. Although the Wetherill material is in storage and not on display, it is "in the process of being made available for research."

37 R. Wetherill, letter to B. Talbot B. Hyde, Esq., December 17, 1893.

38 McNitt, *Richard Wetherill* (pp. 86–88) commends Prudden's understanding of ethnology and archaeology as well as his publications; besides the ones cited in the text Prudden wrote "The Circular Kivas of Small Ruins in the San Juan Watershed," *American Anthropologist,* Vol. 16, No. 1:33–58. *On the Great American Plateau* is a charming and very informative book. Finding no decent maps, he made his own, and despite certain inaccuracies, they were the best archaeological maps of the country up to

that time. See also Charles Avery Amsden, *Prehistoric Southwesterners from Basketmakers to Pueblo* (Los Angeles: Southwest Museum, 1949), a very readable book mainly on Basketmaker culture. Amsden was a Farmington, New Mexico, banker with an abiding interest in archaeology; no other than A. V. Kidder, with whom he worked in the field, wrote the introduction. Harold S. Gladwin, *A History of the Ancient Southwest* (Portland, ME: Bond Wheelwright Co., 1957) is also useful for the general reader. A handsome book with beautiful photographs by David Muench is Donald Pike, *Anasazi: Ancient People of the Rock* (New York: Scribner & Sons, 1974).

Wetherill was shot at Chaco Canyon, June 22, 1910, a tragic and enigmatic murder.

38   Robert Wauchope, "Alfred Vincent Kidder, 1885–1963," *American Antiquity,* Vol. 31, No. 2, Part 1:149–71 (1965), p. 149: "Renowned as a master of field archaeology, scholar of prehistory in two major fields, writer, and administrator, he was also one of the most beloved men of his profession." Wauchope describes Kidder's *Introduction to the Study of Southwestern Archaeology* (New Haven: Yale University Press, 1924) as (p. 154) "a pioneer work of synthesis, making order of the chaos of scattered Southwestern archaeological data." It is still a handsome, useful, and well-reading book, and basic reference for the area.

39   Michael A. Glassow, "Changes in the Adaptations of Southwestern Basketmakers: A Systems Perspective," in Leone, *Contemporary Archaeology,* pp. 289–302: the shift from Basketmaker II to Basketmaker III involved a major shift in the proportions of products extracted from the environment, a shift in technical means used to extract and utilize these products, and a shift in the organization of social groups associated with these activities. William D. Lipe and R. G. Matson, "Human Settlement and Resources in the Cedar Mesa Area, SE Utah," in George J. Gumerman, ed., *The Distribution of Prehistoric Population Aggregates, Proceedings of the Southwestern Anthropological Research Group,* Anthropological Reports No. 1:126–151, 1971, p. 136: the shift in settlement patterns between Basketmaker II and III is "the result of improved cultigens, development or introduction of dry-farming techniques, and development of improved storage structures, allowing groups to spend most of their time on the mesa."

39   Wauchope, "Alfred Vincent Kidder," p. 154: "The first of the famous Pecos conferences was held there in 1927. Like most affairs that Kidder presided over, this was most informally run. I still treasure a snapshot I took—with an old box camera— of A. E. Douglass, his tree-ring chart propped on the ground . . . in a clear space between the piñons. Here the first systematic classification for Southwestern prehistory was worked out, a construct still widely followed, with some modifications, for the northern part of the area."

See also Emil W. Haury, "Tree Rings—the Archaeologist's Time-Piece," *American Antiquity,* Vol. 1, No. 2:98–108 (1953), and David A. Breternitz, *An Appraisal of Tree-Ring Dated Pottery in the South-West,* Anthropological Papers of the University of Arizona, No. 10 (Tucson: University of Arizona Press, 1966), p. 1: dendrochronology "provides Southwestern archaeology with a chronological technique that is both unique and absolute. It is small wonder that archaeological applications and interpretations of tree-ring dates have been developed and most intensively used for the 'dating' of various aspects of prehistory in the southwestern United States." See also Edward Schulman, *Dendroclimatic Changes in Semiarid America* (Tucson: University of Arizona Press, 1956), and Terah L. Smiley, "A Summary of Tree-Ring Dates from Some Southwestern Archaeological Sites," *University of Arizona Bulletin,* Laboratory of Tree-Ring Research Bulletin No. 5 (Tucson: University of Arizona, October, 1951), Vol. 22, No. 4; Smiley estimates that only 5 to 10% of total beam, etc. specimens are datable. Harold C. Fritts, David G. Smith, Marvin A. Stokes, "The Biological Model for Paleoclimatic Interpretation of Mesa Verde Tree-Ring Series," *Memoirs for the Society of American Archaeology,* Contributions of the Wetherill Mesa Archeological Project, Number 19, Vol. 31, No. 2, Part 2:101-21 (1965), contains specific data on what narrow tree rings indicate for individual tree species.

The generally accepted dates for Anasazi culture begin with the postulated pre-agricultural Basketmaker I, for which there is no artifactual evidence; it is now considered to be the local or "Four Corners" variant of the Desert Culture; Basketmaker II, A.D. 1 to 450–550; Basketmaker III, A.D. 450–500 to 700–750; Pueblo I, 700–750 to 900; Pueblo II, 900 to 1100–1150; Pueblo III or "Classic Pueblo," 1100–1150 to 1300, at which time the Four Corners area was largely abandoned; Pueblo IV, 1300 until the Spanish arrival around 1600; Pueblo V, 1600 to present.

40   Keller *et al., Final Report for Surface Cleanup,* pp. 34–35: All the teeth examined displayed wear typical of groups subsisting on stoneground foods. Osteophytosis, small bony outgrowths at the joints, was the most prevalent pathology, aside from fractures, which are generally regarded as a common affliction among the cliff dwellers.

The attitude toward children in a nomadic society differs from that in an agricultural one; in the former, with every member carrying his or her own baggage as they moved from place to place, a mother would have been limited to the number of children who couldn't yet walk that she must carry. Since she was also the predominant provider, extra mouths to feed were not as welcome as in an agricultural society, where children could be left in charge of someone else and were a potential source of more labor. The physical difficulties of nursing more than one child at a time would require that one child be weaned before the next could be properly nourished, a three-year interval between children would be needed. But since conception can occur during nursing, regardless of the physiological needs of the mother, children that could not have survived would have been born into a nomadic society, resulting, as one anthropologist puts it, in "systematic infanticide." Under these stringent conditions, a hunting and gathering population may have just been able to maintain a replacement birth rate. See Lewis R. Binford, "Post-Pleistocene Adaptations," in Leone, *Contemporary Archaeology,* pp. 237–54.

41   For illustrations of Anasazi sandals, see John C. McGregor, *Southwestern Archaeology* (Urbana: University of Illinois Press, 1965), pp. 180 and 340–41. Pueblo sandals are predominantly woven in a twilled weave, of either split or unsplit yucca leaves, in contrast to the finer Basketmaker sandals. Many Pueblo sandals have toe notches for the little toe, and sandals for right and left feet were made.

41   Earl H. Morris and Robert F. Burgh, *Anasazi Basketry, Basketmaker II through Pueblo III: A Study Based on Specimens from the San Juan River Country* (Washington, D.C.: Carnegie Institution Publication 533, 1941) is a thorough and extensively illustrated book on Anasazi basketry. P. 59: "Coiled basketry of the Anasazi is an art old and well perfected as far back as we know anything about it and during the 1000 years from some time in Basket Maker II to the close of Pueblo III, circa 1300, it continued with surprisingly few changes and modifications. The two dominant techniques—uninterlocked stitches on two-rod-and-bundle foundation, bunched, and interlocked stitches on one-rod foundation—lived through the entire millennium, and fabrics constructed according to the second of them from the two extremes, could not be told apart, either by visual appearance or by dissection." Pueblo III baskets were so strong that they estimate that nothing less than two hundred pounds would crush one. Frank Cushing, "A Study of Pueblo Pottery as Illustrative of Zuñi Culture Growth," *Fourth Annual Report of Bureau of American Ethnology* (Washington, D.C.: U.S. Government Printing Office, 1886), p. 491: the boiling basket is known in present-

day Zuñi as the "coiled cooking-basket" and the cooking pot as "coiled earthenware cooking-basket."

43   Quote, Keller *et al.*, *Final Report for Surface Cleanup*, pp. 2–3.

44   See Morris and Burgh, *Anasazi Basketry*, p. 47, and McNitt, *Richard Wetherill*, pp. 33–34, for an evaluation of Wetherill's work. William D. Lipe, "Grand Gulch: 'Three Days on the Road from Bluff,' " n.d. (permission to quote from the typescript graciously given by Dr. Lipe), pp. 45–46, found the field catalogues of Wetherill's expeditions "surprisingly good, considering the time and place they were made. The catalogs list each specimen, note the room, feature, or pit from which it came, and from what depth. The field notes, though brief, have sketch maps adequate to identify the site and most of the places where digging was done." (One needs only to compare these with Graham's notes to appreciate Wetherill.) Lipe's perceptive evaluation is that of a working archaeologist (p. 47): "Through the usually stiff sentences of his letters and notes, one can feel the driving enthusiasm that stood up under gagging cave dust, near-bankruptcy, and long days on the 120-mile trail connecting Mancos and Grand Gulch. Also apparent is his empathy with the Anasazi. Not only had he spent years probing their buried secrets, but he, too, had lived most of his days directly on the land. He, too, knew how it felt to see his crops wither and fail, or to slip on a high ledge and catch himself just in time. He had what we would now call a 'feel' for the pattern of Anasazi life."

Archeomagnetic dating involves encasing a sample of archaeological baked clay in a small metal box and taking a precise compass reading while it is still *in situ*. It is then removed and another reading is made of the residual magnetism. The variation in position of the magnetic poles over time has been plotted; comparison of the specimen with plot-dated samples provides a date for the site. See Frank Hole and Robert F. Heizer, *An Introduction to Prehistoric Archeology* (New York: Holt, Rinehart and Winston, 1969), pp. 227–29.

William D. Lipe, "The Wilderness System and Archeological Conservation," Archeological Report No. 7, USDA Forest Service, Southwestern Region, Dee F. Green, ed., *The Wilderness and Cultural Values: A Symposium* (Albuquerque, New Mexico, 1975), pp. 7–21; and Lipe, "A Conservation Model for American Archaeology," *The Kiva*, Vol. 39, Nos. 3–4:213–45 (1974), p. 213: "Archaeological research on any particular segment of the past is based on a non-renewable resource, and one that is being very rapidly eroded. If archaeological field work is to continue very much into the future, we must slow down the attrition of the resource base and must see that from now on it is expended very frugally.... Sites not immediately threatened with destruction should be dug only when the data needs of a problem cannot be met from the available pool of sites requiring salvage. Such pure problem-oriented research should be conducted so as to leave as much of the archaeological resource as possible for future workers."

44   Christy Turner, *Petrographs of the Glen Canyon Region* (Flagstaff: Northern Arizona Society of Science and Art, 1963) was one of several studies of the survey and salvage operations undertaken by the Museum of Northern Arizona and the University of Utah prior to the flooding of Glen Canyon by Lake Powell. Turner (pp. 6–7) divides the rock art of the area into five styles, of which this panel would contain elements of "Style 5," pre-1050 A.D., and "Style 4," A.D. 1050–1250. Characteristic of the former are rectilinear outline forms, sheep with large rectangular bodies with head, tail, and legs disproportionately small; anthropomorphs with huge elongated bodies, arms and legs minor. Style 4 is characterized by both solid and pecked outline forms; characteristic are birds, flute players, hunting scenes, etc. It is more widespread than Style 5. Another approach is that of LaVan Martineau,

The Rocks Begin to Speak (Las Vegas, Nevada: KC Publications, 1973); Martineau interprets the rock art of Utah in the light of knowledge gained in cryptanalysis in the U.S. Air Force and of his Paiute upbringing.

46   In spite of the extensive research, the origins of maize have not yet been fully deciphered. See A. F. Hill, *Economic Botany* (New York and London: McGraw-Hill Book Co., 1937); Kirk Bryan, "Flood-water Farming," *Geological Revue,* Vol. 19:444–56 (1929); W. Wilfred Robbins, *The Botany of Crop Plants* (Philadelphia: P. Blakiston's Son & Co., 1931). Haury, "The Greater American Southwest," considers that the development of agriculture was encouraged by the range of environments in the Southwest and (p. 108) ". . . the fact that these vegetation areas provide the range of climate, terrain, and plant resources on which man could work out a variety of subsistence activities. The adaptive process in a nearly universally harsh environment was eased because of the varied resources. And somewhere within the area agricultural stimuli, as a prelude to the development of a higher societal order, should have found fertile ground." See also Flannery, "Archaeological Systems Theory," pp. 230–31, and Herbert G. Baker, *Plants and Civilization* (Belmont, CA: Wadsworth Publishing Co., 1970), Kent V. Flannery, "The Origins of Agriculture," *Annual Review of Anthropology,* Vol. 2:271–310 (1973); pp. 279–80: The whole process of disarticulation takes an average of from 1 to 2 weeks, seeds being dispersed one at a time, which prevented the unfavorable conditions which would result if the whole head fell in one place at one time, where half the seeds would never be buried and the rest would sprout in a dense mass of over-competition. If the harvester waits too long, he gets only empty stalks; too early, and not all the grain is ripe. "Being in the right area at the right time is therefore far more important than for collection of wild nut crops, and the harvest may be a fast and furious affair." Harold E. Driver, *Indians of North America* (Chicago: University of Chicago Press, 1975), pp. 69–70: pod corn appeared about 3000 B.C. in the Southwest, and was probably selected against early because the glumes enclosing the separate grains are difficult to remove and would have had little value to Indian economy.

    P. C. Mangelsdorf, R. S. MacNeish, G. R. Willey, "Origins of Agriculture in Middle America," in Robert Wauchope, ed. *Handbook of Middle American Indians* (Austin: University of Texas Press, 1964), Vol. I, pp. 427–45; p. 439: at the beginning both beans and squash were probably more productive than maize, but "maize eventually became the basic food plant of the pre-Columbian cultures and civilizations of the New World . . . due to its remarkable ability to evolve rapidly in a man-made environment." J. G. Hawkes, "The Ecological Background of Plant Domestication," in Peter J. Ucko and G. W. Dimbleby, eds., *The Domestication and Exploitation of Plants and Animals* (Chicago: Aldine Publishing Co., 1969), pp. 17–24; p. 27: ". . . the process [of agriculture], once started, was practically automatic. Good plants appeared, as if by magic or as a gift from the gods, and gathering changed imperceptibly into harvesting and thence into planting." Some 99.5% of man's total period on earth has been unagricultural; fossil evidence of wild maize pollen from peat below Mexico City, radiocarbon dated to 80,000 B.P., shows that maize was available long before domestication took place. A settled mode of existence was needed before agriculture could begin, and man did not develop this until some 9,000 years ago, and then only in certain areas. When this stage of human development was reached, then agriculture could begin if the plants were available. See also Haury, "The Greater American Southwest."

    Albert H. Schroeder, "Pattern Diffusion from Mexico into the Southwest after A.D. 600," *American Antiquity,* Vol. 31, No. 5:683–704 (1966); p. 698: "The type of culture and settlement pattern can reflect new or revised sociological and ceremonial complexes. To move from nomadism to subsistence farming, and later to irrigation farming, requires alterations in the division of labor; new regulatory measures and controls; additional tools and crafts; shifts in ceremonialism; new techniques of adapting to the environment; new concepts on property rights; possible development of social stratification; some new ordering of the social organization; and changes in communication between local groups of a population unit, as well as with non-culturally related groups, through trade channels, either in the process of transmittal (diffusion) or in the reception of an idea (acculturation)."

49 I am indebted for much of this information to Jim Scorup, Jr., of Monticello, Utah, who rode the Grand Gulch Plateau; it was a privilege to listen to the pungent memories of those days told by a gentleman of the Old West, which isn't very far away in Utah. See also Neal Lambert, "Al Scorup: Cattleman of the Canyons," *Utah Historical Quarterly,* Vol. 32:301–20 (1964), and Mary Risher and Bill Mapp, *The Cattle Industry in Southeastern Utah: Dereese Nielson* (Fullerton, CA: Utah State Historical Society and California State University, Oral History Program, Southeastern Utah Project, 1971), copy generously made available by Mr. Nielson. Perkins *et al., Saga of San Juan,* pp. 279–84: By 1892, before the Forest Service had permit charges, a livestock license had to be obtained from the San Juan County Clerk for 2¼ cents per head per year. The Taylor Grazing Act of 1934 gave the Secretary of the Interior authority to limit grazing in the public domain with administration by the Bureau of Land Management. The BLM now administers approximately 2,904,718 acres in San Juan County. See also N. Keith Roberts and B. Delworth Gardner, "Livestock and the Public Lands," *Utah Historical Quarterly,* Vol. 32:285–300 (1964) about BLM history and regulation in Utah.

Upper Grand Gulch

55 Nelson, *Cartier Grand Gulch Expedition, San Juan Country* p. 6.
56 Cynthia Simmons, *personal communication.* There are no records prior to 1974; in that year 753 people hiked Grand Gulch, including those who signed in at Collins Spring (the BLM estimates a 75% visitor contact at that time). In 1975, 669 people signed in; the lesser number was due to a very cold spring that year, the season at which visitor level is normally highest. In 1976, 949 people walked Grand Gulch, and in 1977, 1017 people; figures may be low in 1977 because of severe drought in the area. The BLM now estimates 90% visitor contact. The trend is toward people staying longer per trip, an average of 3½ days. There are six commercial outfitters licensed to bring tourists into Grand Gulch, only two of whom are stock using, Pete Steele and Ken Sleight. There is no regulation of any of the other canyons.

One of the principal reasons for designating Grand Gulch as a Primitive Area in 1970 was to preserve the archaeological resources; under this philosophy archaeological sites will *not* be developed as information centers. Dr. William Lipe, "Wilderness System," p. 14, is of the opinion that the Primitive Area ought to be enlarged to include more of this mesa top and thus more of the prehistoric settlements. Enlargement of the area would also help in management since vehicular traffic could be kept away from the canyon proper, and visitors encouraged to use the main trails rather than seeking shortcuts into the main canyons. Those interested in the designation of Grand Gulch as a Wilderness Area should write to Lester Sweeney, Area Manager, Bureau of Land Management, Monticello, Utah 84535, for information about scheduled hearings. A final draft of the *Management Plan for Grand Gulch Primitive Area and Interim Management Guidance for Cedar Mesa,* March, 1977, is available for $4.20 (for duplicating) from the same address, as well as an informative and attractive brochure (November, 1977), "Grand Gulch Primitive Area."

56 Richard Wetherill, "Field Notes, Grand Gulch, Utah, 1897."

58 See Edmund Naquatewa, "Why the Spaniards Called the Hopi, 'Moqui,' Hopi Customs, Folklore, and Ceremonies" (Flagstaff: Northern Arizona Society of Science and Art, Museum of Northern Arizona Reprint Series No. 4, 1954), pp. 74–79.

58 Nelson's interest in Grand Gulch was awakened by Kidder and Guernsey, the foremost Southwestern archaeologists of the period. The expedition was financed by L. D. Cartier and was in the field September 19, 1920, to January 8, 1921. Nelson, *Cartier Grand Gulch Expedition,* p. 2: "The Grand Gulch region of southern Utah, although one of the most inaccessible in the United States, became known for its antiquities about thirty years ago. Because of its comparative richness in material, the pioneer relic hunters during the early nineties made, it seems, a fairly thorough job of excavation and it is a question whether there is anything left for the archaeologist to learn." Nelson went into the field to ascertain (p. 3) "the number, nature, and condition of its antiquities; the extent of former excavations; and the prospects for future scientific work. In all, some sixty to seventy miles of the canyon and its principal tributaries were mapped and about one hundred and ten archaeological sites definitely placed. These sites comprise several large groups of unusually interesting pictographs, a number of rockshelters showing evidences of 'Basketmaker' occupation, and for the rest cliffhouses ranging in size from one to thirty rooms."

Site notes of October, 1974, for Junction Ruin courtesy of Dr. William Lipe. The Laboratory of Tree-Ring Research report (February, 1975) gives a cluster of dates roughly between A.D. 1055 and 1175.

59 Flannery, "Archaeological Systems Theory," p. 227: A division of labor results when resources are available simultaneously, producing a conflict for the time and labor of the group. One common solution is the division of labor along lines of sex, e.g., men hunting, women collecting. Driver, *Indians of North America,* p. 100, says that wild plant gathering was principally the work of women; women seem to have gathered in groups more consistently than men hunted in groups, probably for mutual protection against intruders. Each woman made seed beaters and basket containers as well as teaching younger girls plant lore, gathering techniques, and food preparation. Edward P. Dozier, *The Pueblo Indians of North America* (New York: Holt, Rinehart and Winston, 1970), p. 129: women undoubtedly assisted men in communal labor tasks, but otherwise there was a fairly rigid division of labor. Men planted and tilled the fields; cut and hauled firewood; hunted; dressed the skins of animals killed; made bows, arrows, shields, and war clubs; wove blankets and sashes. Women cared for children, prepared and cooked meals, made pottery. Men constructed houses, both living quarters and ceremonial chambers, while women did the plastering.

Brew, *Archaeology of Alkali Ridge,* p. 223: masonry techniques vary from "dry masonry technique with voids filled with mud" to "stones imbedded between cushions of mud"; toward the end of Pueblo II times all the many variations existed and persisted throughout Pueblo III. See also Arthur H. Rohn, *Cultural Change and Contintuity on Chapin Mesa* (Lawrence: Regents Press of Kansas, 1977), pp. 47–52. Keller *et al., Final Report for Surface Cleanup,* p. 177: from measurements of bone fragments, the adult male was calculated to average 61.3 inches in height, and adult female, 59.3".

60 Brew, *Archaeology of Alkali Ridge,* pp. 209–11, cites an instance of posts moved outward in the reconstruction of a kiva.

60 Haury, "The Greater American Southwest," p. 124: The kiva was established with the Anasazi by A.D. 600, having diffused from the south to the north. The diagram

is from Junction Ruin; Lipe suggests that it may originally have been a pithouse. See William D. Lipe, "Man and the Plateau: An Archaeologist's View," *Plateau,* Vol. 49, No. 1 (1976), pp. 27–32.

62   Driver, *Indians of North America,* p. 96: Intensive analyses of prehistoric Indian bones and teeth show that those who depended principally on wild foods were healthier than those who lived mainly by farming; the teeth of farmers showed many more cavities than those of wild-food eaters. See also John Yudkin, "Archaeology and the Nutritionist," pp. 547–52, and David R. Harris, "Agricultural Systems, Ecosystems and the Origins of Agriculture," pp. 3–15, both in Ucko and Dimbleby, *Domestication . . . of Plants and Animals.*

Haury, "The Greater American Southwest," p. 133, finds evidence of beans in the Southwest by 1000 B.C.; see also J. Smartt, "Evolution of American Phaseolus Beans under Domestication," in Ucko and Dimbleby, *Domestication . . . of Plants and Animals,* pp. 451–62. Three of the essential amino acids—lysine, methionine, and tryptophan—cannot be manufactured within the human body and must be present in diet. They are deficient in many plants, but nuts, some grains, and legumes provide good amounts. Baker, *Plants and Civilization,* pp. 44 and 96, finds it no coincidence that Indians of both South and North America in agricultural areas settled on a diet made up predominantly of beans and maize.

Dumond, "Population Growth and Cultural Change," pp. 309–10, estimates a 400% increase in population between A.D. 1100 and 1700. Haury, "Post-Pleistocene Human Occupation of the Southwest," p. 110, estimates 75 people per 100 square kilometers in the Pueblo area (which extrapolates to about 1.8 people per square mile, probably the highest density for native populations north of Mexico. See also Lipe and Matson, "Human Settlements." Glassow, "Changes in the Adaptations," pp. 297–98: storage space of late Basketmaker times was probably double that of early Basketmaker times, with more aboveground storage being built. For pollen studies, see Martin, *Last 10,000 Years;* James N. Hill and Richard H. Hevly, "Pollen at Broken K Pueblo: Some New Interpretations," *American Antiquity,* Vol. 33, No. 2:200–10 (1968); Paul S. Martin and William Byers, "Pollen and Archaeology at Wetherill Mesa," Contribution No. 6 of Wetherill Mesa Archeological Project, *American Antiquity,* Vol. 31, No. 2, Part 2:122–35 (1965); and James N. Hill, "A Prehistoric Community in Eastern Arizona," *Southwestern Anthropologist,* Vol. 22:9–30 (1966).

62   Spencer and Jennings, *Native Americans,* p. 286, date the earliest pottery in the Southwest at about 250 B.C.; see also Schroeder, "Pattern Diffusion," pp. 693, 697–700.

Keller *et al., Final Report for Surface Cleanup,* p. 28, note that the stabilization was done in 1974; Lipe "Wilderness System," p. 13: site stabilization "should be as discreet and minimal as possible and should be dictated by specific needs of preserving the site. . . . If a site is threatened and cannot be stabilized without obvious violation of the wilderness character of the area, then salvage may be a preferred alternative."

64   Edmund C. Jaeger, *Desert Wild Flowers* (Stanford: Stanford University Press, 1940), p. 13, lists some of the uses of yucca by prehistoric Indians: the green pods were eaten raw or roasted; fruits to be stored were first dried, then ground and kneaded into small cakes, which were sun-dried; others were made into a conserve to sweeten beverages. The roots yielded soap used especially in ceremonial hair washings. See also Lyman Benson and Robert A. Darrow, *The Trees and Shrubs of the Southwestern Deserts* (Albuquerque: University of New Mexico Press, 1954).

Morris and Burgh, *Anasazi Basketry,* pp. 3–4, used narrow-leaf yucca to make a twilled ring basket, first drying the leaves, then soaking them and weaving them as a flat mat, forcing it while still damp into an osier ring, but found it so time-consuming that they made no comparable experiments with coiled basketry. They suggest that the idea for the ring basket came from suspending a yucca plant by the crown and braiding the leaves, and cite as evidence one such found by Guernsey and Kidder. Once begun, the manufacture of ring baskets continued for fully 15 centuries without interruption.

65 Harold S. Colton, *Potsherds: An Introduction to the Study of Prehistoric Southwestern Ceramics and Their Use in Historic Reconstruction* (Flagstaff: Museum of Northern Arizona Bulletin 25, 1953), pp. 14–15: the prehistoric potter had three kinds of clay to work with: sedimentary, alluvial, and residual; the clays of the plateau area are predominantly from alluvial sources. Anna O. Shepard, *Ceramics for the Archaeologist,* Publication 609 (Washington, D.C.: Carnegie Institution, 1956), is an exhaustive treatment of pre-historic ceramics. William H. Holmes, "Origin and Development of Form and Ornament in Ceramic Art," *Fourth Annual Report of the Bureau of American Ethnology* (Washington, D.C.: U.S. Government Printing Office, 1886), p. 267: "Suitable clay could be found in nearly every valley, both in the well-exposed strata and in the sediment of streams. I have noticed that after the passage of a sudden storm over the mesa country, and the rapid disappearance of the transient flood, the pools of the arroyos would retain a sediment of clay two or three inches thick, having a consistency perfectly suited to the hand of the potter. This I have taken without tempering and have made imitations of the handsome vases whose remnants I could pick up on all sides." Rubbing and polishing gives the vessel surface luster and is important where prehistoric potters did not use glaze. Florence Hawley, "Prehistoric Pottery Pigments in the Southwest," *American Anthropologist,* Vol. 31, No. 4:732–34 (1929): prolonged smoothing brings a thin emulsion of clay particles to the surface that fill in the pores so that the vessel *looks* as if it had actually been coated with the very thin clay suspension known as a "slip."

66 Harold S. Colton, "The Reducing Atmosphere and Oxidizing Atmosphere in Prehis-toric Southwestern Ceramics," *American Antiquity,* Vol. 4, No. 3:224–31 (1939); pp. 230–31; Colton describes his attempts to duplicate Anasazi firing conditions of between A.D. 600 to 1300; most of the gray pottery is found in regions where juniper was the prevalent fuel. Colton, *Potsherds,* pp. 23–25: primitive firing temperatures were never constant; usually an oxidizing atmosphere was present at the beginning, changing to a reducing atmosphere during firing. When iron compounds, either sesquioxide Fe_2O_3 or hydroxide $Fe(OH_3)$ or a mixture of the two, lose oxygen to the outside gases, they are said to be reduced, and the clay fires gray.

68 McGregor, *Southwestern Archaeology,* p. 106: certain key types of pottery can be accu-rately dated to within fifty years, some within twenty-five years or less; pp. 107–108 contains a list of well-known pottery styles and dates. See Breternitz, *Appraisal of Tree-Ring Dated Pottery,* and David A. Breternitz, Arthur H. Rohn, Jr., Elizabeth A. Morris, *Prehistoric Ceramics of the Mesa Verde Region,* Museum of Northern Arizona Ceramic Series No. 3 (Flagstaff: Northern Arizona Society of Science and Art, 1974), p. 53: Abajo Polychrome is Pueblo I, between A.D. 700 and 850, and strikes them as an experiment which never became popular; polychrome pottery is almost or totally absent in the Southwest at earlier or contemporary times. In the illustration, Mesa Verde Black-on-White sherds courtesy American Museum of Natural His-tory; top, left to right, 29.0/5120, 5116; center, 29.0/5118; bottom, 29.0/5120 and 5117.

70 The early government explorations sometimes contain delightful insights into the thoughts of the writers: Holmes, "Origin and Development . . . in Ceramic Art," p. 315: "The fragments are exceedingly plentiful about camp sites and ruins, and

fairly whiten the debris slopes beneath the houses in the cliffs. I found my mind so diverted by these fascinating relics that it was often difficult to keep the geologic problems of the district properly in view."

70   Driver, *Indians of North America,* p. 97: boys were given toy weapons with which to play until they were actually old enough to hunt. Lipe thinks that when the Anasazi living system was working well, as it did most of the time, there was free time for such things as play.

Klaus F. Wellman, "Kokopelli of Indian Paleology, Hunch-backed Rain Priest, Hunting Magician, and Don Juan of the Old Southwest," *Journal of the American Medical Association,* Vol. 212, No. 10:1678–1682 (1970), which explodes the idea that Kokopelli's attributes are caused by tuberculosis of the spine. See also Florence Hawley, "Kokopelli, of the Prehistoric Southwestern Pantheon," *American Anthropologist,* Vol 39:644–46 (1937), and E. C. Parsons, "The Humpbacked Flute Player of the Southwest," *American Anthropologist,* Vol. 40:337–38 (1938).

H. C. Cutler, "Medicine Men and the Preservation of a Relict Gene in Maize," *The Journal of Heredity,* Vol. 35:290–94 (1944): "To the writer it seems likely that the ancient Southwestern hunchback was actually a Callahuayo medicine man bringing to North America the character of tunicate maize which had been introduced earlier in ears selected for food use. If this is the case, the beliefs of these Indians not only preserved this wild relict gene, but made possible for it to spread from its original home to all parts of the Americas."

Mischa Titiev, "The Story of Kokopele," *American Anthropologist,* Vol. 41, No. 1:91–98 (1939), p. 98: "in one manifestation or another Kokopele is still an active figure in Southwestern myth and ritual. . . . In both cases the antics of the performers were lewd and obscene, and notoriously obnoxious to prudish white observers. With the growing influx of outside visitors to Hopi ceremonials, government officials tended to suppress bawdy actions and to punish actors who persisted in maintaining the older tradition. . . . I believe that the scarcity of Kokopele representations in modern times is due less to a diminution of his importance than to restraint imposed by the American government on all erotic and phallic exhibitions." See also Hamilton A. Tyler, *Pueblo Gods and Myths* (Norman: University of Oklahoma Press, 1972), Frank Waters, *Book of the Hopi* (NY: Ballantine Books, 1963), and Charlotte M. Otten, *Anthropology and Art* (Garden City, NY: The Natural History Press, 1971).

Turner, *Petrographs of Glen Canyon Region,* pp. 27–28, suggests petrographs may recall events in winter homes; create sympathetic magic concerning the hunt; practice, create, and remember designs for weaving, pottery, baskets, etc.; teach novitiates about ceremonies; stand as clan symbols to delineate clan lands; be pure creative impulse; serve as propitiatory gestures, fertility tokens, etc; be doodling (although Turner does not think this probable).

74   Ernest Antevs, "Arroyo-cutting and Filling," *Journal of Geology,* Vol. 60:375–85 (1952), and Luna B. Leopold and J. P. Miller, *Ephemeral Streams—Hydraulic Factors and Their Relation to the Drainage Net,* U.S.G.S. Professional Paper 282-A (1956), pp. 3–4, developed a rule of thumb for predicting when flash floods would occur: when there was a rainfall of more than 1.5 inches at the storm center, and the curtain of rain viewed from a distance was too dense to see through. Quote, H. E. Gregory and R. C. Moore, *The Kapairowits Region,* U.S.G.S. Professional Paper 164 (1931), pp. 125–26.

75   Larry D. Agenbroad, "The Alluvial Geology of Upper Grand Gulch, Utah; Its Relationship to Anasazi Inhabitation of the Cedar Mesa Area," in James E. Fassett, ed., Four Corners Geological Society Guidebook, *Canyonlands Country* (8th Field Conference, 1975), pp. 63–65: Preliminary data on the snail sequence in a section of

alluvium in Kane Wash indicate a standing body of water (reflected in an interval dominated by aquatic molluscs) and a much wetter environment with higher soil moisture. This is followed by a drier period, with a terrace containing Basketmaker III cultural materials, with channel deposits giving way to aeolian materials near the surface. Near the close of Pueblo III occupation, this terrace was partially eroded during an arroyo-cutting period, followed by the aggradation that built up the most recent terrace, which is now being cut. The alluvial terrace sequence was noted in the entire drainage network. When walking one can distinguish these terraces by their vegetation: the oldest terrace has moderate sagebrush cover with some piñon and juniper; the middle lacks the tree cover and has instead very dense growth of unusually large sagebrush as well as cottonwood; the youngest is barren or supports willow, tamarisk, and rabbitbrush in addition to sparse sage.

Lipe and Matson, "Archaeology and Alluvium in the Grand Gulch-Cedar Mesa Area, Southeastern Utah," in Fassett, ed., *Canyonlands Country,* pp. 67–69: Prehistoric settlements existed both in the canyons and on the mesa tops, but most of the people were on the mesa most of the time and the canyons were less densely settled; of those, canyons with T_2 were more utilized. Nevertheless (p. 67): "the environmentally distinctive canyons must have been important to the prehistoric occupants. . . . The only permanent surface water supplies are found in the canyons, they have a different and greater variety of plant resources than do the mesa tops, some have alluvial soils, there are many dry ledge and alcove shelters, and rainfall is concentrated by runoff from the walls and ledges, and by floods coming down the canyon floor. In canyons having stable or aggrading alluvium, such floods would spread out over these soils, making them attractive locations for farming." Gregory, *San Juan Country,* pp. 101–102, notes that "where the fill has been removed the bottom of the old canyon is revealed as a floor cut by sheer-walled trenches or by grooves and crossed here and there by ledges over which the streams pass as waterfalls," and estimates that "the amount of fill removed in a typical 1-mile stretch is estimated as 1,000,000 cubic yards for Grand Gulch."

77 E. O. Essig, *Insects of Western North America* (New York: Macmillan Co., 1926), pp. 335–36.

78 Richard Wetherill to B. T. B. Hyde, February 15, 1897; McNitt, *Richard Wetherill,* pp. 158–62. Keller *et al., Final Report for Surface Cleanup,* pp. 62–63: "This disturbance severely limits the research potential of excavation at the site, which must once have had great research potential. Furthermore, the site is obviously multi-component, containing definite evidence of Pueblo II and Pueblo III occupation and probable evidence (provided by the pictographs and by Wetherill's accounts of burial finds) of Basketmaker II and possibly earlier occupation. The extremely irregular floor of the site, with obviously 'pocketed' fill further complicates the picture." Further excavations would only be last-ditch salvage efforts. The kiva is D-shaped rather than circular, a "cliff kiva" backed up against the wall and typical of Grand Gulch, undoubtedly a shape forced by the narrowness of the hardpan floor (there is also a D-shaped kiva at Junction Ruin).

Keller *et al., Final Report for Surface Cleanup,* find the pictographs at this site "its most outstanding feature" for their variety, placement, and unique iconography; they feel that further excavation might be useful because Wetherill's notes can be matched with the artifacts in the American Museum of Natural History, and perhaps "fingerprinting" of dirt on the museum specimens would assign other artifacts to this site.

Quote, Wetherill Field Notes, 1897.

80 Wetherill to B. T. B. Hyde, January 24, 1898.

81   Gregory, *San Juan Country,* p. 27: "The breeding birds most commonly seen are the magpies, mourning doves, piñon jays, sage sparrows, canyon towhees, catbirds, rock wrens, house wrens, sage thrashers, bluebirds, swallows, and chickadees. But the list includes mountain eagles, ravens, ducks, woodpeckers, meadow larks, blackbirds, turkey buzzards, cranes, finches, sapsuckers, flycatchers, grouse, swifts, humming birds, and various warblers. Hawks seem to be always in the sky, and the hoot of owls is the commonest of night sounds." Miser, *San Juan Canyon*, p. 75: "The principal birds noted during the years 1909 to 1913 are the eagle, hawk, nighthawk, raven, wild turkey, crow, two species of duck, white and sandhill crane, piñon jay, three species of owl, catbird, swallow, and rock wren." To these I can add canyon wren, ash-throated fly-catcher, chukar partridge, prairie falcon, marsh hawk, and bald eagle. A more extensive list is that of M. F. Gilman, "Birds on the Navajo Reservation in New Mexico," *Condor,* Vol. 10:146–52 (July, 1908).

85   Ezra B. W. Zubrow, "Carrying Capacity and Dynamic Equilibrium in the Prehistoric Southwest," in Leone, *Contemporary Archeology,* pp. 268–79. "Carrying capacity is the maximum number of organisms or amounts of biomass which can maintain itself indefinitely in an area . . . ;" equilibrium is determined by the maxima and minima of specific resources. "A population will tend to keep reproducing and growing in size until an ultimate limit is reached, which is determined by the supply of nutrients and energy. When there is a change in the supply of nutrients and energy, a change in the carrying capacity results, and there is a consequence [sic] growth or decrease of the biomass until a new equilibrium is reached." Since population growth is not mechanistic, a population does not grow precisely to carrying capacity and then stop. If population overshoots, the result is an increase in mortality rate and out-migration; the standard of living acts as a buffer—survival may result for a population above carrying capacity at the expense of its standard of living. A growth rate that remains positive, despite a decrease in the standard of living, will result in Malthusian starvation.

See also David W. Love, "Dynamics of Sedimentation and Geomorphic History of Chaco Canyon National Monument, New Mexico," in James E. Fassett, ed., New Mexico Geological Society Guidebook *San Juan Basin* III, 1977, pp. 291–300. L. B. Leopold, "Rainfall Frequency—an Aspect of Climatic Variation," *American Geophysical Union Transactions,* Vol. 32:347–57 (1951), showed that years with above-average rainfall have larger separate storms, and correlates periods of heavier rain with arroyo cutting. The situation in Chaco Canyon bears many resemblances to that of Grand Gulch; Love's studies showed a series of alternate scourings and fillings.

Martin, *The Last 10,000 Years,* p. 49: the increase in non-economic pollens was largely in the chenopodium-amaranth species, which prefer fine alkaline soils of flood plains and disturbed ground. Today (p. 69) the same plants grow in low-water-table lands in flood plains, soil with a high salt content, in a climate characterized by summer deluges, and Martin assumes that the same environment existed in prehistoric times. Fritts, Smith, and Stokes, "Interpretation of Mesa Verde Tree-Ring Series," p. 101: Tree-ring chronology A.D. 1273–85 "exhibits a clearly defined drought which exceeds in length and intensity any dry period occurring since A.D. 1673. A comparison of the chronologies from species which are influenced differently by summer precipitation indicates that during this period both summers and winters must have been dry. However, the A.D. 1273–1285 drought at Mesa Verde was surpassed by six other droughts of greater intensity during the period A.D. 500–1300. The A.D. 1273–1285 drought may be only one of several factors in a chain of events which led to the decline of prehistoric population in the Mesa Verde." They also found (p. 119) both summer and autumn temperatures probably unusually high. See also Ernst Antevs, "Late Quaternary Climates in Arizona," *American Antiquity,* Vol. 28:193–98 (1962), and "Geologic-Climatic Dating in the West," *American Antiquities,* Vol. 20:317–35 (1955), and Stephen A. Hall, "Late Quaternary Sedimentation and Paleoecologic History of Chaco Canyon, New Mexico," *Geol. Soc. Am. Bulletin,* Vol. 88:1539–1618 (Nov., 1977). William Lipe and R. G. Matson, "Archaeology and Alluvium in the Grand Gulch . . . Area," p. 68: The first time Cedar Mesa was abandoned was around A.D. 700, years which "show the most consistently narrow growth rings in any century in the record, suggesting persistent drought conditions. Since Cedar Mesa is environmentally marginal for farming peoples, owing to the fact that annual precipitation is from about 10 to 13 inches, depending on location and elevation, drought conditions would have made the area very unattractive." The abandonment persisted until A.D. 1000; pp. 70–71: "There are some indications that as the Pueblo occupation drew to a close, perhaps because of droughts in the 1200's, the canyon environments became more important to the Anasazi. If this is so, and if arroyo cutting occurred in alluvial situations during the early or middle 1220's, this destruction of alluvium would probably have contributed to the final abandonment of the area. It is very unlikely, however, that arroyo-cutting by itself was the primary cause of this abandonment." See also Douglas W. Schwartz, "The Postmigration Culture: A Base for Archaeological Inference," in William Longacre, ed., *Reconstructing Prehistoric Pueblo Societies* (Albuquerque: University of New Mexico Press, 1970), pp. 175–93, and William D. Lipe, "Man and the Plateau: An Archaeologist's Viewpoint," *Plateau,* Vol. 49, No. 1., pp. 27–32 (1976).

89   This discussion is based on Colton, *Potsherds,* Shepard, *Ceramics for the Archaeologist,* and Bunzel, *The Pueblo Potter, A Study of Creative Imagination in Primitive Art* (New York: Dover Publications, 1929), who describes corrugated ware, p. 73: "In this type the coiled technique was utilized for decorative purposes. These vessels were made of exceedingly fine coils and the corrugations were not smoothed out as in the painted types. The coils were further ornamented with regular flutings and patterns made by indentations in the soft clay. This ware reached the highest stage of technical excellence, and a good piece of coiled pottery is among the finest ceramic productions of the Southwest. This ware persisted for a very long period, and is found in greater or less quantities in all prehistoric pueblos." Shepard, *op. cit.* pp. 66–67: in present-day San Ildefonso Pueblo, a gourd-rind scraper is used to shape the vessel and also to smooth the surface immediately after the last coil is added; after the vessel is dry, the surface is dampened and scraped again to remove support marks and thin the walls, and then dampened again and rubbed hard with a wet cloth.

In interviewing modern Pueblo potters, Bunzel (p. 6) found that they had "no idea whatever of the proportions of tempering they use in the clay. In mixing the paste, they are guided entirely by their tactile sense." When asked how she approached making a pot, one woman replied (p. 52): "This is a new design. I learned the different parts of it from my mother, but they are put together in a new way." All women learned from their mothers not only the technique of pottery making, but the particular designs and style of decoration, but they also had other sources of inspiration, such as dreams, "seeing" the design in the shape of the pot, or learning from other pottery designs.

JOHNS CANYON

95   F. A. Barnes, *Canyon Country Hiking and Natural History* (Wasatch Publishers, Inc., 1977) is a skeletal guide to the entire San Juan County.

97   Nielson (in Risher and Mapp, *Cattle Industry,* pp. 51–52) describes Jimmy Palmer: "He would steal horses around here and take them down into Johns Canyon. He moved from here down to Bluff and was around there for awhile, then he moved down into Johns Canyon. He had a real good deal there for stealing; it was really convenient. He'd steal these horses and put them into Johns Canyon, then he had made this steep trail up onto our range. At one time, he had forty or fifty stolen horses up on our range . . . and my uncle told him he'd better get his horses off our range. Palmer told him that it wasn't any more our range than it was his. They got into a feud and he told my uncle he was going to kill him. . . . Palmer never did kill him, but he put his horses up on the range and after he had killed Norris and Bill, he was chased out of the country."

99   There are some very strong feelings about helicopter patrols over wilderness areas; according to the Salt Lake *Tribune,* April 23, 1973, a ranger lost his job because he refused to fly "Big Brother" flights. Misuse of helicopter patrols "runs the risk of alienating the very people whose cooperation is a must." James E. Fassett, *personal communication.*

99   Russel M. Potter and George R. Rossman, "Desert Varnish: The Importance of Clay Minerals," *Science,* Vol. 196:1446–48 (February, 1977); scanning electron micrographs shows desert varnish to be a surface deposit. See also D. D. Engle and P. R. Sharp, "Chemical Data on Desert Varnish," *Geological Society of America Bulletin,* Vol. 69:487–518 (1958); E. Blissenbach, "Geology of Alluvial Fans in Semi-Arid Regions," *Geol. Soc. Am. Bull.,* Vol. 65:175–90 (1954); and C. B. Hunt, *Cenozoic History of the Colorado Plateau,* U.S.G.S. Professional Paper 279, 1956, and *Physiography of the United States* (San Francisco and London: W. H. Freeman & Co., 1967).

100 Donald L. Baars, "Permianland: The Rocks of Monument Valley," in H. L. James, ed., New Mexico Geological Society *Guidebook of Monument Valley,* 1973, and Baars, ed., Four Corners Geological Society's *Geology of the Canyons of the San Juan River,* 1973; W. L. Stokes, "Continental Sediments of the Colorado Plateau," in Albert F. Sanborn, ed., Intermountain Association of Petroleum Geologists', *Guidebook to the Geology of the Paradox Basin,* 1958, pp. 26–30; J. D. Sears, *Geology of Comb Ridge and Vicinity North of San Juan River, San Juan County, Utah,* U.S.G.S. Bulletin 1021-E, 1956; and James Fassett, *personal communication.*

103 Roger W. Barbour and Wayne H. Davis, *Bats of America* (Lexington: University Press of Kentucky, 1969) illustrates every species with colored photographs and discusses habits and ecology. See also Grover M. Allen, *Bats* (Cambridge: Harvard University Press, 1939), a delightful book, and Donald R. Griffin, *Echoes of Bats and Men* (Garden City, NY: Doubleday & Co., 1959). For more local information, see Hugo G. Rodeck, *Guide to the Mammals of Colorado* (Boulder: University of Colorado Museum, 1966) and Vernon Bailey, *Mammals of the Southwestern United States with special reference to New Mexico* (New York: Dover Publications, 1971).

106 E. G. Woodruff, 1912, *Geology of the San Juan Oil Field,* Utah, U.S.G.S. Bulletin 471, 1912, was the first field examination of the oil potential of the region; pp. 96–97: "it is believed that the chance of finding oil is better in the syncline than it is in the anticline, because in this region there is very little precipitation and there is ample opportunity for the water in the rocks above river level to escape into the canyons. The accumulation of the oil is also unusually influenced by the canyons, whose effect in draining water and oil from the strata demands the most careful consideration. Such deep incisions in the strata afford ample opportunity for the escape of all fluids from the strata adjacent to them."

See also George H. Hansen, "History of Exploration in Southeastern Utah," in Intermountain Association of Petroleum Geologists, *Geology and Economic Deposits of East*

Central Utah, 1956; pp. 23–25; Gary C. Huber, "Mexican Hat Oil Field," in Baars, ed., *Canyons of the San Juan River,* pp. 51–54; and R. B. O'Sullivan, *Geology of the Cedar Mesa–Boundary Butte Area, San Juan County, Utah,* U.S.G.S. Bulletin 1186, 1965, pp. 110–18; the last-named contains a log of the wells drilled prior to 1964. Gregory, *San Juan Country,* p. 111: "After discouraging efforts, funds necessary to develop the claim were obtained in 1907 [near present Goodridge bridge], and on March 4, 1908, oil was struck at a depth of 225 feet—'a gusher, throwing oil to a height of 70 feet above the floor of the derrick.' The success of this pioneer well (Crossing No. 1) led to the drilling of more than 50 wells in the Goodridge field and adjoining regions and to the study of oil possibilities in all southeastern Utah. Most of the geologic investigation and most of the development has been along the San Juan River . . . some hundreds of claims have been staked on northern Sage Plain, Grand Gulch Plateau . . ."

George D. Fehr and J. R. Williams, "Oil and Gas Leasing in the Paradox Basin," in Albert F. Sanborn, ed., *Geology of the Paradox Basin,* pp. 241–46; p. 242: The 1908 discovery of oil at Mexican Hat "created the first big rush to the Paradox. At that time promotors and stock companies by the dozens were filing oil placer claims, leasing lands for miles around, hauling oil field equipment by wagon train down the tortuous route through McElmo Canyon from Cortez, Colorado, and printing bales of stock certificates in what was for those times an oil stock boom of rather large proportions."

A. A. Baker, *Geology of the Monument Valley–Navajo Mountain Region, San Juan County, Utah,* U.S.G.S. Bulletin 865, 1936, p. 98: "Until test wells are drilled it is impossible to determine the extent to which water in the oil-bearing strata may have influenced the accumulation of oil. . . . Such systematic prospecting would not only be expensive but would meet with difficulties in this arid country remote from railroads." See also H. D. Miser, "Geologic Structure of San Juan Canyon and Adjacent Country, Utah," in K. C. Heald and W. T. Thom, Geologists in Charge, *Contributions to Economic Geology 1923–1924. Part II. Mineral Fuels,* U.S.G.S. Bulletin 751, 1925, pp. 115–55. Miser, *San Juan Canyon,* p. 144: "The difficulties of exploration in this rough arid region, 150 to 200 miles from a railroad, are many. There are few inhabitants, so that most laborers must be imported. All so-called roads west of Bluff and north of Kayenta are poor indeed and at times impassable for wagons and automobiles. Most parts of the canyon country are not traversed by roads. The rainfall does not exceed about 6 inches a year, so that water for drilling as well as for drinking is scarce and generally has to be hauled or carried long distances. No timber is available for fuel except driftwood along the San Juan and scrub cedar and piñon on Cedar Mesa and other mesas of similar height farther west. The principal fuel for drilling is oil from the small producing wells in the San Juan oil field. The cost of hauling coal into the region from the vicinity of Monticello, Utah, or from other places is prohibitive."

109 Gregory, *San Juan Country,* pp. 115–16: . . . "The position of springs is determined by topography and the stratigraphic sequence of beds; their number, permanency, and size by the amount of rainfall received by the aquifer at nearby or distant places and by the effectiveness of evaporation. . . . On canyon floors and along washes most of the springs are at the contact of alluvium and bedrock. For the region as a whole these division planes between relatively porous and relatively impervious formations are the spring zones, but some springs emerge directly from formations that as a whole are watertight: their position is determined by thin beds or lenses of limestone or dense sandstone that lie below layers of porous sandstone. Controlled by this arrangement of subordinate beds, springs issue from the Hermosa

formation . . . above the mouth of Slickhorn Gulch; from the Halgaito member in Johns Canyon. . . . Many of the springs that issue from these generally impervious formations are connected by joint cracks with water-bearing beds from which their supply is derived. . . . Some of these springs yield small perennial supplies, but most of them are tiny seeps tucked away in alcoves and tunnels high on canyon walls and flow only during the night or during cold months. On hot days evaporation removes the water at a surprising rate. A spot on a bare wall marked at the daytime only by efflorescence and patches of vegetation may yield at night water sufficient for camp needs."

110 Samuel Rowley, on the Mormon trek in 1879–80 (quoted in Miller, *Hole-in-the-Rock Expedition,* p. 189): "Traveling up Grand Gulch, at noon of the second day we stopped at a pool of highly-colored water in the wash, which proved to be so minerally we could not use it . . . We soon found a pool of rain-water, which had run down from the cliff some time before, it being literally full of pollywogs. However, it answered our purpose after undergoing a separating process."

115 Stebbins, *Field Guide,* p. 96, cites a subspecies of *Holbrookia maculata* in Utah, ssp. *approximans.* Kenneth S. Norris, "Color Adaptation in Desert Reptiles and Its Thermal Relationships," in William W. Milstead, ed., *Lizard Ecology, A Symposium, Kansas City, 1965* (Columbia: University of Missouri Press, 1967), pp. 162–229, is a fascinating study that attempts to quantify the amount of radiation reaching a lizard's body and the color changes that take place in response; he notes that color functions both as an adaptation assisting body temperature regulation and as camouflage, and (pp. 165–66) "there is often a complex relationship between the use of color as a temperature regulator and as concealment." See also Angus Bellairs, *The Life of Reptiles* (New York: Universe Books, 1970).

116 Cronquist *et al., Intermountain Flora,* p. 59: Alice Eastwood explored the southern part of Utah in May–June, 1892, and returned in 1895. On both trips she collected numerous species, many of which are endemic to the San Juan drainage, such as *Penstemon utahensis, Cryptantha wetherillii, Enceliopsis nutans, Astragalus eastwoodii* (a complete list can be found in Alice Eastwood, *Report on a Collection of Plants from San Juan County, in Southeastern Utah,* California Academy of Science Proceedings, 2nd Series, Vol. 6:271–329, 1896). See also Carol Green Wilson, "The Eastwood Era at the California Academy of Sciences," *Leaflets of Western Botany,* 1953, pp. 58–64, and *Alice Eastwood's Wonderland, the Adventures of a Botanist* (San Francisco: California Academy of Sciences, 1955). Quotes are from Eastwood, pp. 278–79, 280–81, and Wilson, *Leaflets,* pp. 61–62.

119 Gregory and Moore, *Kapairowits,* p. 23.

120 Marie Morisawa, *Streams—Their Dynamics and Hydrology* (New York: McGraw-Hill Book Co., 1968), and Luna B. Leopold, M. Gordon Wolman, and John P. Miller, *Fluvial Processes in Geomorphology* (San Francisco and London: W. H. Freeman and Co., 1964). Gregory, *San Juan Country,* pp. 96–98: "The streams are young and, though intermittently powerful, have so far been unable to grade their floors. In cutting their immediate runways deeper and wider they increase the height and maintain the steepness of the bordering walls. Under these unfavorable conditions the reduction of cliffs and canyon walls to slopes with mature profiles seems almost impossible. . . . Johns Canyon, Grand Gulch, and some smaller tributaries terminate as ephemeral waterfalls 30 to 80 feet high over relatively resistant rock strata. . . . Many tributaries of the second and third order occupy hanging valleys in hard rocks and soft rocks alike, and where valleys are poorly defined ephemeral sheet streams drop water directly into box-headed canyons."

121 James R. Beebower, *Field Guide to Fossils* (Boston: Houghton Mifflin Co., 1971) and

Carroll L. and Mildred A. Fenton, *The Fossil Book* (Garden City, NY: Doubleday and Co., Inc., 1958).; F. J. Pettijohn, *Sedimentary Rocks* (New York: Harper & Row, 1957), pp. 225–26, 687: limestone does not contain enough magnesium to be considered dolomite ($CaMg(CO_3)_2$) so the magnesium is presumed to have come from surrounding sea water; it involves large-scale recrystallization. The term "dolomite" was first applied to certain carbonate rocks in the Tyrolean Alps now known as the Dolomites. Marvin J. Weller, *Stratigraphic Principles and Practice* (New York: Harper & Row, 1960), pp. 62–63, 312–13: the brownish cast of dolomite comes from small amounts of oxidized ferrous iron that may be substituted for some of the dolomite during recrystallization. A. A. Baker, p. 123, lists fossils collected from the Hermosa Formation.

Eastwood, *Report on a Collection of Plants,* pp. 278 and 280–81.

An excellent guide is Peggy Larson, *The Deserts of the Southwest* (San Francisco: Sierra Club Books, 1977), which contains a thorough chapter on "Man, Heat, and Dehydration," pp. 177–88.

SLICKHORN CANYON

131 Miser, *San Juan Canyon,* uses "Slickhorn Gulch" as does Gregory, *San Juan Country,* and A. J. Eardley, "Physiography of Southeastern Utah," in Sanborn, ed., *Geology of Paradox Basin.* Current U.S.G.S. maps, published in 1963, print "Slickhorn Canyon." Webster defines "gulch" as a "deep or precipitous cleft in a hillside: a ravine or gully, *esp:* one that is short, steep-sided, and occas. occupied by a torrent." A canyon is "a deep narrow valley with precipitous sides characteristic of regions where downward cutting of the streams greatly exceeds the weathering." I leave the choice to the reader. Gregory, *San Juan Country,* p. 116: the springs in Slickhorn emerge directly from what as a whole is a watertight formation; they are probably determined by thin beds or lenses of limestone or denser sandstone that lie between layers of porous sandstone.

131 It is inexcusable that so many people go into the wilderness without being aware of proper sanitary precautions, and many guidebooks tend to ignore this necessity. All feces should be buried, all toilet paper burned *completely.* At least 200 feet from a water source is sacrosanct.

131 Miser, "San Juan Oil Field," in Gregory, *San Juan Country,* pp. 111–12: "The seeps were observed on the right bank of the river. . . . The oil comes up as bubbles in the water and as minute streams through sand and also through boulders of sandstone and limestone at the edge of the water. The boulders, which have fallen from the adjacent cliffs, are cut by cracks through which the oil passes. The drops of oil break on reaching the surface of the river and spread as thin iridescent films. The oil is a brown liquid that flows easily, and although its odor is strong the odor of gasoline is not noticeable. . . . At one seep a film of oil covering several square feet of a sand bar is used by flies as a breeding place, and hundreds of larvae live in the oily substance on the bare surface of the sand bar, in spite of the intensely hot rays of a summer's sun which beat down on them during the day." See also D. L. Baars, ed., *Canyons of the San Juan River,* a river guide which gives current information about these oil-bearing strata; quote from Miser, *San Juan Canyon,* p. 28.

137 Stebbins, *Field Guide,* pp. 110–11; Jaeger, *Desert Wild Flowers,* p. 188; see also Donald W. Tinkle, "Home Range, Density, Dynamics, and Structure of a Texas Population of the Lizard *Uta stansburiana,*" in Milstead, ed., *Lizard Ecology,* pp. 5–29, and Norris, "Color Adaptation," p. 211: *Uta stansburiana* is active on cool days and often throughout the winter, using very restricted microclimatic situations to reach activ-

ity levels on "truly forbidding days." When found active in this situation, they are very dark and (p. 214) "must be especially conspicuous, and hence the very high heating increment conferred upon the animal by color change must be of great selective value." During warming the lizard is at its most vulnerable; not only is reaction time impaired by low body temperatures but color matching is usually wholly absent or less than precise because the body is darkened in order to gain heat as fast as possible.

141   Arthur Bent, *Life Histories of North American Nuthatches, Wrens, Thrashers and Their Allies* (New York: Dover Publications, 1964), p. 279: "We saw or heard a long list of interesting birds, but the gem of them all was the canyon wren. Its wild, joyous strain of sweet, silvery notes greeted us as we passed some steep cliffs; they seemed to reverberate from one cliff to another, to fill the whole canyon with delightful melody and to add a fitting charm to the wild surroundings." Bent quotes a Mr. Hoffman, who said its song (p. 284) "pours out a cascade of sweet liquid notes, like the spray of a waterfall in sunshine."

141   George Olin, *Mammals of the Southwest Mountains and Mesas* (Globe, AZ: Southwest Parks and Monuments Association, 1971), p. 74: porcupines, because of their low reproductive rate, do not do permanent damage; Rodeck, *Guide to the Mammals,* p. 23, disagrees: "Where Porcupines are too abundant they may do serious harm to the forest by girdling and thus killing many trees."

142   Bailey, *Mammals of the Southwestern United States,* pp. 385–86: the pipistrelles *(Pipistrellus hesperus)* "perhaps more than any other bats are canyon dwellers, being rarely found far from the rocky walls of canyons or cliffs."

144   Bailey, pp. 160–61: the canyon mouse *(Peromyscus crinitus)* often favors pueblo ruins and "their whole range is closely associated with the region of abundant prehistoric cliff houses."

145   Bates E. Wilson and Lloyd Pierson, "Arches and Natural Bridge National Monuments," in Sanborn, ed., *Geology of Paradox Basin,* p. 17: the difference between bridges and arches is that the former actually spanned ancient stream channels whereas arches are formed by jointing and processes of weathering.

146   Pete Steele tells me that horns of sheep in Anasazi times tended to remain firm-pointed at the ends, whereas those of modern mountain sheep are blunted and ragged because of insufficient calcium in their diet. Keller *et al., Final Report for Surface Cleanup,* p. 21: bighorn sheep in the early 1970s were not common in the area although some may still enter the lower parts of Grand Gulch from the canyon to the San Juan River. Olin, *Mammals of the Southwest Mountains,* pp. 2–4, describes their eyes "as a clear, golden amber with a long oval, velvety black pupil. Credited with telescopic vision, they must be some of the most useful as well as beautiful eyes to be found in the animal kingdom." Miser, *San Juan Canyon,* p. 307, saw seven along the San Juan between Honaker Trail and Olijeto Creek and conjectures that they "have survived here for the reasons that much of this part of the canyon is inaccessible to persons on foot and that few people have ever descended the canyon in boats."

150   Kidder's comment quoted by Wauchope, "Alfred Vincent Kidder," p. 149.

151   When asked if government could decide that they needed the range for something else, Nielson replied (Risher and Mapp, *Cattle Industry,* p. 35): "Yes, for parks and things, and it will probably happen someday. . . . These Sierra Clubs have a lot of pressure and a lot of backing . . . We've put a lot of money into this range of ours for reseeding, reservoirs, trails, water troughs and fences; we've put thousands and thousands of dollars into it in the past years. I don't see how they could take it away without paying us a little something for it, but they might."

STEER GULCH AND WHIRLWIND DRAW

162 W. H. Bradley, "Factors That Determine the Curvature of Mud-cracked Layers," *American Journal of Science* (5)26:55–71 (1933).

164 Carl O. Dunbar and Karl M. Waage, *Historical Geology* (New York: John Wiley & Sons, 1969), p. 298: The amount of salt that formations in southeastern Utah contain presupposes times of excessive heat and evaporation. Such an arid climate is also implied by both plant and animal fossils; see Peter Paul Vaughn, "Vertebrates from the Cutler Group of Monument Valley and Vicinity," in James, ed., *Guide to Monument Valley*, pp. 91–105.

165 Gregory, *Geology and Geography of Zion Park Region*, pp. 182–83: "Observation of streams during floods shows that after a period of violent agitation much of the sand and gravel is swept away from the saucerlike depressions but that many of the deeper pits retain their grinding loads. Doubtless the abrasive materials remain in some holes until their rims are lowered nearly to their bottoms. The vigor and persistency of pot hole erosion is well shown by the rate of drilling and by abandoned pits on canyon walls."

166 Lloyd Kaufman and Irvin Rock, "The Moon Illusion," *Scientific American*, Vol. 207, No. 1:120–30 (July, 1962); p. 120: The "apparent-distance theory" seems to go back to the "second-century astronomer and geometer Ptolemy. He proposed that any object seen through filled space, such as the moon seen across terrain at the horizon, is perceived as being more distant than an object just as far away but seen through empty space, such as the moon at the zenith. If the images of these objects in the eye are in fact of equal size, the one that appears farther away will seem larger."

169 Nelson, *Cartier Grand Gulch Expedition*, p. 6.

170 Gregory, *San Juan Country*, p. 26: "During the field work the mammals most frequently noted at lower altitudes were several kinds of rats, grasshopper mouse, white-footed mouse, harvest mouse, meadow mouse, pocket mouse, prairie dog, spotted squirrel, banded squirrel, pocket gopher, rock chipmunk, jack rabbit, cottontail rabbit, and cave bat. A few coyotes, skunks, and ring-tailed cats were seen on Sage Plain, muskrats and beavers along the San Juan River, and otters in Glen Canyon." Miser, *San Juan Canyon*, p. 74: "Among the larger indigenous animals . . . are the rabbit, prairie dog, coyote, trade rat, field mouse, snakes of several species, including abundant rattlers, and a large variety of lizard; brown squirrels and chipmunks are found in the forests, where also wild cat, porcupine, wolf, fox, and bear are occasionally met." See Olaus T. Murie, *A Field Guide to Animal Tracks* (Boston: Houghton Mifflin Co., 1954).

174 Concerning desert pavement, see Kirk Bryan, *Pedestal Rocks in the Arid Southwest*, U.S.G.S. Bulletin 760-A, 1923, p. 7.

174 Gregory, *San Juan, Country*, p. 99: "So completely do the surfaces on one side of the canyon seem to merge into those on the other that the canyon itself appears only on close approach. Within a mile of their rims the presence of even such profound gorges as Dark Canyon, San Juan Canyon at Polly Mesa, and Glen Canyon at Trail Cliff are not clearly revealed by the topography. Likewise the surfaces that at a distance seem broad and smooth are intricately dissected or broken into long platforms by canyons, some of them hundreds of feet deep." *Deseret News* quoted by Perkins *et al.*, *Saga of San Juan*, p. 9.

177 Gregory, *San Juan Country*, p. 106: "No large dunes or large areas of persistent small dunes were seen in the San Juan country. Here and there on the generally bare rock surface of Red Rock and Grand Gulch Plateaus sand dunes form and migrate, and

on the floors of washes they are common. During the infrequent but severe wind storms great quantities of dust are swept from the ground and carried high into the air, but most of the wind-blown sand accumulates about the base of shrubs and trees or in the sheltered places on canyon walls. The topography is unfavorable for large-scale wind erosion or deposition."

177   William E. Safford, *Daturas of the Old World and New: An Account of their Narcotic Properties and Their Use in Oracular and Initiatory Ceremonies* (Washington, D.C.: Smithsonian Institution, Annual Report for 1920). Its name in India, *dhatura,* was Latinized by Linnaeus for the genus name.

    Datura's other common name, jimson weed, is a corruption of "Jamestown weed." Troops were dispatched to Jamestown, Virginia, to put down an uprising known as "Bacon's Rebellion" in 1676. Perhaps feeling the need for some fresh greens, or mistaking it for another plant, or perhaps having heard of its peculiar properties from local Indians, the troops cooked up a big batch, with disastrous results. They spent eleven days in a "frantick Condition" and all had to be locked up for the duration. The event was of enough note to be recorded in Robert Beverly's contemporary *History and Present State of Virginia* written in 1705. See also L. S. M. Curtin, *Healing Herbs of the Upper Rio Grande* (Los Angeles: Southwest Museum, 1965).

182   See also F. G. Poole, *Stream Directions in Triassic Rocks of the Colorado Plateau,* U.S.G.S. Professional Paper 424-C, 1961; John H. Steward, "Triassic Strata of Southeastern Utah and Southwestern Colorado," in James A. Peterson, ed., Intermountain Association of Petroleum Geologists, *Geology and Economic Deposits of East Central Utah,* 1956, pp. 85–92, and *Origin of Cross-strata in Fluvial Sandstone Layers in the Chinle Formation (Upper Triassic) on the Colorado Plateau,* U.S.G.S. Professional Paper 424-C, 1961.

185   P. J. Mill, *Respiration in the Invertebrates* (New York: Macmillan, St. Martin's Press, 1972) and Pennak, *Fresh-water Invertebrates,* pp. 326–34: "Except for the immature stages in some families of insects, this is the only major taxonomic category found exclusively in fresh waters in the United States." Waldo L. Schmitt, *Crustaceans* (Ann Arbor: University of Michigan Press, 1965), p. 45: desiccation is required before development: "Nearly all, if not all . . . —living in evanescent bodies of water—are endowed in the egg stage with a remarkable drought-resisting faculty. It is probable that with rare exceptions eggs not subjected to some sort of drying fail to hatch—a most providential arrangement, for if it were possible for eggs to hatch without undergoing the apparent vicissitude of a drought, such eggs as remained when the pool became dry—and when the adults, in consequence, died off—might not have the resistance to endure until the next rainy season. Thus the species would be wiped out with the first complete evaporation of its particular little puddle cosmos." See also Rowe Findley, "Miracle of the Potholes," *National Geographic,* Vol. 148, No. 4:570–79 (October, 1975).

185   This view was forecast by Miser, "Erosion in San Juan County, Utah," *Geol. Soc. Am. Bull.,* Vol. 36, pp. 365–378 (1925), pp. 376–77: "If the proposed storage and power projects on San Juan and Colorado rivers are carried to completion, the mad chase of the San Juan will in part be ended, rapids will be silenced, and the region, with its wild beauty, will become accessible to tourists. Then the canyon, with its now turbulent waters, will be partly filled with the placid waters of huge reservoirs."

186   The generic name of sagebrush, *Artemisia,* is the ancient name of sagebrush, given in memory of the wife-sister of Mausolus, King of Caria, who built for him the funerary tomb known as a mausoleum, one of the Seven Wonders of the World in ancient times. Paul A. Vestal and Richard E. Schultes, *The Economic Botany of the Kiowa*

Indians as It Relates to the History of the Tribe (Cambridge: Botanical Museum, 1939), p. 56.

188 Cronquist *et al., Intermountain Flora,* p. 37: although Fremont lost some of his collections, he managed to send over 1,000 species to John Torrey and Asa Gray, who along with various English botanists identified and named many species familiar in San Juan country: piñon *(Pinus monophylla),* bladderstem *(Eriogonum inflatum),* saltbush *(Atriplex confertifolia),* peppergrass *(Lepidium fremontii),* cottonwood *(Populus fremontii),* bitterbrush *(Coleogyne ramossissima),* etc.

189 H. D. Harrington, *Western Edible Wild Plants* (Albuquerque: University of New Mexico Press, 1972), p. 125;

190 Gregory, *San Juan Country,* p. 21: "For the San Juan country as a whole soil is deficient in amount and in fertility. Over large areas it is merely shallow filling of disintegrated material in depressions between projecting rocks, sand temporarily holding its position on wind-swept rocks, or deposits left by storm floods only to be moved by succeeding floods. . . . Most of the flat-lying surface rock is siliceous sandstone deficient in mineral plant food. . . . The low ground-water tables, the short-lived heavy showers, and the scanty vegetation are unfavorable for the decomposition of rocks and the retention of soil in place."

191 Bailey, *Mammals of the Southwestern United States,* pp. 318–19: 70 years ago there was no bounty on coyote fur and they were left undisturbed; the Navajo Indians who lived in the area believed that Coyote Man was one of the powerful ancestors and would not hunt them.

HONAKER TRAIL

198 Perkins *et al., Saga of San Juan* pp. 75, 266; Miser, *San Juan Canyon,* p. 28: "The trail was built in 1904 by gold prospectors, who were attempting to work the placer deposits in and near the river channel. The canyon wall descended by the trail is only 1,235 feet high, yet the trail is so crooked that it is about 2½ miles long. The trail was built with the intention of using pack animals on it, but the only horse ever to attempt the descent fell off from a particularly steep, narrow stretch known as 'The Horn,' and its bleached bones may still be seen lying at the base of the cliff. Before 1904 prospectors reached this part of the canyon by descending the river from Goodridge and Bluff or by ascending the canyon from Clay Hill Crossing or the mouth of Slickhorn Gulch. Also for some time they used ropes for lowering themselves and supplies into the canyon at the Honaker trail. The ropes were used over the high impassable pink cliff that is about halfway down from the rim." E. G. Woodruff, "Geology of the San Juan Oil Field, Utah," in Marius R. Campbell, *Contributions to Economic Geology (Short Papers and Preliminary Reports) 1910,* U.S.G.S. Bulletin 471 (Washington, D.C.: U.S. Government Printing Office, 1912), p. 79, calculates the drop at 1,400 feet. Newbury quote in Macomb, *Report on the Exploring Expedition,* pp. 103–04.

201 Kenneth E. Carter, "Stratigraphy of Desert Creek and Ismay Zones and Relationship to Oil, Paradox Basin, Utah," in Sanborn, ed., *Geology of the Paradox Basin,* pp. 138–45.

202 Windstorms are so notable in this country that nearly every traveler has left an account. Miser, *San Juan Canyon,* p. 17, descending the San Juan River: "The river fell several inches during the daytime on September 17, 18, 19 and rose a corresponding amount at night. This coincidence of the fall and rise of the river with the activity and pause of the windstorms indicates that they were due to the extreme evaporation of the water during the storms in comparison with the little evaporation during the pauses." He describes the storm itself: "It began to blow from the south between 9

and 10 A.M. on September 18 and continued without cessation from this direction until 5 P.M. It blew in gusts and picked up sand and fine yellow dust, which were carried up into the air for hundreds if not thousands of feet. The wind shook Mr. Trimble's plane table so violently and blew so much sand into our eyes that at 11 A.M. we discontinued the descent of the canyon. The beating of the wind against the canyon walls roared like an enormous waterfall or the din of a forest storm.... On all three days considerable sand and fine dust were carried in the air. On the mornings after the sand storms much of the cloudless sky was streaked by thin light-gray to cream-colored bands that were probably composed of impalpable dust."

William Y. Adams and Nettie K. Adams, *Inventory of Prehistoric Sites on the Lower San Juan River, Utah,* Museum of Northern Arizona Bulletin 31 (Glen Canyon Series No. 1) (Flagstaff: Northern Arizona Society of Science and Art, 1959), p. 8: "High winds, usually occurring in a succession of stiff gusts, are encountered in all seasons of the year but are most common in the spring and fall. As a result sandstorms are frequent during these seasons, and especially so in the fall when numerous sandbars are exposed by receding water in the river. Prevailing wind direction throughout the area is from the southwest." See also Gregory and Moore, *Kapairowits Region,* p. 23.

203   Richard Jeffries, *Field and Hedgerow, Being the Last Essays of Richard Jeffries* (London: Longmans, Green, and Co., 1889), p. 269.

208   Miser, *San Juan Canyon,* pp. 77–78: "Drinking water for the Trimble party was obtained mostly from the San Juan.... The water thus obtained was generally free from noticeable quantities of mineral matter in solution, but it all was charged with so much silt that the bottoms of our two water pails, after being filled with water, could seldom be seen. In fact, the river was muddy at all times during the descent of the canyon from July 18 to October 3, 1921, yet the river water left standing in the pails over night would clarify by the complete settling of the silt. Water clarified in this way was used as much as possible in filling our canteens and water bags when it could not be had from other sources." The San Juan transports an unusually high amount of silt; the average silt content is 1.41% by weight or a little over 1% by volume; during flood the river carries 12.75% by volume. Miser, "Erosion in San Juan Canyon," pp. 374–75: "the water is always muddy. It is usually gray to buff in color, but during low stages, it assumes a milky color, and during the falling stages of some floods it becomes brick red in color. On one occasion I saw the river run with a smooth, oily movement, like that of molten metal, so red was it and so viscous with silt." The Bureau of Land Management estimates that the San Juan carries 24,000 acre feet of silt per year.

209   Essig, *Insects of Western North America,* p. 364; these water striders are probably *Gerris marginatis,* which are only half as large as the more familiar and widespread *G. remigis.*

210   James E. Fassett, ed., *Canyonlands Country,* p. 1, speaking as a petroleum geologist and devoted backpacker, puts the dilemma well: "How to provide access to the unique wonder of southeast Utah and at the same time preserve its loneliness? ... And how about the mother lode or the giant oil field that turns up in the middle of a wilderness area; should a unique scenic resource be destroyed for a gob of grease or a pellet of U_3O_8? Many of us geologists are becoming increasingly impatient with the restrictions placed on mineral exploration by the BLM in southeast Utah, but can we tolerate the alternative; totally uncontrolled access to our precious canyon country by anyone who can afford to hire a caterpillar tractor and wants to blade a new road?"

Quote, Lipe, "Grand Gulch," p. 51

Roderick Nash, *Wilderness and the American Mind* (New Haven: Yale University Press, 1967), p. 273: "Still, the idea of the intense control that quota systems entail is difficult to square with the meaning of wilderness. Essentially, a man-managed wilderness is a contradiction because wilderness necessitates an *absence* of civilization's ordering influence. The quality of freedom so frequently associated with wilderness is diminished, if not destroyed, by regulation. Campgrounds become sleeping-bag motels with defined capacities and checkout times. The point is underscored by the fact that wilderness, in the final analysis, is a state of mind. It is a resource, in other words, that is defined by human perception. Simply to know that one visits a wilderness by the grace of and under conditions established by governmental agencies could break the spell for many people. Yet, considering both the gains in appreciation for the wilderness and the losses in the amount of wild country left to appreciate, it is increasingly evident that the future of the American wilderness depends on American civilization's deliberately keeping it wild." Quotes in text, pp. 264 and 272.

Lipe, *The Wilderness System,* p. 19, sees the same specter on the horizon for Grand Gulch: "It may be that eventually only a certain number of persons per day will be permitted to enter the area, or that parties will be requested not to enter certain ruins. There already are restrictions on the size of hiking and horseback parties."

I would hope that those of us who walk the quiet might somehow find sensible solutions.

Acknowledgments

In writing this book I have been unusually fortunate to have professional readers who are not only experts in their respective fields, but perceptive nit pickers and merciless critics: Dr. Richard Beidleman, ecologist and essayist, Professor of Biology at The Colorado College, besides extended comment on the manuscript gave bibliographical help; James E. Fassett, District Geologist, Conservation Division, U.S.G.S., Farmington, New Mexico, checked portions on geology and made other suggestions; Dr. William D. Lipe, Professor of Anthropology, Washington State University, an archaeologist who has done definitive work on Cedar Mesa and its canyons, read the passages on the Anasazi, loaned material, and gave extensive background on an area with which he is most familiar. All loaned material to which I would not otherwise have had access. Timilou Rixon, grammarian and lover of words, spent hours shoring up my syntax; Anne Cross was a knowledgeable critic and friend. Any errors that remain after all their fine-toothed combing are entirely my own embarrassment.

Dr. and Mrs. Edwin Way Teale gave invaluable suggestions for organization and new insights into old problems, and for their support and encouragement I am deeply grateful. Millet Gray, an experienced outdoorswoman, offered valuable suggestions, especially on the last chapter. Linda Powell, a superb wildlife artist, gave advice and help on the animal drawings; I could not have done them otherwise. I also thank Marshall Sprague, whose expertise in Western history was of great value.

I appreciate the guides with whom I've worked, each exceptional in his or her own way: Patrick and Susan Conley of Wild and Scenic Expeditions; Frank and Dave Nordstrom; Clair Quist and Pam Davis of Moki-Mac Expeditions; Pete Steele of Horsehead Pack Trips. They generously shared their knowledge and love of the canyons. When I went with them, I traveled with the best.

Time in the canyons is essentially solitary time, and I've been privileged to walk with others who felt the same. I would especially like to thank the following for the gift of their company on some memorable trips: Bob and John Bell; Ernst Chilton; Anita Greenfield; Mike Good; John, Jim, and Lisa Hosbein; Virginia Kavanaugh; Charlie Litton; Bill Maierhofer; John Running; Rick Smith; Jim Ward; Bob Whitney; Buz Wyeth; and most especially two wonderful daughters, Sara and Susan. Although Jane could not go, she was so often in my thoughts that it almost seemed as if she had.

For time spent in the field there is much more time spent doing research. I am particularly indebted to The Colorado College Tutt Library for expert help: Dr. George Fagan and his staff: Rosemae Campbell, reference librarians Kathy Kaufman and Susan Myers, and particularly to Sally Payne Morgan, Charlotte Tate, and Donna Jones, whose unfailing cheerfulness, courtesy, and thoughtfulness are so very much appreciated.

At the American Museum of Natural History in New York, I thank Dr. David Thomas and Barbara Conklin of the Department of Anthropology, who allowed access to the Wetherill and Nelson material and provided sherds for drawing.

Otis Dock Marston most graciously loaned his typescript, "James White's Grand Canyon Cruise????" Others who added to my reading are Adam Csoeke-Poeckh, Verne Huser, and Walter Loope (who generously sent me his plant list from Canyonlands National Park). Cynthia Simmons, BLM ranger at Kane Ranger Station, helpfully provided BLM statistics and other information, as did Larry Teeter, BLM Recreation Specialist; my thanks also to Lester Sweeney, BLM District Manager.

Jackie Steele of Monticello, Utah, made it possible for me to interview some of the men who still remember the days on the open range, among them Brig Stevens, Dereese Nielson, and Clarence Rogers; I especially thank Jim Scorup of Monticello, Utah, for an evening of lively reminiscences.

For a great deal of efficient help in manuscript preparation I am grateful to Louise Keber of Copy Cat Reproductions and her staff: Penny and Pat Belville, Vickie Fulgenzi, and Roberta Ring.

Others have helped more than they may know although they don't fit into any category; I would just like to acknowledge them and hope each will know their special contribution: Shirlee Carsell, Karen Engle,

June Lipe, Louise Marshall, Dick and Judy Noyes, Eileen Padley, Pina Ruiz, Carol Snow.

For editorial help, I value the long-suffering patience and precise suggestions of Buz Wyeth and Corona Machemer, and the expert assistance of Kathleen Hyde and Judy Graham, all of Harper & Row. I am privileged to have a sensitive copy editor, Margaret Cheney, and an understanding, perceptive agent, Fran Collin.

A backpack trip does not begin with suddenly being dropped into a canyon; I thank Judy Nordstrom most affectionately for her hospitality and friendship, and kindness to me and my family.

It pleases me to be able to say publicly a thank you to a special husband who flew me to halfway beyond and picked me up at some equally remote runway, who bore with patience and forbearance the eternal clacking of the typewriter and who helped in innumerable thoughtful ways.

And, last but not least, Sara Zwinger, who helped immensely with proofreading and the Index, and Sara and Stephanie Noyes, who pitched in at the last panicky moment to help in collating the final manuscripts. Bless them both.

ANN H. ZWINGER

Colorado Springs

Index